Praise f

House of the Moon
Surviving the Sixties

"Donna Conrad's *House of the Moon* is raw, unpredictable, powerful, and all too difficult to put down. … Sex, drugs, and rock and roll are only the beginning of her stories about her upbringing in the heart of the sixties. Conrad's writing is authentic and unforgettable, vivid and captivating."

"This book is riveting! I couldn't put it down. It's so vivid and real - as though I was part of the story - watching from a distance, but being able to hear every word that everyone said. It's definitely a book that everyone should read. You won't be able to put it down. LOVE IT."

"A fast paced and compelling memoir for anyone interested in the real cultural history of America. A must-read in every sense of the phrase."

"Grab this for your book club because this Go Ask Alice meets Glass Castle is prime for further discussion. Take a 'trip' through a unique world. It's a wild ride you won't want to miss!"

"I really loved this book. … Love how it shows that, despite a life of turmoil, it's those experiences which shape you, make you stronger, and become the person you are to be."

"This book is POWERFUL. From the very first chapter, to the end … following along with Donna from an innocent girl to a fully realized woman, and all the characters along the way."

Bill,
Enjoy The Ride!

House of the Moon

Surviving the Sixties

Donna D. Conrad

Donna D. Conrad

Cold Creek Press Inc.

USA

Cover Design: Monica Dodd, 10 Knots Design
Cover Model: Kayla Anchell
Cover Photograph: © 2016 Steve Anchell

Published by Cold Creek Press Inc.®
www.coldcreekpress.com

Library of Congress Control Number: 2013955969

ISBN 978-0-9723443-1-9

1. 1960s—History—United States 2. Women's issues 4. Sixties Counterculture 5. Drugs 6. Vietnam War Protest—History 7. Summer of Love 8. Biography and Memoir

www.House of the Moon.com

E-mail: info@coldcreekpress.com

10 9 8 7 6 5 4 3

Cold Creek Press Inc.

This is dedicated to the one I love.

... buy the ticket, take the ride.

–Hunter S. Thompson

Fear and Loathing in Las Vegas

Barking Mad
October 1971

Suggested listening:
Album—Cheap Thrills, Big Brother and the Holding Company

The house is dank and shabby with a low-slung porch that groans under the overhanging shake roof. Preacher brakes hard and swerves the back tire of his BMW in the dirt of the long driveway before walking it back against a rotted wood fence.

You sure? he asks me.

Yeah, I tell him from the backseat of the bike.

These guys aren't like the acidheads you hang with, he adds.

I wrap my arms around his waist, slide my hands up his tight belly and say, You aren't like the acidheads I hang with and we're doing alright. I cock my head and look over his shoulder.

He turns in the curved seat and nuzzles my neck under my long hair. We do okay, he says and tries to kiss me.

I nip his lip. He smiles and tells me, Come on then. I'll keep the guys in line.

I climb off the Beemer, stamp my heels back down into my over-the-knee black suede boots, and take off my short leather jacket. He climbs off the bike, hangs his goggles over the handlebars and walks back to me at the tail. He presses against me and I wince when his hipbones grind against mine.

You need some meat on you, girl, he says.

You should talk. You're all gristle, I tease.

He silences me with a kiss then slaps me hard on the butt and heads toward the house.

I walk behind him and retie the leather strap of my headband. A gunshot rings out from behind the house followed by loud cussing and the sounds of a fight. I pause and Preacher turns and looks at me, shaking his head. Just messing around. Nobody gets hurt bad … not that kind of party, or I wouldn't have brought you.

I stand rooted to the spot and reach behind me to tighten the strap that runs under my breasts and holds the suede halter in place. Preacher walks back to me and pulls the leather belt on my mini-skirt a notch tighter around my hips.

You sure? he asks again.

Yeah. Let's go. I tell him and smile.

But I'm not sure at all. It's been almost three years since I was gang raped with my best friend. I think I should be over it. Think I should be braver than I am. Think I should be safe with Preacher. Think a biker party in the woods should be fun.

A man bigger than I can imagine is standing next to the front door. His tattooed shoulders look wider than the door and his head crests the top. Preacher reaches for the door and a thick, greasy arm blocks the opening.

She legal? the guy asks.

Yeah, legal, Preacher answers and takes the guy's wrist in his hand and pulls it off the doorframe. She's my problem, Slammer.

Nice little problem, Preacher.

I tug my short skirt down, which only makes it slide lower on my hips. Slammer puckers a kiss at me and I follow Preacher inside.

The smell hits me first, then the heat, then the noise. So many unwashed bodies crammed in the low-ceilinged room makes me nearly wretch.

Preacher pulls me under his protecting arm and says quietly, They know me here, but still … don't stray too far. Women are open game. Got it, Kool Aid?

Got it. I answer, wishing I'd taken at least a couple of reds to steady my nerves. But Preacher isn't big into drugs—just a few joints, nothing more.

Skanky guys in dirty leathers and jeans nod or give Preacher the high sign as we wade through the room. Preacher keeps a tight grip around my waist. His hand feels warm against my skin. I don't see many women, but the ones I do see are slutty and crass. One has her hand down a guy's pants beating fast strokes while the guy keeps on talking to a shirtless dirt-bag sitting next to him.

We make it to the kitchen and Preacher pops the tops off two bottles of beer. I want his hand back around my waist and so take the beer quickly and snuggle close.

You sure you wanna stay? he asks.

I down the beer and nod. How bad can they be? They're your people, I say in a hushed voice.

He pulls me full against him and I feel a hard shaft though his jeans, which means I've pleased him … though pleasing Preacher isn't too difficult.

Fucking Becker! A voice booms from behind us. And a sweet honeycomb, the voice coos. A big, meaty hand grabs my ass.

Hands off, Dutch, Preacher warns. The biker drops his hand and takes a step back.

And here I thought you'd brought us a nice young piece to play with.

The guy's taller than Preacher by at least a head and wearing Hells Angels' colors on his sleeveless denim vest. His arms bulge with muscles and are covered with tattoos of naked women and skulls and dragons.

I look at Preacher and sense a power I've felt before but never really understood. I know Preacher gave up motorcycle gangs when he left the Pagans on the East Coast. But here he was hanging with Angels as if he were one of their own. I can sense the respect they have for him. But why? I flash back to when I first met him in the college library only a month ago. Even then I knew he was more than just an ex-vet working off his tuition as a German tutor.

Then it dawns on me: Just below the calm surface there's a cold, calculating violence that doesn't need a loud voice, cuss words, or even a gun to wreak havoc. I feel it now and sense the Angels feel it too; respect it. Perhaps all the women who find Preacher irresistible sense it in him as well.

You got enough here to keep you busy, Preacher tells Dutch in a level voice. This one's solo mio.

Dutch grabs Preacher around the neck and drags him into a head lock, lands a punch to Preacher's ribs with his free hand that knocks the wind out of me just watching. Preacher doesn't seem fazed.

Solo, Dude, Dutch says and laughs. I'll spread the word.

The Angel blows a too sweet kiss at me and leaves.

I really want those reds now. I look around and it hits me—I don't know anyone but Preacher, and I sure as hell don't know him as well as I thought I did. To top it off, I hadn't told anyone where I was going. And the guys crowding in around me make the ones that gang raped me look like monks.

Honor among thieves? I ask hopefully.

At least among bikers, Preacher answers and leads me back into the living room.

Take it, you'll like it. Not too much psycho stuff floating around here, but this should set you up.

I don't ask what it is, just put the rolled hundred dollar bill he offers up my nose and suck up the white powder.

And for desert … he pulls a pipe out of his vest pocket loaded with what is either hash or opium. Either is okay by me.

Preacher had left me in the care of Jackson, a lanky blonde from somewhere in the Deep South, and told him to keep me out of trouble. He'd then walked up to a stacked redhead and slid his hand up her skirt without asking. She'd pushed her hips towards him, grabbed his long hair and kissed him full on the mouth.

I'd stood there feeling like a fool. My boyfriend was finger-fucking a woman right in front of me and twenty other guys. And I was supposed to do what? We'd agreed we weren't going steady; agreed we weren't stuck with each other. But I would never think of doing it with another guy right in front of him.

The redhead had pulled Preacher by the hair and backed through an open door off the front room with his hand still up her skirt. He'd kicked the door closed behind them without looking back, leaving me standing next to the window with Jackson and a roomful of grunting, squabbling hogs that smelled worse than they looked.

I stick the pipe in my mouth and inhale deeply as Jackson holds the match over the bowl. Opium … nice … I hand the pipe back to Jackson.

Jackson takes a hit and a thin wisp of pale blue smoke rises from the bowl. It holds its own for a moment against the thick tobacco haze. I watch it mingle, merge, then vanish. I feel a fragile kinship with the opiate cloud—too weak to hold my own for long in the world that swirls around me.

Jackson hands the pipe back and I take another hit. The room wavers, calms. I lean against the window, the cool night nuzzling my bare back through the glass.

Preacher comes out of the room followed by the redhead. I look her up and down and realize Preacher's taste runs to hefty women. Fuck him! Thin and tight is better than stacked and fat!

You got that straight! Jackson says and I realize I've been talking out loud. Just like you, Sweet Cakes. He sighs and shakes his head soulfully. Solo. Damn we could have had us some fun, me and you.

Whatever Jackson gave me is starting to buzz. I lean against him, his hand on the small of my back. Don't make this any harder than it already is, Sweet Cakes, he says and I burst out laughing. Not hard like that … well yeah, guess it is hard like that, he adds and laughs.

Thanks for watching her, Jacks. Preacher slides his hand around my neck, pulls me close and kisses me; Jackson's hand still resting on my back.

He pulls away and slams both palms into Jackson's chest. What the fuck did you give her?

Some blow and some dragon, dude. Be cool now.

I'm cool, baby, I say to Preacher and try to kiss him. I feel the bottom of my feet start to float away from the ground and grab hold of Preacher's vest.

Take me with you, I beg Preacher.

No.

A few minutes earlier the room had cleared, everyone heading down a long hallway. I could hear whoops and whistles coming from the end of the dark passage. Preacher kisses me and pats my ass and tells me to stay put.

The blow has worn off and the opium is slipping away. I don't want to lose Preacher, too. What are they doing in there?

Nothing for you to see, Kool Aid.

I pout and drop into an empty chair next to the front door. Preacher kneels in front of me. I said you could come with me if you did what I said and kept out of my way. I didn't know they were doing anything special tonight or I wouldn't have brought you. I'm not missing this and you're staying put. No more discussion! Slammer's watching you so don't try anything. He nods at the giant standing in the open doorway.

At least find Jackson before you desert me, I tell him. Slammer nods towards the kitchen.

Fuck all bitches as whores, Preacher curses and walks into the kitchen. A moment later Jackson appears as Preacher throws his arm around a bare-breasted woman with a skirt almost as short as mine. They head down the hallway together.

Jackson already has his pipe out and is rolling an oily nub of opium between his thumb and forefinger. Lost the dragon already, darlin'? he asks and kneels at my feet.

Must be a cheap grade, I tell him.

He puts a hand to his heart as if he's been wounded. Well, just so happens this dragon has a friend. If he can't satisfy you, his friend's sure to. Here, take another hit as an appetizer. I smile and take a hit off the pipe.

I don't do horse, I say on the exhale. Don't mainline anything.

Whooo, Whooo, a cunt with scruples! Well then, darlin', you got nothing to fear, I don't do horse neither. He pushes up the sleeves of his shirt and turns his arms over. See, clean as a baby's behind. He leans in close and whispers, Wouldn't want to ruin my good looks.

I look into his eyes, silently daring him to kiss me. No, No, NO, he backs away. You're likely to get my ass snuffed, Sweet Cakes. Preacher says solo, and that's how you're staying.

Fuck the bastard, I groan.

Probably what he has in mind for later, Jackson says as he reaches in his hip pocket and pulls out a folded piece of waxed paper. But the man said nothing about tripping. He smiles. I reach for the paper. Jackson pulls it out of reach and looks up at Slammer, who's watching the whole exchange. Just a little piece ... as a thank you? He waggles the packet between two fingers in front of Slammer. Slammer turns his back with a snort and Jackson leans in closer, his other hand already up my skirt. His fingers slip under my cotton panties and stroke me before I can protest.

He pulls his hand out from under my skirt, waves it under his nose and sighs, then drops the packet in my lap. Sweet, sweet, sweet, he says and grabs his bulging crotch. Solo. Fuck me running! He turns to leave and adds, Enjoy.

I unfold the paper and lick the small mound of pale yellowish powder from the center, then run my tongue over the entire square of paper, from corner to corner, just in case I've missed some. I fall back against the overstuffed chair and try to settle into the opium haze nibbling away at my anger.

I feel a hand on my leg—open my eyes to find Jackson leaning over me, the back of his hand lazing up and down my thigh between my boots and the edge of my skirt. I smile and close my eyes again; the dragon calming me enough to let him.

When I open my eyes again, I'm alone. The front door is closed and neither Slammer nor Jackson are anywhere in sight. Blaring music, whooping and hollering, dogs growling and barking, comes from down the hall. I wonder how long I've been floating. I check my skirt and underwear and find them as I left them. I'm relieved nothing happened while I was out. I look around the empty room and damn Preacher again for not letting me go with him.

Fuck him if he thinks I'm staying put, I say out loud and start to push out of the chair.

Slammer opens the front door and leans into the room. Do as Preacher says and there won't be no trouble.

Just then several bikes roar into the front yard. Slammer steps back outside and pulls the door closed behind him. I jump out of the chair and make a beeline for the hallway. The door at the end is locked so I slip outside through a side door and around to a set of sliding doors. I quietly slide one open, slip in behind the drawn curtains, and slide it closed behind me.

The absolute darkness surprises me. The curtains are thick and spongy and coated with what feels like rubber. They press me against the glass. I wait, stilling my breathing, though I could cough and no one would hear me over the noise.

Janis Joplin is belting out *Piece of my Heart*, guys are shouting, Go, Go, Go, Yeah! Dogs are growling and yipping, fists are beating on the walls making the glass doors vibrate in time with the music. I want to duck back out, but am too curious about what's happening on the other side of the curtain. I edge along feeling for the split between the panels when something slams into me at knee height. Teeth dig into one of my boots and start tugging at me. Hands pull me from behind the curtains.

I kick at the brindle dog that still has my booted leg in his mouth. A man yells something and the dog lets go, but doesn't stop growling. I look around as I'm being pulled away from the curtains.

The room looks to be a converted garage, the concrete floor covered with old scraps of greasy carpet, the walls with cheap wood paneling. Long fluorescent light fixtures hang from the ceiling casting an eerie greenish pall over everything.

Dozens of guys are backed against the walls holding dogs of varying breeds and sizes with studded collars on leather leads. There are women in various stages of undress scattered among them. In the center of the room men are crowded around a pool table with its legs sawn down.

Before I can think of what to do, the overhead lights begin pulsating in time with the music, the room swells and contracts as if it's breathing, the dogs start singing the words to the song. I realize the yellowish powder Jackson gave me must have been some kind of acid.

I'm slammed against a wall and a bare arm with a writhing dragon pins me tight. A husky voice barks, Preacher, your bitch is here.

The pack of men part in slow motion, look over their shoulders toward me. I duck my head, but a hand yanks my chin up. You wanted to see, well take a look, Honeycomb! My eyes fly open at the sound of Dutch's voice coming from the other end of the arm.

A pool table flies towards me, the red hair of the woman who'd pulled Preacher into the bedroom vivid against the green felt. She lies naked on the table, her legs hanging over the edge.

She turns her head and looks at me and suddenly I'm next to her. I feel her breath on my cheek, smell the Southern Comfort she's been drinking, taste her sweat. The next instant I'm up among the rafters watching from the heights as men grab her hands from either side of the table and pull tight.

A biker at the foot of the table scoops dog food from a can and rubs it between her legs. A black dog with an enormous head is loosed from the wall and rushes the table. It licks her exposed cunt where it perches on the thick ledge. The redhead groans and spreads her legs wider. Two men grab her knees and lift them even with the table, keeping them spread wide. Her lips part and a man pours

Southern Comfort into her mouth. Another is rubbing her clit hard and fast. He nods at the dog's handler and shouts, She's ready!

The owner picks up the mastiff's front paws and plants them on the rim of the table between the woman's legs. The men howl, the other dogs bark and strain at their leads, the mastiff hunches its back to mount her and starts humping, faster and faster. The redhead's hips strain to meet each thrust as I crash back against the wall crying, willing my eyes to close. They remain open.

The mastiff drops back to all fours and a wiry-haired mutt is held squirming in front of the woman's spread legs. His tiny dick wiggles and squirts a cloudy bit of cum.

I throw up. No one notices.

The owner laughs and reaches between the dog's legs and starts jerking him off, yelling, Warm her up! He's got more than one shot in him!

The man at the end of the table renews rubbing her clit and the redhead moans loudly. I begin floating towards her. The thick arm still has me pinned against the wall—but flesh has no power over acid and I fly to her side.

I feel the exhilaration throbbing in her. Know the thrill of being the one everyone is watching—share her disdain for these men. Feel the power she has over them—if only for this moment.

She cries out. The room blinks out of existence.

I'm on my back in the damp grass, Preacher on his knees straddling me.

I told you to stay put! he screams. Jesus Christ! You're lucky they didn't throw *you* on the damned table!

I twist and try to break his hold on my wrists.

Stop it! No more hysterics! he snaps at me.

I keep struggling as a deep purple cloud descends, obscuring everything except Preacher and me. I try to reason with myself, tell myself I can trust Preacher; that this is all just a bad trip—decide to be good if he'll just let me go.

I watch as furred legs materialize out of a swirling green-gold mist where his arms should be. Enormous, claw-tipped paws spring from the wolf-like limbs that pin me to the ground. Behind the paws is the muzzle of a great wolfhound, growling and snapping.

I try to scream, but have no voice. I try to kick and roll away.

The world goes black when a hammer-like paw slams into my jaw.

Take the Ride
April 1966

Suggested listening:
Album—Do You Believe in Magic, The Lovin' Spoonful

It began with a bust.

Covina, California in the 1960s was a clean, white place to live, just twenty-four miles east of downtown Los Angeles. A maze of three-bedroom, two-bath housing tracts with wide streets and narrow minds. Perfect for the family of an undercover agent for the State, his wife, son, and two daughters. But the son was sent to war in '64, the wife was a fall-down drunk, and the daughters prime candidates for a cultural revolution that was gathering recruits with every toke.

Weed, Mary Jane, pot—smoked in a reefer, a joint, a doobie—hand rolled and thick as your little finger. Not in Covina, my dad tells us over dinner. I believe him. Shirley, my older sister, knows better.

Just after school opens in September 1965, I come home to find my dad's car in the driveway. Dad, Muzzie, our nickname for our mom, and Shirley are at the kitchen table. I know there's trouble, but dad isn't yelling. I'm confused because he's always yelling, especially when there's trouble.

I'm exiled to my room. When I'm summoned to the living room, the jury is in and the verdict is banishment for my sister. I'm told she's going away. I'm not told why. I'm not told where. I'm not told for how long. My father's not the kind of man who feels the need to give answers. I've learned not to ask questions.

I break into tears and can't stop crying. Dad starts yelling and I'm hurried back into the bedroom with Shirley's arm around me. She lets me sob until I start hiccoughing and then tries to scare the hiccoughs away. I shriek and start crying again, but the hiccoughs are gone.

Most things scare me: The dark, an open closet, shadows that move, nightmares where my family has no faces—a father who beats our mother and runs around the house with a loaded shotgun shouting, *A dead man has no cares!*

My brother is eight years older than me and my hero. He's tall and strong and honest and my protector. When children at school tease me for being fat, Terry sits on the bed next to me and says he'll beat them up. I tell him he can't beat up a fifth-grader. He asks if they have older brothers he can beat up.

I don't think he's ever hit anyone. He's a gentle giant. At 6'4" he's larger than life and too much older for me to know very well. He follows in my father's footsteps and joins an elite branch of Army Intelligence when I'm eleven.

Hey, Punk, he says as he's leaving. I'll see you in no time and I'll write every week. Don't worry about me. This is better than being drafted and sent to Nam.

Terry has always looked out for both his little sisters, but he and Shirley are closer in age, and so closer. Shirley loves him more than anyone. When he leaves, Shirley is cut adrift. She finds a safe harbor with other rejected teens whose parents moved to the "burbs" to keep their children safe. When Shirley enters Charter Oak High School she finds her niche—until the principal finds a joint in her purse the second week of her sophomore year.

She's the first student to have dangerous drugs on campus; the first one they catch, at any rate. The School Board feels her expulsion will serve as a warning to others—Charter Oak will not tolerate drug fiends.

Shirley's banishment destroys my last vestige of security. It is Shirley who holds me every time I have a nightmare. Shirley, who leads me into our bedroom and closes the door when our parents start fighting. Shirley who shares the secret that she shoplifted all the clothes she claims are borrowed from friends.

Shirley who tells me why she's being sent away.

After she leaves, no one is there to wake me up when the nightmares come. When Muzzie throws a skillet and hits Dad on the back of the head, when Dad hits her so hard she slams into the wall and doesn't get up—no one is there to take me to my room. I crouch in a corner and close my eyes so I won't see the blood; clamp my hands over my ears so I won't hear the screaming.

Winter passes and Shirley and I talk on the phone as often as long-distant rates will allow. But it's the family phone and I know Shirley can't tell me the truth. Instead she tells lies that will satisfy our dad listening in on the extension.

After one such call I'm told that I am to visit Shirley during Easter vacation. I've just turned thirteen and have never been away from home without my parents. My dad drives me to Los Angeles and puts me on a Greyhound bus bound for San Francisco. The driver promises my dad he'll watch out for me and deliver me safely. I see folded cash change hands.

The door snaps closed and the driver tells me to sit up near the front. I've never seen L.A. after dark before. The streets look sad and lonely. Old men in threadbare suits, a few lucky ones in overcoats, sit huddled on the sidewalks, their backs against the stone buildings. The traffic lights blink from color to color and the woman next to me turns on the overhead light and takes out a book. I hadn't thought to bring one, so I stare out the window until the last signal turns green and the bus eases out onto Highway 101 and the black countryside that surrounds the City of Angels.

Each time a city blazes into sight the bus slows and then stops at a station. People grab their suitcases and leave; new ones find a seat and stash their smaller bags overhead. The driver always finds a middle-aged woman to sit next to me, when the previous one reaches her destination. We have fifteen minutes at each stop. The women escort me to the women's lounge, make sure I wash my hands after using the toilet, and take me back to our seats. More often than not they buy me candy and a soda. I stay awake all through the night and eat a pre-dawn breakfast at the counter of the bus station in San Jose with the driver, because no women are going further than San Jose.

He waits for me outside the door to the women's lounge and asks if I washed my hands. He puts me in the front seat to his right and doesn't let anyone sit next to me. As the bus climbs a steep hill and drops down the other side, the sun's first rays illuminate Shangri-La, the place where my sister is waiting for me—San Francisco.

The bus driver makes me wait until everyone else is off the bus and he's unloaded the stowed luggage. I'm bouncing in my seat, looking for Shirley. Everyone collects their luggage and walks around the front of the bus and vanishes. After nearly forever the driver pokes his head inside and tells me to come out.

I promised your father I'd make sure you find your sister, so let's go find her. What does she look like?

I think for a moment then answer, Tall and thin, and she has really long, really thick hair.

That doesn't help much …

There, there, there! I run ahead of him and throw myself into Shirley's arms.

He catches up and asks, Are you her sister?

Shirley doesn't let go of me. No, we just met. She tucks me under one arm. Of course I'm her sister!

I sniffle and nod. This is my sister. Thank you for bringing me here.

The driver looks Shirley up and down, noting her long straight hair, the black leather jacket, the black and white checkered, vinyl mini-skirt, the knee-high boots, the lit cigarette. You old enough to smoke? he asks.

You a cop? she answers, and I duck a little bit behind her.

The driver shakes his head and bends down to ask me, You gonna be all right? I nod. Be sure to tell your father I got you here safe and sound. I nod and smile. He sets my suitcase next to me and shakes his head and mutters, Damned hippie, as he turns away.

Asshole! Shirley spits at his back, then grabs me and hugs me tight, twisting back and forth. She's warm and real and alive. She's my big sister and I know everything will be all right now that we're back together.

Wanna see the City? she asks. We have all day. I don't have to be back 'til nine tonight.

All day and all night? Without anyone watching us?

Ya, it's cool. Let's go. We stuff my suitcase in a locker and Shirley leads the way out of the bus terminal and onto the streets of San Francisco.

Wanna puff? Shirley asks and passes me her cigarette. I pause a second, then take it. I'm still coughing when we climb onto the cable car and start up the hills.

The newspapers are full of stories about Hippies, Love Children, Drug Addicts, Radicals, Draft Dodgers; none of them positive—but I think hippies are really cool. Even at thirteen I know my parents are square; know there has to be a better way to live in a world where good people like my brother are sent off to kill for something I know is wrong.

Every time someone with jeans or hair below their ears comes into view I tap Shirley on the arm and ask, Is that one? She slaps my hand away and tells me to stop pointing. But the next pair of jeans has me tapping and asking. I've never seen a hippie, but I know Shirley has to have seen one, maybe even knows one.

Finally, to get away from my tapping, Shirley soars out over the street, holding on with one hand and one foot, and whoops and hoots until the brakeman tells her to shut up, get inside, or get off.

We get off at the next stop and walk down the long stairs on

Lombard Street. We turn onto Columbus. Guys and girls dressed mostly in black are sitting on the street with guitars, harmonicas, and bongos, singing and swaying to the music. I tug on Shirley's coat. Are they hippies?

No they're Beats. They're weird. I don't hang here much, but I know a guy who might be at the park over there.

Is he a hippie?

Stop asking! I'll show you one when I see one, she adds and crosses the street. I wait for the light to turn green.

We don't find her friend. Shirley lights another cigarette and we walk back the way we came. We stop and stand on a corner waiting for something. I don't ask what.

A bus pulls up and we hop on. Shirley pays our fare. The bus drops us at the corner of Haight and Ashbury, and I don't need to ask anymore. They're everywhere, and everything I'd ever dreamt of—holding hands, kissing, smoking, drinking, playing music. The guys have hair down to their shoulders and the girls wear hardly anything at all, not even bras. I try not to look, but can't help myself, wondering if I'll ever have boobs that bounce when I dance.

We wander into the notorious Golden Gate Park, past a group of people drumming on huge conical shaped drums. People are dancing and chanting and kissing and touching each other and I move a little closer to Shirley. A guy with hair halfway down his back and a multicolored beaded headband gives her a hand rolled cigarette. She kisses him on the mouth. I'm stunned and can't seem to move as she dances away down the path. After a moment I realize I'm all alone and run to catch up with her.

We cut off the main path onto a dirt trail that runs under enormous trees that almost touch overhead. She lights the cigarette and sucks hard. She doesn't offer me a hit, so I ask, feeling that one coughing fit shouldn't keep me from trying again.

No way! She spins around and points the cigarette at me. Don't you *ever* touch this stuff, you hear me? I nod, willing back the tears; not understanding why she's suddenly so mad at me. Her face softens and she takes another puff. Punk, this isn't tobacco, she says sucking in more air and not exhaling.

Is that marijuana? I nearly shout.

She coughs up a huge cloud of pale blue smoke and smacks me on the head. Shut up, you jerk! Damn, I knew I shouldn't bring you here. You always fuck everything up!

I can't stop the tears.

Don't start crying! Shit! You always start crying. Ok, Ok, Ok. She's on her knees in front of me. Just stop crying, ok? I didn't mean it. I'm glad you're here. I love you. You're my little sister. Come on. She kisses my cheek and smells like something I've never smelled before.

Is that marijuana? I whisper.

Pot. It's called pot—unless you're a Narc.

What's a Narc? I ask, watching her take another deep drag.

Dad, she says, taking in more air, then holding her breath.

Oh. I don't ask any more questions.

I sez to myself, Self, those are two nice looking chickies. Why not ask them to walk with us, instead of by themselves. And Self sez, why not?

I try to ignore the two guys walking behind us, especially the one talking to himself. Shirley stifles a giggle and walks a bit faster. I almost have to run to keep up.

Self, I sez to myself, why are they running away? We just want to rap and maybe smoke with them. It's groovy to rap and smoke with beautiful chickies.

Shirley stops suddenly and turns around. The guys stop dead in their tracks. You wanna rap? You wanna smoke? You got any smoke? They both shake their heads. Didn't think so, Shirley says.

What harm is there in being groovy, chickie? Self asks.

None, Shirley answers.

Cool, then you keep walking and we'll keep walking and we'll all be groovy in the same place, at the same time.

Groovy, Shirley says and the guys walk between us through the park and ride back to the cable cars with us on the bus. They hang off the cable car with Shirley and no one tells them to stop. I keep both hands on the rail and both feet on the floorboard.

They tire of the sport and swing back inside and flop onto the wooden bench. The silent one looks over at me and asks, How old are you?

Shirley stands up and walks along the ledge and pushes between the silent one and me and sits down. Too young, she says.

What's too young?

Shirley yanks the wire running above our heads and pulls me to my feet.

Now why are they running away? Why? I ask myself. Self sez, I don't know.

Because you're a fucking freak, Shirley shouts.

The brakeman raises an eyebrow. They bothering you, Miss?

Stay the fuck outta my life, jerk, Shirley tells the brakeman and pulls me off the cable car before it stops. She swings around and points a long tapered finger at the two guys. Stay the fuck away from us, freaks.

Self doesn't say anything. The brakeman doesn't stop until three blocks away.

I follow Shirley up hills and down alleys and somehow we end up back at Haight Street. She looks back over her shoulder and hisses, Assholes, and tucks me under her arm and laughs. Gotta watch out for my little Punk, now, don't I. I nod, too confused to say anything.

Angel! Shirley screams, and tears off down the sidewalk and straight into the arms of a tall, Negro man with a glistening shaved head. I don't move, can't move. I've never been close to a Negro man before, but know from my dad that they can't be trusted; they're dangerous, violent, filled with hate for anyone who's white.

He picks Shirley up in a great bear hug. She leans into him and bends her knees, curling them out behind her. The street tilts slightly and goes silent. People passing by are moving in slow motion. Some look at me. Some laugh. Some flash me the two-fingered peace sign. One flips me off.

Shirley breaks away and time snaps back in place.

The Negro asks, That's her?

Yeah, Shirley smiles and waves me forward. I take a step.

You have got to be kiddin', he adds.

I stop.

No. She's cool, Shirley tells him.

I walk over, but keep my distance. He looks me up and down. I follow his eyes and see my stained shirt, my fat belly and flat chest straining against the buttons. I blush and look away.

It's cool, sweetie, he says to me. I can't look him in the eyes and so study his knee-high moccasins. It's cool. I dig where you're comin' from. Just be cool and everything will be groovy. He takes Shirley's hand and heads off down the street, with me stumbling along a few steps behind.

We turn onto Page Street and walk a few doors down. Shirley and the Negro hop onto the first stair of a broken down old house. They kiss again and Shirley throws her arms around the Negro. I look away. She's not how I remember her.

I look up at the house directly across from us. A woman is dancing naked in the window of a second floor room. Her long hair flying as she swings her head around in circles. I look away and don't know where to look any more.

Hey! Come on.

I turn back and Shirley and the guy are at the top of the stairs and she's waving at me. Hurry up, she shouts and stamps a foot. We go inside and up three flights of dimly lit stairs, down a musty smelling, narrow hallway to the back of the house. The door at the end is open. I wait in the doorway, not sure what to do.

The room is filled with a smoky haze, like the sky in Covina on a hot summer day. The music is loud and people are packed together, on overstuffed couches or on the floor; smoking, drinking, some dancing. The Negro reaches for me and I back out in the hall.

Oh Christ! He turns to Shirley. Get her fat ass in here now! I do not have the time to waste messin' with your nigger-hatin' little sister.

I feel my face flush and step inside the room. Shirley shakes her head and a finger at me and takes a step closer and tells me, Stop being a jerk. Everything's cool. Go get a drink and sit down somewhere. I'll be right back.

She leaves me alone and goes into another room with the Negro and closes the door behind them. I'm too afraid to look for the kitchen, or the bathroom, which I really need, so I pick the closest corner and slide down the wall and sit with my knees pulled in tight against my chest. What I see doesn't make any sense, but it's wonderful. Kids come and go, hugging each other, kissing, drinking out of the same bottle, smoking from the same hand-rolled cigarettes—joints, I correct myself and smile that I know they're called joints. I bet no one else in my junior high knows they're called joints.

I stay in the corner, my favorite spot in any room, and pretend to be invisible; my favorite thing to do when I'm scared. All the girls are beautiful, with long hair and multi-colored dresses or skirts and t-shirts or bikini tops made out of leather. None of them wear bras and their breasts bounce and sway when they move. One even takes off her clothes right in front of everyone. She doesn't have anything on under a long poncho and I try not to look at the bushy black hair where her underwear should be.

The girls are nice to me and give me brownies and tea after I tell them Shirley's my big sister. The guys ignore me.

After a long, long time Shirley comes out of the side room. When she sees me it's like she doesn't know me. She stops in the middle of the wide, light-filled room and just stares at me. She blinks and looks around. Shit! Did I leave you here all alone? I nod. Fuck, Punk. I'm sorry. She kneels in front of me and brushes my short cropped hair out of my eyes. You okay? I nod again. Anyone hassle you? I shake my head. Good. She turns around looking for something and says, I'll be right back and we'll get something to eat. Stay there.

She doesn't come back for half an hour, and when she does her eyes are red and glassy, but she's smiling. Cool isn't it? she asks. I nod. You see enough hippies? She laughs and grabs me by the hand and hauls me off the floor.

Shirley falls asleep before the bus leaves the station. I look past her and out the window, watch San Francisco fly by. It doesn't look quite real. The colors are deep and pulsating. The hushed voices on the bus are sharp and irritating. I feel the stirrings of a headache and will myself not to cry.

I sip on my Double Cola and nuzzle against Shirley. I'm happy she's sleeping. This new Shirley scares me a little, but I know it will be different once we're alone, just the two of us, without the Negro and the hippies.

Images of kids smoking pot and loud music and dancing throb in my head and I prop my Double Cola between Shirley and me and try to fall asleep. Next thing I know Shirley's shaking me awake. We're in Napa, the small town of her exile. We walk the long blocks to the McAdams' home.

Shirley stands on the corner and unwraps a stick of cinnamon-flavored gum. Hides the smell of pot and beer, she says, and hands me one.

I take the gum and look around the tidy, wide street and say, This could be Covina. Could be our street.

Yeah, weird isn't it, Shirley says looking around. Freaks me out every time I walk up the sidewalk. I keep waiting for Dad to start yelling and ground me every time I walk through the door.

Does Mr. McAdams yell at you?

Naw. They're all great. But you got to remember that your bus didn't get in until tonight.

What?

You don't think they'd let me spend the day in the City alone with you? They think your bus got in at seven tonight, not this morning. So don't blow it by saying anything about what we did.

They don't know?

Of course not! She walks up the driveway, pulling her hair into a pony tail then unrolling the top of her skirt so the hem is down to her knees.

I realize this is no different than Covina—that she needs to lie to keep the adults happy here, just like she did at home. I catch up with her and ask, Can we go back to the City again before I go home?

You bet we can. We'll head back as soon as I figure out a good story to tell them, she says nodding at the house. Watch and learn, Punk, watch and learn.

I lick my fingers and wipe them over my flyaway hair, brush the crumbs off my shirt and put on a happy face for the McAdams.

My education has begun.

1966 in the news

❖ President: Lyndon B Johnson

❖ Vice President: Hubert H. Humphrey

❖ The national debt is 319.9 billion

❖ The population of the United States is 196.56 million

❖ Life expectancy is 70.2 years

❖ Average income per year is $4,940

❖ Minimum wage is $1.25 per hour

❖ Average cost of a new house is $23,300

❖ A gallon of gas costs $0.32

❖ First Class postage is $0.05

❖ *The Sound of Music* wins Best Picture

❖ The following TV shows debut: *Star Trek*; *The Monkees*; *Batman*; and *Mission Impossible*

❖ The Beatles give their last public performance in the U.S.

❖ Grace Slick performs live with *Jefferson Airplane* for the first time

❖ Pakistan and India reach a peace accord ending their 17-day war

❖ The unmanned Soviet Luna 9 spacecraft makes the first controlled rocket-assisted landing on the Moon

❖ 20,000 Buddhists march in demonstrations against the military government in South Vietnam

❖ The Uniform Time Act sets daylight savings time standards for the country

❖ President Johnson increases troop strength in Vietnam throughout the year; first to 190,000 and to 389,000 by year's end and orders the bombing of targets in and around Hanoi, North Vietnam

❖ The Supreme Court rules that the police must inform suspects of their rights before questioning them. These become known as Miranda Rights

❖ Former actor Ronald Reagan is elected Governor of California

❖ Dynamic Random Access Memory (DRAM) in a single cell is developed paving the way for more powerful computers

Spin the Bottle
April 1966

Suggested listening:
Album—Lesley Gore Sings of Mixed-Up Hearts, Lesley Gore

It's the first time I've kissed a boy. I don't even know his name; but the bottle pointed at me so I have to. His breath smells like stale bubble gum and sour beer. His lips part, the tip of his tongue pokes at my closed mouth. I break away and scoot back to my place in the circle; hope I don't get picked again.

Spin, spin, spin, spin, everyone in the circle chants. I look around and see they're all looking at me, all of Shirley's friends here in Napa. Shirley juts her chin at the bottle and tells me to spin it. I feel my face flush.

I get on all fours and stretch to reach the empty Schlitz bottle. It doesn't quite spin, does more like the half turn of a Lazy-Susan in a Chinese restaurant.

You gotta spin it harder, two or three kids tell me. It's got to go around the circle at least once!

Rules? I didn't know there were rules. No one told me there were rules. I feel stupid and know I'm blushing.

Spin, spin, spin.

I tuck my hair behind my ear and give it another spin. The bottle wobbles and veers out of the center of the circle, but just clears me. It points to the girl next to me.

Ewww. Yuck. No way!

It's understood that girls don't have to kiss other girls. I'm relieved my turn is over and that she has to spin the bottle. I start to back into my spot in the circle. Everyone starts clapping in time and chanting, Spin, spin, spin …

You have to spin again, the boy I just kissed tells me.

I stay frozen on my hands and knees, looking at the bottle, too embarrassed to look up.

Spin, spin, spin!

I look at Shirley to save me. She pushes me back down and grabs the bottle.

My turn! She takes a hit off her cigarette and looks slowly around the circle. Who should it be, she says out loud and winks at a guy with sandy blonde hair and a thin mustache opposite her. The bottle spins fast and sure and makes it around the circle at least three times before it settles on the same guy I just kissed.

Your lucky day, Larry, Shirley tells him.

They meet in the center and kiss for a long time. I see Larry's lips part, see Shirley lean closer and open her mouth. Everyone cheers. I look away.

I have to use the bathroom, I whisper in Shirley's ear when she settles back down next to me.

Well go already. You know where it is.

I blush again and know everyone must be looking at me. The bottle twirls past me and I back out of the circle on my hands and knees.

Alright! Larry shouts, and starts to crawl across the circle.

You alright? Shirley asks through the locked door.

Yeah, I say from my perch on the toilet. Fine … just … you know …

Oh. Yeah, okay. Just checking.

I hear kids laughing and shouting from clear in the living room and decide to stay put. Decide I don't like kissing boys, and that I especially don't like kissing Larry. I wonder how long I'll have to stay in the bathroom. How long they can keep spinning that stupid bottle and kissing each other.

My legs start to go all numb and tingly.

That's enough, Shirley yells through the door. You've been in there half an hour. Open up!

I unlock the door and open it. She looks over at the closed toilet lid. I thought so, she announces. What's wrong? Don't you like my friends?

I look away and say, No ... I mean yeah, they're great. I just don't really fit in ... you know ... they're older and mostly guys and you all know each other and I don't think they really like me ...

She lifts my chin and looks me in the eyes. You're my little sister and they'd better like you. Did anyone hassle you? I shake my head. Then get out there. You can't always hide in the head. She pauses for a minute then laughs. Christ. I sound like the old man. "What you doing in the bathroom all day. Get the hell outta there!" She shakes her head and takes me by the arm. Come on. Let's get outta here. You ever had a beer?

Yeah, in Germany.

Christ. That long ago? Wait a minute, you can't remember Germany. You were only a baby.

But I remember it clearly. I remember most things that happen to me. I wish I could forget some of them. But Germany is a happy memory, with everyone smiling and dancing and singing and being nice to me—even my dad. He seemed happier there. I don't remember him ever yelling. He and Muzzie had lots of friends and parties at our house, and at a nearby tavern.

We had a hamster, Hammy, who would climb up the side of my dad's beer stein and actually drink the beer. Whenever people came to the house Dad would pull Hammy out of his cage and set him on the kitchen table. Hammy always performed to perfection, no matter how many people were watching him. One time I asked what Hammy was drinking. My dad handed me his beer stein and said, Here, give it a try. You're half German, you should like this!

I didn't. It smelled like someone's underwear. I took a big gulp anyway, not wanting to be outdone by a hamster. Everyone laughed and some man hollered, That's the way, Condie. Start her off young with the good stuff.

After that I didn't envy Hammy's fame—never really wanted to drink beer again. But if Shirley's offering, I can't refuse.

She throws an arm around my shoulder and laughs, Let's get you a real beer, not that German crap.

No. It's not flooding here, just on the way back down there. No, no. They're fine with her staying longer. Really. Shirley puts her hand over the mouthpiece and whispers, I think they're gonna fall for it. Then takes her hand away from the receiver and says, I'm here. Must be a bad connection.

They fall for it—our little lie—and I get to stay with Shirley and miss a whole week of school. The McAdams have been gone for the last two days and think that I left the day after them. But I didn't leave. It took us the last two days to come up with a good story.

We had been trying to think of a way for me to stay longer when Shirley's friends showed up and the bottle started spinning. It was only when it started pouring rain and everyone rushed home that we got the idea. But we had to wait to make sure the rain didn't stop. It didn't. There was some flooding, enough to cause stories on the evening news—enough to make our story believable—enough to keep me in Napa with Shirley.

I don't know. I'll ask. Shirley looks over at me. Muzzie wants to know if you have enough of your pills for the next week. She puts her hand over the receiver, What pills?

They're nothing, I tell her, and say loud enough for Muzzie to hear, Yes, I have plenty.

I hear Muzzie say, Okay. Well, take care of each other and don't get wet. I'll tell your dad to pick you up Saturday night instead, Punk. Love and Kisses!

Shirley hangs up and spins around shouting, I can't fucking believe she fell for it!

We're lucky Dad wasn't home, I add.

Yeah! What you wanna do?

I shrug and look outside. It's still raining. Wanna watch some TV?

Groovy. Want a beer?

I shake my head.

Hey, what pills are you taking?

Just stuff from the doctor, to make me lose weight. I'm a little hurt that Shirley hasn't noticed I've lost weight.

Really? Let me see. Pull up your shirt.

No way!

Pull it up! I don't care about your little titties. Let me see.

I pull up my baggy shirt and try to suck in my stomach. My slacks slip down and I drop my shirt to grab them.

Wow. You have lost weight. How much?

Twenty pounds, the last time we were at the doctors. Maybe more by now. I lift up my shirt again and turn around, proud that it shows.

Lemme see the pills.

I drop my shirt and go dig the little yellow bag that has all my pills out of my suitcase. I hand her one of the small, sealed envelopes and realize I really do have plenty for the next week. She rips open the bag and pours the rainbow selection into her hand.

Wow! She looks at me. These look like uppers, she says, separating out the three small white pills I take first thing every morning. Don't know what these yellow ones are, but the black ones look like downers. You take all these?

I nod. The white ones in the morning, the yellow and the purple ones at lunch, and the black and the green ones right before bed.

Wow. And Muzzie knows?

I nod. She takes me to the doctor every Friday. The doctor gives her shots every time. He only gives me pills.

You got enough to last you for more than a week? I nod. She pops the entire handful into her mouth and downs them with a swig of beer.

I reach for her and shout, No! Those are for all day! I run for the kitchen. You need lots of water. You need to barf them up.

Shirley follows behind me. Chill out! It's cool.

You took too many! You might die!

For fuck sake! Chill. They can't be too strong or a doc wouldn't give them to someone your age. Does Muzzie take the same pills along with the shots?

I nod.

I left home too soon, she says and leads me into the den.

We sleep together on the davenport each night. Sleep all tangled together like we used to before Shirley was exiled. I'm happy when we're in bed together, when it's just the two of us. I sleep all through the night. No nightmares. I don't even care that the closet door is open; that there's no nightlight; that I'm in a strange house. I sleep deeply without remembering any dreams. That's why I don't hear the car, the front door opening; why I don't know the McAdams are home two days early until Mr. and Mrs. McAdams are standing in the den doorway.

What is she doing here? Mrs. McAdams asks. I hear the disapproval in her voice.

I hide under the covers as Shirley tries to explain. Even I know she's doing a bad job.

The bus ride back to L.A. is long. The driver has the sealed envelope my dad gave me for the return ride when I left L.A. The older women buy me candy and soda at each stop and make sure my hands

Donna D. Conrad

are washed.

I'm passed from woman to woman, never asking their names. I still don't have a book, so I stare out the window. It all looks so different in the sunlight. All the tidy little towns with their trimmed lawns, freshly painted houses, neatly dressed children walking to school—just like Covina—just like home. The bus stops for a red light and I look down into a car, see a father lean back over the front seat and slap a young girl whose bouncing on the backseat.

Just like home, I think and close my eyes. Just like home.

Girls Night Out
April 1966

Suggested listening:
Album—Beach Boys' Party, The Beach Boys

School days are predictable; raising my hand a lot because I always know the answer; scurrying from class to class; avoiding the bathrooms because the tough girls are in there, girls that tease me about being fat and smart and not rich; staying in the library during lunch, so the same girls can't pinch me and call me names.

I hurry home after school, relieved when no one is waiting to pick on me along the dirt path that cuts across the school yard to the back gate. I never cry in front of them because Muzzie told me it makes them think they've won. I don't ever want them to think they've won. But I cry once I get home.

I'm usually alone. Muzzie isn't passed out on the couch like she used to be every day. She's working day shifts at the telephone company so she can be home in the evenings to cook dinner and get me ready for school the next day.

The house is always dark, the shades drawn to keep the heat in, or out, depending on the season. I head straight to the bathroom, and then let Laddie, our collie, in through the sliding glass door. He's not allowed in the house and so is always happy when I let him in. I snag Toll-House cookies out of the jolly teddy bear jar and munch on them while I do my homework on our pale green, speckled Formica kitchen table. I watch my allowed half hour of TV, clean up the kitchen, iron my dad's white shirts and handkerchiefs, and then tidy my room.

All that's the easy part of the day. It's after my homework is done, after Laddie settles down, after I run out of chores—that's the tough part of the day. I start to think about Shirley and San Francisco; of kissing guys and drinking beer like I was a big kid. I think about Terry, wondering where in the world he might be stationed, re-read his latest letter. I think about the long night ahead; hope my dad doesn't start yelling; hope there's no fighting; hope the night will be quiet.

But Friday nights are different. Muzzie and I have a standing date, every Friday night—the best night of the whole week. She calls it *Girls' Night Out* and tells Dad every Thursday night that he's not invited. He laughs and says, Wouldn't dream of intruding on a girls' night out. They say exactly the same thing almost every week, but I like it anyway.

Friday night is my time alone with Muzzie. It's the one night I can count on—the one night I never want to change. First we head to the diet doctor in Azusa. We both get weighed and congratulated for losing more weight. Muzzie gets a shot and I get a new bunch of envelopes.

Muzzie and I hold hands and cross the wide street, heading for El Patio, the Mexican restaurant caddy-corner from the doctor's office. I always order two tacos with beans and rice, Muzzie gets chile rellenos and a large side-order of guacamole and chips. I sip on a Coca-Cola and munch on the chips and guacamole and tell her about all the great things I did during the week. My report card is always filled with *A's* and *Outstandings*, so she believes the stories I make up about all my friends and all the clubs I belong to—I'm even president of one.

She always orders a margarita with an extra shot and I always wonder why she wants another shot when she just had one at the doctors. The waitress never brings a syringe to the table so I figure it's just a joke and chuckle every time Muzzie places her order. We eat and I talk. She pays the bill and says, See you next week, Rosa, to the round Mexican woman who always serves us. The woman always smiles and nods and says, Gracias. Adios.

She sounds so exotic.

Our next stop is the Crest theatre in Monrovia. Friday night before six costs 25 cents for kids under sixteen, so we always rush to get there after the doctor's and El Patio. Doesn't matter what's playing. If it's a comedy, Muzzie laughs real loud and slaps my leg. Sometimes I get the jokes, most time I laugh just because she's laughing. If it's a sad movie, we hold hands and share a handkerchief.

After the movies we head to the In-N-Out close to our house. In-N-Out's Terry's favorite place. One time I order a double-double and try to eat it all like Terry always does—once! I stick to a regular burger and fries now. Muzzie does the same.

We always talk about him while we're eating in the car. She tells me stories about my big brother that I've heard before, but I like them all the same. I always wish I could remember something she doesn't already know so I could tell her a new story. But I always come back to telling about the time my best friend, Sylvia, got stuck up on the roof. Terry told her to jump down to him. She did—he caught her in his arms. It's the best story of all.

One warm, summery Friday, Muzzie passes over my burger and fries and coke just like always. It's all perfect, just like it always is— except Muzzie isn't eating—she's just looking at her burger.

Sometimes I think he'll never come home, she says, and I know she's talking about Terry. Why in the world would he want to? she asks.

I sit very still; don't know what to say; don't like the sad sound of her voice; don't understand why Terry wouldn't want to come home—to Muzzie—to me.

Remember when he picked your dad up by the shirt and held him against the dining room wall? she asks and looks at me out of the corner of her eye, still holding the uneaten burger in both hands.

I remember.

Donna D. Conrad

Dad looks so small next to Terry, his feet dangling a few inches off the floor. Terry! Put me down! Stop this! You have no right … Shirley and I are watching from the living room; watching Dad struggle. It seems like time stands still—like Terry will never turn him loose.

If you ever hit her again, I'll kill you, Terry shouts. His face is so close to Dad's I can see little specks of spit spatter Dad's glasses.

Put me down! Dad orders.

Terry blinks and looks around, sees Shirley and me watching; looks over his shoulder at Muzzie, who's still on the floor, her nose bleeding. He looks back at Dad and lets go. Dad lands hard on his feet and goes to slap Terry across the face; but Terry has already turned away and is walking to his room.

I remember, I answer.

He was protecting me, Muzzie says. He was always such a gentle boy. It was so unlike him to do something like that. Her voice fades away. She sighs and bites into her burger. Ummm, this is the best ever. Try yours, she says. It's even better than last week's.

I take a bite of my burger and pretend this Friday is like all the other Fridays—a night for fun—not a night to remember.

1967 in the news

❖ The national debt is 326.2 billion

❖ The population of the United States is 198.71 million

❖ Average income per year is $5,213

❖ Minimum wage is $1.40 per hour

❖ Average cost of a new house is $24,600

❖ Average monthly rent is $125

❖ A gallon of gas costs $0.33

❖ A movie ticket costs $1.25

❖ *A Man for All Seasons* wins Best Picture

❖ *Michelle* wins Best Song

❖ *Strangers in the Night* wins Best Album

❖ The following TV shows debut: *The Flying Nun; High Chaparral; Carol Burnett Show; Ironside; Mannix; The Smothers Brothers;* and *Phil Donahue*

❖ Lester Maddox is elected Governor of Georgia on a segregationist platform

❖ *Rolling Stone* magazine debuts

❖ The waterbed is created by a design student at San Francisco State University

❖ Super Bowl I is played with the Green Bay Packers defeating Kansas City

❖ Astronauts Gus Grissom, Edward Higgins White, and Roger Chaffee are killed aboard the Apollo 1 spacecraft during a launch pad test

- ❖ Israel defeats Egypt, Syria and Jordan in the Six Day War
- ❖ Muhammad Ali refuses military service on religious grounds
- ❖ The first automatic cash machine (ATM) is installed at Barclays Bank in England
- ❖ Public Broadcasting Act establishes the Corporation for Public Broadcasting (PBS)
- ❖ Race riots erupt in 127 U.S. cities, some lasting several days
- ❖ The National Organization for Women (NOW) is formed and holds its first national conference
- ❖ The world's first heart transplant is performed in Cape Town, South Africa, by Christiaan Barnard; the patient lives 18 days

Baby Steps
April 22, 1967

Suggested listening:
Album—Revolver, UK Release, The Beatles

It's my first real babysitting job, real in that it's not for free. Her name is Miss Woods, which confuses me because she has two kids, which would make her a Mrs. even if she's divorced. She wants me to call her Barbara, but I just can't—it wouldn't be right to call an adult by her first name, even if she asks you to. A friend of Muzzie's at work recommended me to Miss Woods. She seems nice; but both her kids are babies and I haven't really taken care of many babies.

Kelly and Christopher are already fed and put down, so they shouldn't give you any trouble, Miss Woods tells me as she's putting on a colorful-waist length jacket that matches her paisley-print skirt. If Kelly wakes up she can have a glass of warm milk and one cookie. Make sure she eats it and doesn't just hide it under her pillow. Christopher might wake up for changing. You've changed diapers before, so that shouldn't be a problem.

Sure. Lots. I'm not completely lying, I tell myself. I did change diapers before the McNary's two-year-old got potty trained.

There's a bottle on the table next to the crib if he's hungry. Everything else you need's in their room. Food's in the fridge. Help yourself to anything, watch TV, listen to some music, do whatever you like. Miss Woods smiles at me and adds, The place is yours. I'll be back around ten.

She flies out the front door, then pops back in. Forgot my purse, she tells me and grabs a small sparkly clutch off the narrow table next to the door. Bye-bye.

I wait a minute to make sure she's really gone.

The old house is silent, but I can hear cars zipping by on Covina Boulevard and people talking to each other as they walk past on the sidewalk. I tiptoe into the kids' room. The little girl looks like a china doll, her almost white hair curling around her little face, her cheeks rosy and chubby, her thumb just outside her puckered lips. Her little brother is so tiny, three months old, Miss Woods told me. I've never seen anything so small. His hair looks black, but there's so little of it you can see right through to his head. They're lying at opposite ends of the same crib, with matching blankets and jammies.

I hope they don't wake up.

I pull the door mostly closed and go to the kitchen. There's a bucket of Kentucky Fried Chicken, open cans of peaches, chili, and something with the label missing, a gallon of milk, and a whole shelf of beer in the fridge. There's a box of donuts on the counter along with an open bag of potato chips. I start with a donut.

The house smells funny, like a wet dog or something, but Miss Woods doesn't have a dog. I wander into the living room and stand looking at the TV. I'm only allowed an hour a day on weekends and I watched cartoons this morning. I wonder if it counts if I'm not at home, decide it would still have to count.

I wander over to the stereo and flip through Miss Woods's albums. They're arranged by bands and still have their plastic covers on. I find the Beatles and flip to one I've never seen before: *Revolver.* I'm disappointed—was sure Muzzie had bought me all their albums.

The cover is strange, black and white drawings, like in art class, with people and things coming out of the Beatles' heads. I love the Beatles—I even went to the movie theatre and saw a closed-circuit broadcast of one their concerts. I screamed myself hoarse and nearly fainted, along with Sylvia, when Paul shook his head real fast during *I Want to Hold your Hand.*

I really love the Beatles. Thinking about them makes me miss Shirley even more. We used to listen to all their 45s on our little record player, tucked away in our bedroom. It was just me and Shirley, and John, Paul, George, and Ringo. Now it's only me. Shirley took the record player with her and I haven't saved enough from my allowance to buy my own.

I take the album out of the stack, tip the cover and let the LP slide out, like Shirley taught me. It slips past my fingers and bounces a couple of times on the shaggy rug.

I scoop it up and dust it off with my shirt-sleeve, and put Side One up on the tall spindle. I wait for the stereo to warm up then push the lever to "play." The turntable spins, the album drops, the needle levitates before it drifts over and drops on the outer loop of the album.

A man counts, *One, two, three, a four.* I don't even recognize the voice. I look at the album cover. It says The Beatles. Someone coughs while the man counts and the drums start up fast. They're all singing about taxes, the guitars are squealing, and George sounds mad at someone. I turn the volume down and just stand there watching the album go round and round; not sure what I'm hearing. Then there're violins and a big orchestra that sounds like something my dad and Muzzie listen to. I look at the cover again. This can't be my Beatles. Then I hear the words, *All the lonely people, where do they all come from. All the lonely people where do they all belong.*

I step away from the stereo and sit down on the couch; ignore the donut on the table. I realize I care about Eleanor Rigby even though I don't know her; that I'm sad no one came to her funeral—wish my Beatles had never made this song. Before I know it the violins are gone and my Beatles are back with a love song. But *All the Lonely People* keeps circling in my head and I don't want to think that I'm one of them—but I know I am.

The next song has me running to the stereo. A high-pitched twanging jumps out and I feel like someone's running their fingers down a chalk board. I snatch the needle off the album, scratching a deep groove. I turn everything off and stuff the album back in the jacket and re-file it at the back of the Beatles group, not knowing how they could change so much since I last heard them on the radio.

Someone gives a little cry. I look at the bedroom door hoping this new kind of Beatles didn't wake the kids. Another whimper, I hurry into the room. Kelly is standing up, hanging on to the wood railing. She takes one look at me and bursts out crying. Christopher snaps awake and joins in.

It's okay, I tell them. I'm supposed to be here. You're mommy asked me to take care of you. I walk over and brush back Kelly's hair. She slaps at my hand and cries even louder, adding Mama, Mama between sobs. Christopher is simply screaming. I don't know which one to pick up first. Settle on Christopher because he can't slap me.

I cradle his head and slip my hand under his bottom. It's soaking wet. I lift him out of the crib and then start looking for the diapers, cooing to the little thing; trying to get him to stop crying. I flip on the room light with my elbow and see a waist-high table with rails against the far wall. The baby stops crying and grabs two big chunks of my hair with his pudgy little hands.

What a strong little boy, I tell him and hope he doesn't yank any harder. He giggles and kicks his legs.

By the time we make it to the table I'm almost ready to cry. Kelly is hiccoughing between cries for her mama and I set Christopher down too hard and he lets out a frenzied scream and starts crying again.

Please, please. Please please please, I beg him. Shush, shush, it's okay, it's okay. Christopher quiets. Kelly plops back down in the crib whimpering, but at least she's not crying anymore. We'll get you changed, little boy, and then get the big girl a cookie, I say over my shoulder, with one hand pressing Christopher against the table top.

Oook? Kelly asks me through the bars on her crib.

Cookie, I tell her very slowly.

Oookee, she answers.

What a smart girl you are, I tell her, really amazed that such a little girl can understand what I'm saying. You get a cookie just as soon as I get your little brother changed.

Oooookkkeeeeee! Kelly screams and climbs back up hanging onto the railing. That starts Christopher crying again. I can't believe anything this small can make so much noise. I pat his tummy with one hand, opening the drawers under the table with the other. I finally find clean diapers, but they aren't folded right. They're in squares. Even I know they have to be in triangles, very tiny triangles for such a little baby. I feel tears coming on.

You can do this, I tell myself. Just think. Doesn't matter how small he is, diapers work the same. Just don't bang his head on the table again. I look over and make sure Kelly isn't able to climb out of the crib and blow kisses at her. She giggles and bounces on her little legs.

I take off Christopher's diaper and shrink back at the greenish gunk. The baby laughs and gurgles and Kelly starts shouting Oooookkkeee, Oookkkeeeeee.

Diaper changed, hands washed, twice, cookie eaten and warm milk drunk—everyone tucked in and I'm back on the couch. I look at the TV and decide I deserve to watch a little extra. I turn the knob on the console, make sure the sound is turned way down, and throw myself on the couch, more tired than I thought I could ever be.

Mama! Mama!

Please, no! I climb off the couch, turn the TV off, and peek in the room. Kelly is bouncing up and down, pushing against the rails and moving sideways, getting closer to a sleeping Christopher with every bounce. I dash across the room.

I'm too late. She lands on Christopher's leg. It all starts again and I don't know what to do anymore. I can't hold them both. I can't get Kelly to lie down and I can't get Christopher to stop crying no matter how many times I tell him he's a good boy, no matter how good I rub his tummy and pat Kelly on the head.

They hate me.

I look at the clock—eight o'clock—I'll never survive until ten. Tears well up, spill over and run down my cheek. Kelly reaches out and touches the tears. She puckers her little mouth and stops crying, looking at me like she's a real person.

No saaaa, she tells me and touches another tear. Christopher quiets at the sound of Kelly's voice.

I sniff back the tears and tell Kelly, No. No sad. It's all okay, little Kelly. No sad.

She giggles and bounces once. I catch her before she lands on her brother.

Now go to sleep, I tell her and tuck her in at the other end of the crib. I pick up a rabbit, a mouse, two bears, and a kangaroo off the floor and tuck them all in with her. She drags the rabbit under her blanket, sticks her thumb in her mouth and falls instantly to sleep. Christopher gurgles and reaches for me. I find another bear, almost as big as he is and tuck it next to him. He tries to keep his eyes open but can't; falls asleep sucking the bear's floppy ear.

I'm saved. I chance a kiss on Christopher's forehead. He sucks on the ear a little harder. I tiptoe out of the room and don't even think of turning on the TV. I sit on the couch and listen to the traffic splashing water out of puddles; realize it must have started to rain since I got here. I curl up on the couch and hope everyone stays asleep for just a little while.

Someone's gently rocking me. I think it must be Muzzie.

Donna. Wake up, sweetie.

I open my eyes. It takes me a minute to focus on the beautiful blonde woman leaning over me. Her hair is piled high on top of her head with sparkling berets and hairpins holding the big curls and swirls. Her eyes are outlined in black with long curled eyelashes and bright blue eye shadow.

I jump off the couch, realizing its Miss Woods—that I'm asleep on the job.

Hey, hey. It's okay. Really. She pats my arm and sits me down with her on the couch. Guess they weren't too much trouble, she says, nodding towards the bedroom.

No. None at all, I lie and try to hide a big yawn.

Miss Wood laughs and pats my leg. Well, I'm glad they didn't give you a hard time. Sorry I'm late. She gets up and walks into the kitchen. That's five hours as I make it, she says and I hear the fridge open; hear the top of a beer being popped; only then notice a man in an overcoat standing next to the front door.

Oh. Uh. I look at the clock, it's quarter to eleven. Not quite five, I say.

She walks back into the living room and hands the beer to the man. This is Michael, she tells me. And this is Donna, she tells him. He smiles and nods to me and tips the bottle way back. I look away, wishing Miss Woods had told me his real name—hoping she doesn't want me to call him Michael.

He'll drive you home.

I look back at the man. He smiles and says, Ready? He downs the rest of the beer and hands the bottle back to Miss Woods.

Sure, I say and look around for my sweater.

Here it is, sweetie. Miss Woods holds out my thick sweater. You're gonna need it, she adds. It's raining cats and dogs out there.

I take the sweater and thank her, then just stand there, not knowing how to ask her for my money.

Oh shi … I mean … sorry … I forgot to pay you. Hold on a minute. She grabs her little sparkly purse and digs in it for a minute. You got a few bucks, Mick? I'm short.

Sure. Here. Let me get her. The man pulls a silver money clip, like my dad's, out of his pants pocket and flips through twenty-dollar bills until he gets to the ones. How much? he asks.

Four, Miss Woods tells him. I start to tell her it's only two-fifty, but she winks at me and wobbles her head for me to keep quiet. He whips four dollars out of the clip and hands it to Miss Woods.

She passes it over to me. There you go.

Thank you, I whisper, not sure if I should take more money than I earned.

You are more than welcome, my fine, fine little babysitter, Miss Woods says. Why, not a child stirring and the house all tidy. You earned every penny. She kisses the top of my head. Next Saturday? Same time? she asks.

I nod and walk under the man's arm that's holding open the door—wish I could count all four dollars right then and there, but know that would be rude.

I spend the short ride home figuring out how many more Saturdays I'll need to baby sit before I can buy my own record player.

Summertime Blues
June – July 1967

Suggested listening:
Single—*I'll Give You a Stone if You'll Throw It*, Janis Ian

I graduate Junior High with honors. Muzzie gives me a string of real pearls. Dad congratulates me and tells me I'm all grown up now; he has tears in his eyes as he hands me twenty dollars and tells me I can spend it on whatever I like.

Now there's nothing for me to do—no summer school, no homework, nobody to talk to. Sylvia's gone to stay with her Uncle, who's not really her Uncle, way out in Altadena. She won't be home all summer. Muzzie started drinking again a month or so ago, so I can't even talk with her during the day; and every night she and Dad fight. We don't even have Girls' Night Out anymore on Fridays because Dad won't let her drive, except to go to work—but she doesn't work very often.

I lie in my room and wish I were anywhere else; wonder if the folks would send me to stay with Shirley for the summer. Dad doesn't even think about it before he says *No!* I go back to my room and throw myself on the bed and am so lonesome I can't even cry.

Then the fight starts. Muzzie tells Dad he should let me go see Shirley. Dad slams something down and starts yelling that they don't even know where the hell Shirley is anymore. That the last they heard from Jack, Mr. McAdams, she was living in some dive in Haight-Ashbury with a pack of hippies. Probably stoned all the time and screwing anyone that comes along. Muzzie starts to protest and Dad screams, Why shouldn't she? She's just like her tramp of a mother, isn't she! Muzzie spits something back at him and I plug my ears.

All I can think of is that Shirley is living in Haight-Ashbury. That means she's with friends, with all those beautiful women dancing, spinning bottles whenever she wants to kiss a guy, never having to listen to fights because everyone in Haight-Ashbury is into love. I hope they never find her.

The fight's over. I scoot up on the bed, lean back against the wall and pull my book out from under the pillow. *Rosemary's Baby*—I had to tell the librarian it was for my mother before she'd let me check it out. Said it wasn't appropriate for someone my age. I promised her I wouldn't even open the book. I read the first chapter sitting at the A&W root beer stand next to the library.

I flip to my place—happy I don't live in a haunted apartment building with weird people who are in league with the devil. Living here is bad enough.

I wake up before dawn, I'm completely dressed and my reading light is still on. No one came in to check on me. That means the fight was real bad, that Muzzie is passed out and Dad is gone. I wonder where he goes; wonder who he knows that lets him spend the night; wonder if he yells at them too.

I creep across the hall to the bathroom. I try to pee quietly, just in case someone is home. I quickly wash my hands and face. Something in the mirror stops me. I rarely look in the mirror, never like what I see. But this time I look different. I reach up and touch the ends of my hair. It's below my shoulders now. When did it grow? I remember it being short and stringy. I pick up a comb and run it through my hair. It shines, little glints of red inside the brown—just like Muzzie's.

The front door slams. I drop the comb and sneak back into my room, dive under the covers. The bedroom door squeaks open and I know Dad's standing there, watching me. The door closes and I know he won't come back until ten o'clock. I get to sleep until then when I'm not in school, but no later.

Late in the day, Muzzie comes out of her room. I've already finished all my chores and am reading in the living room. Dad went out without saying anything, so the house is quiet.

Muzzie sits next to me on the couch and pats my leg. Your dad and I had a long talk last night.

I don't believe she can call what I heard a "talk." But, I close my book anyway and look over at her. Her eyes are all puffy and her hair and skin look dull and lifeless. I wish she'd just pack us up and leave. Lots of kids have just one parent now days. I don't care if we don't have much money. Anything would be better than her getting yelled at all the time, let alone when Dad hits her.

She pats my leg again and smiles. We decided it would be best if Shirley comes back home. Would you like that?

I can't believe what she's saying. You mean come home here … to stay?

Yes. To stay.

I drop my book on the floor and hug and kiss her over and over again. She hugs me tight against her. I thought that would make you happy, she says, sniffing back tears.

Can we have Girls' Night Out again and take Shirley with us?

Muzzie kisses the top of my head and tells me the three of us will have the best Girls' Night Out ever, as soon as Shirley's back home.

And I know everything will be okay—better than okay, now that Shirley's coming home.

Summer of Love
July 1967

Suggested listening:
Single—*San Francisco*, Scott McKenzie
Album—The Grateful Dead, The Grateful Dead

The song *San Francisco* comes out before I graduate junior high and the radio can't play it enough for me. It's a call to everyone under thirty, and my sister's living there, in San Francisco, the summer of 1967—The Summer of Love. The singer tells us to wear flowers in our hair. Nobody was wearing flowers when I was there a year and a half ago. But that doesn't matter; I just know they're wearing them now.

I had hoped I could go stay with Shirley, but now the folks are planning to bring her home. Every time the radio plays *San Francisco* I almost cry. I have to get back there before Shirley comes home for good.

But how?

I don't like the idea of her riding down alone, my dad tells Mr. McAdams. They've been talking on the phone for a really long time, right in the middle of the day when rates are the highest.

We couldn't even be sure she'd stay on the bus. But I can't take any time off and I wouldn't ask you to drive her down. OK. Thanks Jack. We'll come up with something. Yep. Goodbye. My dad hangs up the phone and I dash back down the hallway and hop on my bed, my heart racing.

That's it! I tell myself. But how do I convince dad I'm the solution to his problem? I get up and go into the big bathroom; dare to look in the mirror.

If you're going to San Francisco, be sure to wear some flowers in your hair, I softly sing to myself and pull my hair out of the rubber band and part it down the middle. It's well below my shoulders now and perfectly straight, except for a ridge left over from the rubber band.

I close my eyes and imagine myself decked out in flowers, a big crown of daisies, with small yellow roses tucked behind each ear and a string of violet pansies around my neck.

Don't let losing all that weight go to your head. My dad's voice breaks the spell.

I whip around and find him standing in the bathroom door, smiling. I know I closed it and feel my face heat up I'm so mad he'd open it without knocking first.

I ... I was checking for pimples, I stammer.

Naw. You have beautiful skin, just like your mom used to.

I can't believe he's being so nice; wonder why. We both just kinda stand there, not saying anything for a minute and I know it's now or never. Dad? I start and his smile fades. I was kinda wondering ...

Speak up, Punk. No point mumblin'.

I was wondering, I say really loud so he can hear. I really liked taking the bus trip last year ... and ... and ... I was thinking that with Shirley coming home ... she ...

Spit it out for Christ's sake, my dad tells me and takes a step towards me.

Could I go up to Napa and help Shirley move back home and we could ride the bus back together and it would be so great if we could and I'm not in school so I don't have any homework and I'd do all my chores before I leave and double chores when we get back. It all comes pouring out. I only stop 'cause I have to take a breath. Then I hold it, squint my eyes almost closed waiting for him to explode.

But he laughs. Laughs—right there in the bathroom door and I don't know what to think. I'll have to talk to your mother, but you might just have solved a little problem, Punk.

I let out a big breath and actually smile at him, see his eyes water up like they do whenever they play the National Anthem on TV at the beginning of a ball game. I hate it when he starts to cry and honks his nose in his handkerchief. But this time he just sniffs and smiles at me and says, My little Punk is growing up, and walks away.

I remember to take a book this time and am so glad I did. The trip takes forever and the old women the bus driver sticks me with set down so many rules I can't possibly follow them all. I try to ignore them and their stinky perfume. I take extra-long in the bathroom just to be alone for a few minutes.

After breakfast in San Jose I drift off to sleep and wake up just as we're pulling into the bus station. I can't believe I missed seeing the city at dawn. Wish I'd seen it all pale and shiny like it was the first time. Dad is making us come home tomorrow morning, so today will be my only chance to see San Francisco again—probably for my whole life.

I brush past the driver, hop down the steps and run straight to Shirley, who's wearing a bright orange and red mini-skirt and fringed moccasins that come up to her knees. She has to be the coolest sister in the whole world.

Hey! Look at you, she says and twirls me around. Good god, you're almost as tall as me and almost as skinny. Shit, how much weight you lost?

I feel myself blush and tuck in my shirt and straighten the collar. All together? I ask.

She nods and taps a cigarette outta the pack and lights it.

Sixty-five pounds.

She coughs and a big cloud of smoke billows out of her mouth. Sixty-five? That's a lot. Wow, groovy. She looks me up and down and adds, We have to get you some cool clothes.

I don't have any money, I tell her, wishing I'd gone shopping with Muzzie before the trip. All my clothes are too big for me and I have to pull the belts really tight to keep my pants up, and the blouses are all baggy and too long to tuck in very well.

Who needs money, she laughs. Money is square. She juts her chin toward the bus. Better grab your shit from the Man before he calls the cops.

I turn and see the bus driver holding my overnight case, tapping his foot. I almost skip back over to the bus. That's my sister, I tell him. Thank you for bringing me here.

His eyes narrow. Your dad know she's like that? he asks.

Like what? I turn back and look at Shirley who's blowing smoke rings and looking all tough with one hip cocked up. I know my dad doesn't know she's changed this much. But I'm not telling the bus driver that. Sure, I say. She's coming back home with me tomorrow.

He bends over a little to look me in the eyes. You watch out for yourself. There's a bad group in town. You seem like a nice kid. You're lucky to have a dad that cares so much about you. He hands me my bag.

He says something else, but I'm not listening. If he thinks my dad cares about me, he's out of his mind. I look over at Shirley and know she's the only one who really loves me. I say goodbye and walk away from the bus and its driver. Shirley drapes an arm around my shoulder and tells me today is gonna be the best day of my life

We stash my bag in a locker. Shirley tucks the key into her moccasin and steps back and looks at me again. First, let's get you some new rags, she says and pulls me by the arm out of the bus station.

We walk along the main street for a long way and then cut through a few alleys that stink of pee and beer. After what seems like forever, Shirley stops and points to a street sign that reads Haight Street. The Promised Land, she announces and takes my hand. I almost run to the corner, pulling Shirley along. I swing around the corner, but there's nothing there, no hippies, no music, no flowers; just a bunch of run down old houses and bums asleep on the sidewalk.

Where's everyone? I ask, almost ready to cry I'm so tired and thirsty.

She lightly smacks the back of my head and tells me, We still have a ways to go. But at least we're getting close, and takes off down the street.

I would have preferred a Double Cola, but the cold beer is better than nothing. The foam makes my nose tickle. I sneeze and everyone in the quiet room looks at me. One guy smiles and gives me the peace sign. I chug the beer and tuck my feet under my crossed legs and lean back against the wall. I wish the cut-off jeans we got from the Free Store weren't quite so cut-off; it's almost like wearing a bathing suit, especially with the paisley halter top. Shirley said they were definitely groovy. I wouldn't let her leave my old clothes at the store like we were supposed to do, because I definitely can't wear these shorts on the bus ride home, let alone back in Covina.

The guy who smiled at me picks up a guitar and starts strumming a slow song real quiet. Kids settle back into each other's arms and drift off again. Shirley puts an arm around my shoulder and pulls me against her. I unfold my legs and curl up with my head on her lap and think she was right; this is the best day of my life.

It's noon when we wake up. The room's almost empty, my head aches, and my mouth tastes like a toilet. Shirley pushes me off her legs and stretches like our cat Patches used to do before he ran away.

I need to use the restroom, I whisper.

At the end of the hall, she tells me, then adds, Call it the head.

What?

The bathroom, call it the head.

I nod and climb to my feet. I don't dare look at myself in the mirror. I squat over the toilet, remembering that Muzzie always tells me to never sit on a public toilet seat, and even if this is a house, I don't know who's sat on it before me. I wash my hands, rinse out my mouth, and splash my face. There's no glass so I hold my hair back and put my mouth under the faucet.

There's a knock at the door. I open it and the guitar player brushes past. His hand curves around my waist and across my stomach. I giggle and try to get out the door, but he turns me around and leans in close. There isn't a bottle being spun, but I don't care. I let him kiss me, then spin around and duck out the door, closing it behind me.

Hey, be cool now, chickie, he says through the closed door. I almost go back in, but know I shouldn't.

Shirley's standing at the end of the hall, watching me; and I know she knows about the guitar player. I feel myself blush all over and wish I were wearing more clothes than I am. She doesn't say anything, just drapes an arm over my shoulder and heads us toward the front door.

Let's grab some grub and head to the park, she says and leans over a little to look at me.

I nod but can't meet her eyes. I have some money, I tell her.

Stop with all the money bullshit! I told you, money is square. We don't need the Man's money. She stops on the bottom step and faces up the street. All we need is love! she yells and takes off running.

The park is bigger than I remember. We stop and talk with all kinds of hippies; Shirley calls them Freaks, says hippie is the Man's word for us—actually says us—and I feel like I belong. She doesn't offer me any pot and shakes her head no to a guy with hair down to his butt who pops a small white pill in her mouth, then looks at me.

I tug on her long floppy sleeve when he leaves. What was that? I ask.

Nothing for you.

I know but what was it?

Acid. She stops and looks at me. We're almost eye level and I realize I must have grown a whole bunch in the last year. Don't take anything from anybody! You hear me. She grabs my arm and shakes me a little.

I shrug away, rubbing my arm. Sure. I'm cool. I don't want anything anyway, I tell her.

The band is like nothing I've ever heard before. Going on and on and on, until it seems the whole day has to have passed and they're still playing the same song. But when it ends, there's still more of the day and more songs. It's like time stops when the Grateful Dead is playing and I wonder if that's what death is like—going on and on without time ever really moving.

Shirley never stops dancing, even when there's no music, her long thick hair flying, her arms floating like snakes suspended in air. Other freaks dance all around her and I keep stepping back and back until I can't see her anymore for all the people dancing. But for once in my life, I'm not afraid. I know she'll find me and that I'm safe surrounded by people I don't even know.

The waitress almost doesn't let us in the door, but I tear up and she says okay, but makes me show her my money first. I hold out three dollars and she tells us to sit in the back so people walking by don't see us. I grab Shirley by the arm and lead her to a table back by the kitchen. She follows along behind me, smiling and blowing kisses to nobody in particular.

I'm not as happy as she is. It's been dark for a while, so I know it has to be late. We were supposed to be on the six o'clock bus to Napa, but I don't have a clue where we are or how to get to the bus station. Every time I ask Shirley, she kisses me and tells me everything is groovy or cool or trippy or something and never tells me how to get back to the bus station.

I figure we need to eat before the bus ride back to Napa and so tell Shirley I'm starving. It's the only way I can get her in this place. I just hope she doesn't give the waitress a hard time or we might just get kicked out before I figure out how to get us to the bus station.

There's no time to change clothes before the last bus to Napa leaves the station. I hand the driver our tickets and steer Shirley to the back of the bus and shove her into a seat next to the window so she can't dance up and down the aisles like she did in the coffee shop.

Way cool ... She swings her head away from the window and tries to focus on my face. I can tell she can't. All the little people ... She swings back to the window, jabs a finger against the glass and taps it really fast. They're so little, she says and swings her head back around and looks at me. Why are they so small and I'm so big?

I close my eyes and am too tired to cry; don't know how we'll get past the McAdams without them knowing Shirley's stoned.

Sweet baby Jane, she coos and kisses my closed eyes. Sweet, sweet baby Jane.

I feel something smack against me and open my eyes. Shirley's head's on my shoulder; a tangled mass of hair covering her face. I say a little prayer of thanks and hope she wakes up when we get to Napa. Trust that after everything Mr. and Mrs. McAdams have gone through they'll make sure we get on the bus at seven in the morning even if they have to carry Shirley to the bus and put her in a seat.

Mr. and Mrs. McAdams take us to the bus station in the morning and give me ten dollars for the ride home. Shirley doesn't say anything the whole time. I say too much, trying to make it all right—Shirley running away from them, us showing up five hours late with Shirley so stoned they had to pick us up at the bus station even though it was only a few blocks away. I feel sorry for them. They took care of

Shirley when she had no place to go and now she won't even say goodbye.

She climbs on the bus without looking back and finds a seat on the far side. Mrs. McAdams gives me a quick kiss on the cheek and tells me to make sure Shirley eats something when we stop in San Jose. She looks over at Mr. McAdams and back, then adds, Make sure you stay with her at the bus stations. Don't let her wander off, now.

I wonder why she thinks Shirley would wander off. I put on my biggest smile and tell her I'll take care of my big sister. I can't think of anything else to say and so tell them I should get on so I can find a good seat. They don't mention that Shirley's already saved our seats and I realize they're just as anxious for us to leave as I am to get back to Covina—something I never thought I'd want to do.

High Times
Late August 1967

Suggested listening:
Album—Sound of Silence, Simon & Garfunkel

The dress is new, a pretty red paisley with a high scalloped neck, long sleeves with slightly ruffled cuffs and an empire waist. I can't believe it's a size six, that I've lost fifty pounds and grown almost two inches in just the last year; that it's Freshman Orientation Day; that I'm about to start high school.

Muzzie drops me off in front of Charter Oak High. Kids are everywhere, walking in doubles, small groups, chatting, laughing. I don't recognize any of them from junior high, but then I didn't really know many kids when I was at Cedargrove—only Sylvia, who was my best friend, and Debbie Morris, who was my worst nightmare.

Debbie Morris is tall and blonde and "built," according to Sylvia. She's a bully, according to Muzzie. Either way, she's made my school life hell since sixth grade. *Fatty, fatty two by four, can't get through the bathroom door*—her standard taunt. When we moved to the junior high side of Cedargrove, she started shoving me. In eighth grade she cornered me whenever she could and slapped me and knocked me down. Once she even kicked me. She never got caught, always had a group of girls that followed her around, covered up for her, did whatever she said.

I know she'll be here today. I feel like I might throw up and turn to run back to the car, but Muzzie has already driven away and I'm left alone to face Debbie Morris.

I keep looking at my registration card as I inch my way closer to the office window. I'm only five kids away from the window when someone cuts in front of me, then someone else, then someone else. I want to push them out of line, tell them to wait their turn. I shoot daggers at the back of their heads and try to think of something to say. I stare at the clump of blonde hair bobbing back and forth and suddenly realize it has to be Debbie Morris; she always wears her hair in a high ponytail anchored at the crown of her head. I look back at my registration card and hope she doesn't turn around.

Hey. Hey. Is that you? I try to ignore the girl who's stopped next to me. I'm only three away from the window. I just want to get this over with and go home before I really throw up.

It is you. Wow! You look so different. What happened? Debbie, look, it's Conrad.

My eyes snap up and see Debbie turn from the window. She looks around and asks, Where?

Here, the short blonde next to me tells her.

Debbie looks me up and down and says, No it's not. The woman stamps her registration card and she walks away from the window. I move a step.

Is, too. The girl leans in front of me and looks up at my face. It's you. What's it? What's it? She snaps her fingers and announces, Donna. Donna Conrad!

I want to run, but I'm next in line. Debbie stops next to the first girl and looks at me. So she got skinny and tall. She's still trash, Debbie says just loud enough so we can hear but the woman in the office can't. She leans in close and whispers, I'll kick your ass in high school just like I did in junior high, only worse. She turns and walks away, slapping the other girl on the arm. Come on, Kathy.

Go on, Kathy tells her. I'll catch up.

She's a piece of trash.

Yeah, well … go on, I'll catch up.

I slide my card into the metal tray under the window. The woman looks through a stack of long, narrow cards and pulls one out. You're assigned to the Gymnasium, she tells me and slides the schedule card back through the tray.

I stand there not knowing what to do. If I leave I have to face Kathy and most likely Debbie Morris. Go on, over there. The woman points behind me. I don't move. Next in line! she calls out and I'm shoved aside.

Hey, it's cool, Kathy says.

I chance a look at her. I recognize her freckled face and remember her always standing outside the ring of girls when Debbie picked a fight. I remember her trying to talk to me during P.E. in eighth grade, but I was too afraid to talk with her, thought she would tease me and set me up for Debbie Morris.

I nod and walk around her.

Hey, I'm sorry for all those times I didn't do anything.

I stop but don't turn around.

I'm going to the Gym, too. Wanna walk together?

I look at Debbie Morris waiting with a hand on her hip half-way to the Gym. What about her? I ask.

She's a bitch, Kathy says flatly. Your dress is totally groovy, she adds with enthusiasm. And I like your hair long.

I don't say anything, study my shiny black shoes—hope she'll go away.

She doesn't.

Kathy follows me home to meet Shirley.

She lived in Haight-Ashbury? How groovy! Kathy digs in her purse and pulls out a pack of Pall Malls and stops to light up. There's a breeze so it takes her four matches. Want one, she offers. I nod. She hands me the longest cigarette I've ever seen. I wonder how anyone could smoke the whole thing and decide to pass. She shrugs and tucks it back in the pack and we start up again, walking the long way to avoid crossing the Junior High field.

Shirley's in our room listening to Simon & Garfunkel. Her hair is to her waist now, a thick, brown blanket. I wish my hair were thick.

You're back early. How'd it go? Shirley asks. She looks from me to Kathy and back to me.

Oh, uh, this is Kathy, I tell her.

Kathy almost jumps across the narrow space between the door and our double bed. Wow, you lived in Haight-Ashbury? she blurts out. That has to be the coolest thing ever!

Shirley smiles and nods. Yeah, real cool. She takes in the room with a glance and adds, But I'm back in Covina now, which is not cool at all.

Kathy flops down on the bed and curls her legs under her. What's it like? I mean, is it like on the news? You look so cool. I love your hair. She reaches out and strokes a long strand.

Shirley moves back a little on the bed and looks at me, ignoring Kathy. Why're you home so early? Didn't the seniors take you out?

I shake my head.

What assholes!

They're cheerleaders, Kathy says. They only take out other cheerleaders.

Fucking bitches! Shirley says, looking at Kathy. They're supposed to take you out someplace special today! What bitches.

Yeah. Kathy pulls out her cigarette pack. Can I smoke in here?

Fuck no! Shirley tells her. I'm not even eighteen and you're what, fourteen?

Yeah. So?

My purse slips out of my hand and smacks against the hardwood floor. They both look up at me, then back at each other.

Oh fuck it. Let's go over to Eric's, Shirley tells us and stands up. Fucking bitches, leaving you on your own. She throws an arm around my shoulder and kisses my cheek. Can't let my little Punk down.

Punk? Kathy squeals. I roll my eyes at Shirley and feel tears welling up.

Yeah, Blondie. You got a problem with it? Shirley drops her arm to her hip and looks all tough at Kathy.

Blondie? Blondie. I like it! Kathy smiles and flashes Shirley the peace sign.

Sandy's the fattest person I've ever seen. A lot fatter than I ever was. Her upper arms are bigger than my thighs when I was fat. Her butt and stomach hang down on her thighs. And her chins, more than just a double chin, cover her throat. When she laughs everything jiggles.

She's Shirley's best friend.

This is her, my baby sister, Shirley tells Sandy.

Sandy's dark green eyes look right into me and I find myself smiling. Hey there, Baby Girl, you're a real stunner, she tells me. My smile widens. Sure she's *your* sister? she asks Shirley.

Fuck you! Shirley says and opens a can of beer.

Sandy erupts in laughter and pulls me into a bear-hug. It's like diving into a featherbed, all soft and warm.

And you are? she asks Kathy, still clutching me.

Blondie! Kathy chirps with a big smile.

Well named. Very well named. Come on over here Blondie and get a hug. Sandy turns me loose and envelopes Kathy. I can hear a faint giggle from Kathy, whose face is buried in Sandy's ample bosom.

Shirley's boyfriend Eric walks into the living room with a baggy full of dried, dark green leaves. I've never seen loose pot before, but think this might be it. Shirley opens two more beers and tells Kathy and me to help ourselves.

A little smoke to go with the brew? Eric asks.

Not for these two, Shirley tells him and sits on the arm of the couch.

Why not? Eric asks.

They're fucking fourteen, dipshit!

If that's all then they shouldn't be drinking either, Sandy adds from the kitchen. Or smoking cigarettes.

I hide my cigarette behind my back. Kathy takes a big hit off her Pall Mall and blows a giant smoke ring.

That's different, Shirley protests.

How? both Eric and Sandy ask at the same time. Sandy busts out laughing and grabs both Kathy and me by our arms and walks us into the living room.

Now, here we have two fourteen-year-olds, Sandy says very seriously, like she's a news reporter. They are drinking alcohol, obviously *not* for the first time. However, if we're lucky, we might witness the first time they smoke marijuana, devil weed, the scourge of our times—witness their transformation from clean-living, all American teenagers into drug-crazed hooligans, hell-bent on living a life of depredation!

Oh give me a fucking break. She juts her chin at my sister. Get off your dad's high horse and let the girls have a little fun! You're starting to be a real bummer!

I look everywhere but at my sister. She doesn't say anything for a minute, then says, Shit. Go ahead. What the fuck. Why not?

Sandy is triumphant as she steers us over to the couch. Looks like we got us two young'uns to corrupt today, Eric, my man. Roll up a big one. Roll up a big fucking fat one for the virgins!

Down and Out
Early September 1967

Suggested listening:
Album—Farewell Angelina, Joan Baez

High school is horrifying. I've spent eight years waiting to be grown up. Dreamed of choosing my own classes and going to dances and having my very own locker where I keep my very own books—of being valedictorian—of proving to everyone that I'm someone special now that I'm not a kid anymore.

But it turns out that I'm just another kid; a kid with a big sister who caused the most trouble ever known at Charter Oak High School.

Conrad?

Here, I answer the teacher of my first class, the first day of my first year in high school.

The teacher looks over her glasses to find me. Conrad?

I nod and leave my hand in the air.

Are you related to Shirley Conrad?

I nod and answer, Yes, ma'am. Thinking how great it is that she remembers Shirley.

I don't want any trouble from you, Miss Conrad, she tells me. I drop my hand.

I'll be keeping my eye on you and I will not tolerate one misstep. But ... I ...

No back talk! she interrupts me. I will not put up with unruly behavior. Now be quiet or you'll be sent to the office.

I'm too stunned to pay attention to the teacher's orientation lecture and so don't know where to go when the bell rings. I stay at my desk as everyone rushes for the door. I follow at the back of the group, look at my class schedule, try to figure out where the D-wing is.

The morning only gets worse. It's like all my teachers are the same teacher, each one calling my name, asking about Shirley, issuing warnings, ignoring me even when I have the courage to raise my hand.

I don't know anyone in any of my classes. They're all really smart; at least as smart as me. They all know each other and slip notes across the narrow aisles when the teacher's back is turned. The guys are all wearing narrow ties and the girls have matching purses and shoes which all look brand new. My dress and shoes are new, but not new like theirs.

Muzzie shops at Robert Hall's. It's a yearly ritual, buying all my school clothes at one time in late August. I take my money from babysitting and my graduation money. I tell her I want the red, paisley dress.

You can only wear that once a week at the most, Punk, she tells me and holds up a cream colored blouse, a dark brown blouse and two plaid skirts. If we buy these four, and say a couple of sweaters, you can wear some combination all week long—and all of these cost less than that one dress.

I clutch the dress and won't put it back on the rack.

I understand, darling. But we can't afford it. She lowers her voice. I wish we could. It looked lovely on you, but ...

I can pay for it, I interrupt.

She reaches for the dress and I take a step back. If you want it that much we'll just make it work. Come on, it's okay. We'll make it work.

I have enough money saved, I tell her.

You can't spend your money on clothes!

It's okay. I want to. It's something special. You shouldn't have to spend your money on special stuff.

She looks away and I know she feels bad she can't buy me what I want.

Lemme try on those skirts. They look real cute, I tell her. She perks up and hands me the armload of practical clothes.

They're perfect, she says and pulls the drape across the dressing room. Thank god your feet didn't grow anymore; you can still wear last year's shoes. We'll need to get a good pair to go with your new dress, but that's all. Maybe next summer we can get you all new ones.

I zip the skirt, tuck in the blouse and really hate them.

How are they, Muzzie asks through the curtain.

They're perfect, I tell her and the big lump in my throat gets even bigger.

The whole first week is a nightmare. I try to behave, try to fit in. But, the teachers don't care at all and the other students care too much. I'm not one of them. The cheerleaders and pep squad girls make it very clear I'll never be one of them. During third period the pep squad leader passes me a note telling me if I answer one more question she'll beat the tar out of me. I crumple the note and try to swallow, but my mouth has gone dry.

Miss Conrad, what is that in your hand?

The pep squad girl is glaring at me and I know she'll beat me up even worse if I fink on her.

Nothing, I tell the teacher.

It looks like something to me.

I tuck the crumpled note in my purse and shake my head.

Show me what is in your purse, Miss Conrad.

I shake my head again and study my hands.

You leave me no choice, the teacher tells me and I hear paper ripping from a pad. Go to the office.

I stand up and watch my folded hands all the way to the desk.

I am very disappointed in you Miss Conrad, not even a week and you've already been sent to the office three times. I look up at her, surprised. How did she know about the other times? Oh, we talk, all the teachers. We are all very disappointed in you. But then it's only to be expected. She sighs and turns back to the blackboard.

I turn and walk blindly down the aisle. I trip on something and almost fall. The class erupts in laughter and I can't stop the tears from welling up.

Miss Conrad! None of your antics! Get to the office now!

I grab my books off the desk and hurry from the room. It's true; this will be my third time at the office and I don't understand why. It all seems so unfair and there's no one I know that can help. I can't tell Shirley; she'd feel terrible that she's the cause of all of this. I can't ever find Kathy between classes or at lunch. Muzzie's been drinking again and Dad is never an option. He'd tell me to keep my nose clean and try harder, then ground me for being sent to the office. He'd never understand that I'm trying as hard as I can—that they all hate me.

Just one more class and it's the weekend, the thought keeps me going. But all I want to do is skip sixth period. It's full of jocks and cheerleaders. I slam my locker closed and turn the combination lock; remember too late that my homework is in my other folder. The bell rings and everyone starts flocking to the winged buildings that run from the center quad area and make a semi-circle of brick and glass, with concrete sidewalks wide enough for three students to walk together side by side.

Someone shoves me against my locker and a bunch of girls burst out laughing. Better get a move on, Conrad, Debbie Morris calls back and I lean my head against the locker and try not to cry. She's everywhere, in three of my classes—in sixth period, even though she's not a cheerleader yet.

I dial the combination: 10-8-49, Shirley's birthday, and grab the right folder and slam the door just as the second bell rings. Late, just what I need. And of course sixth period is at the far end of the F building, the furthest room from my locker. I run down the hall hoping the teacher won't send me to the office.

The teacher doesn't even look around when I walk in. I slip into my seat at the back of the room and hope I finally got away with something.

Not a chance!

Thank you for joining us, Miss Conrad, he announces, still looking at the blackboard. I sink down in my seat. Debbie Morris and her friend snicker and the teacher turns around. Miss Morris! That is quite enough. One more sound and you'll get detention.

My mouth drops open. The teacher looks over at me and points to the blackboard. Miss Conrad, please come forward and work out this problem for us.

Me?

If you'd do us the honor. He bows slightly and taps the piece of chalk on his desk. Now, if you don't mind.

I jump up and knock my books off the desk.

Leave them, the teacher tells me. I'm sure Mr. Walters will pick them up for you.

I flush and know my face has to be bright red. James Walters is the captain of the wrestling team and the biggest jock of them all.

The answer is easy and I already know how to write well on a blackboard, from junior high. I show all my work in clear strong lines and step back from the board and study what I wrote. I think this is correct, I tell the teacher.

He smiles at me and says, Yes, I'm certain it is. Take your seat.

I walk down the aisle in a daze. I was right! The week just turned out to be great. There's a note on my seat, waiting for me. *Right after class, creep.* I look over at Debbie Morris. She points her finger at me and then draws it across her throat.

I can't keep my mind on the lesson and miss chances to answer questions the teacher throws out to the class. The bell rings way too soon for class to be over and I stay seated until everyone leaves.

That's it for this week, Miss Conrad, the teacher tells me. Good show today.

Thank you, I say and climb slowly to my feet. I know Debbie and her friends are waiting right outside the door. Know if I walk past them they'll just follow me home and catch me where no one can see. I take a deep breath, pile my books in my left hand and press them tight against my chest. If they're gonna hit me, I want a hand free.

The hall is clear by the time I leave the classroom, clear except for Debbie and two of her friends. I take another breath and close the door behind me.

I don't want any trouble, I tell them.

I bet you don't. Doesn't matter though 'cause you got trouble, Debbie says and grabs for my hair.

I don't jump away, like I usually do. I move in closer and stick my right fist in her stomach and push real hard, all at once, like Terry taught me. Debbie collapses around my fist and I pull it back out real fast. Debbie starts gulping air and I think she might faint or something. She looks up at me with a strange look on her face. She gasps and then throws up on her girlfriend's shiny white shoes.

I don't know what to do. Her friends just stand there, looking at me, ignoring Debbie, who throws up again. I push past them and walk real fast up the hall and turn the corner. No one follows me. I lean back against the wall and remember to breathe.

Hey! Where you been? Haven't seen you all week. Kathy stops in front of me, her hand on her hip, just like Debbie Morris. Hey, you okay? She leans in close. You don't look so good.

I just hit Debbie Morris, I whisper, afraid to say it too loud.

Where?

Down there, I point to the hallway.

Kathy takes off down the hall. I head the other way, not bothering to go back to my locker. I'm not home long enough to change my clothes when there's a knock on the door. I'm afraid it's Debbie Morris. I creep into the kitchen and drop to the floor. Crawl over to the sink and try to look out the window without being seen. My eyes clear the sink and there's Kathy, chewing gum and looking around the closed-in porch.

I drop back down and crawl out of the kitchen, stand up and brush down my blouse and skirt before opening the door.

Hey! Where'd you go? I came back looking for you, even went to your locker and you weren't anywhere. She smacks her gum, blows a small bubble, pops it and puts a hand on her hip, waiting for an answer.

I … came home.

Yeah. So I see. Can I come in?

Sure. I step back and Kathy walks in looking around like she's never been here before.

That was so cool. Where'd you learn to fight like that? You really flattened Debbie. She was still puking when I got there.

Did the teacher see her?

Yeah. He told her to go to nurse's office and have them call her mom to pick her up. Told her she shouldn't be in school if she's sick. We all cracked up, except Debbie.

Oh shit! She's gonna kill me now.

No way! Kathy says and walks into the kitchen and opens the fridge. Got anything good to eat?

Yeah, sure. Anything. Go ahead. But why won't she kill me?

Are you kidding? She's scared shitless. Nobody fights like that; no girl at least. All her friends are scared, too. Kathy pulls a package of lunchmeats out and kicks the door closed. Where's your bread?

I point to the roll-top bread box on the counter.

She'll keep clear of you now. She never loses a fight, but boy did she lose that one! You gotta teach me what you did!

I lean against the sink counter and can't believe I fought a girl, made her throw up, didn't get caught, and might even be tougher than Debbie Morris. I like it! Wish I'd listened to Terry all those years ago when I was in fifth grade.

What you smiling at? Kathy asks, and takes a bite of her sandwich.

I think I like being tough.

Yeah. It beats the hell outta being everyone's punching bag. Hey, I brought some reds. Want some?

What are reds?

God, you are so lame! Reds are downers. They're red so that's what you call 'um. I got 'um from my brother. I thought we could try 'um, you know, to celebrate getting through the first week of school and all. She reaches in her coat pocket and holds out a handful of bright red capsules with pale lettering.

Sure.

Groovy! Three for you, three for me.

My bedroom looks all lopsided. The walls aren't quite straight and the closet doors are definitely off their tracks. Kathy and I are lying on the bed, trying to read some comic books, but the pictures don't go with the words. We've read the same page three times, but neither of us can make sense out of the story.

Jughead needs to get laid, Kathy announces and sends the comic books flying off the bed. He's so weird. She rolls over and throws an arm across my stomach. There aren't any cute guys in any of my classes 'n I hate hanging out with my stupid brother's stupid friends all the time at home. They're so lame. All they talk about is music and cars and the girl's they're screwing. She flops back on her back and slides off the bed, hits the floor hard.

I crawl over and offer her a hand. She's lying flat on her back laughing so hard she's braying like a donkey. I start laughing too, though her falling out of bed shouldn't be funny. She takes my hand and yanks me down with her. We both snort and laugh and try not to crush each other as we roll on the floor.

What the hell are you doing? Shirley yells from the doorway. I roll off Kathy and try to stand up, trip over her and fall hard against Shirley, knock her back out the door and land on top of her in the hall.

She pushes me off and jumps to her feet. What the fuck are you on? Get the fuck back in the room before someone sees you!

I weave back into the room wondering who would see me. Dad won't be home for a couple of hours and Muzzie just left for the second part of her split shift. I try to say something but it all comes out at once, all jumbled up. My mouth feels funny and my tongue's fat and lazy.

What the fuck did you take? Shirley shouts.

Oh wow! You a pig or something? Kathy whines from the floor.

Shut the fuck up, Kathy. Shirley advances on me and I bump up against the bed and sit down hard. So?

Nothin'.

Nothing?

I shake my head. Nothin'.

Don't lie to me, you little shit. Shirley turns to Kathy and gives her a light nudge with her foot. Got any more?

Kathy digs in her pocket and then pouts and tells Shirley, Geesh, we took 'um all. But I can have my brother bring more over ... if you want.

Shirley rounds on me and I'm thinking, She can't tell me what to do. Who does she think she is? A pig? My mother? NO! I stand up fast and smack straight into her hand as she's raising it to point at me.

My face stings and I fall backwards onto the bed. I jump back up and bump straight into Shirley, who's leaning over trying to help me. As I slip off the bed I grab the nightstand and knock the lamp off on my way down.

What the fuck are you doing? Shirley screams.

I try to get up and something else falls off the end table.

Stay there! she shouts. For Christ's sake, you're gonna kill yourself. You two are in big trouble!

I've never seen her so mad.

What the fuck did you take! She demands.

Kathy stops laughing and slurs out, Jus' a few redz.

Reds? Shirley shouts. Are you crazy? Get your asses on the bed!

I don't understand why Shirley's so upset. Her boyfriend gave us pot and she was okay with that.

Kin't, I mumble.

I'm yanked off the floor and start swinging wildly. A hand slaps me across the face and I open my eyes wide and stare at her for a moment, not sure what just happened. I lean towards her, smile and try to kiss her. She looks so upset and I want her to be happy.

Stop it! Get in bed and stay there.

Sure! I flop next to Kathy, who's flat on her back, snoring loudly.

And don't go anywhere.

I start laughing at the thought of trying to even stand up, let alone go anywhere.

Issa deal, I mumble and fall back against the lovely soft pillow.

People are Strange
September 17, 1967

Suggested listening:
Album—The Doors, The Doors

Sunday night is family night at our house—once the summer re-runs are over and regular programming is resumed. Ed Sullivan is the show we always watch. We assemble in the living room; Muzzie on the couch, Dad in his overstuffed chair, Shirley and me sprawled on the floor with bowls of vanilla ice cream topped with hot fudge.

We actually feel like a family on Sunday nights.

Dad twists the knob on the television, waits for the tubes and speakers to start humming, and then adjusts the volume. We have the best color TV on the block, according to Dad. Inside a wood cabinet, with cloth panels hiding the speakers, the console sits proudly in the center of the far wall, with matching orange and green glass lamps hanging above either end from swag hooks in the ceiling.

This is our first family night since I started high school. Our first family night since I started smoking pot. The first family night that Shirley's been at since she was sent away a year and a half ago. It's a big family night for our family.

We all settle down when Mr. Sullivan walks out from between the stage walls. It's always going to be *a really big show*. We all smile and look over at each other whenever Mr. Sullivan says that. Shirley and I look at each other, surprised, when he announces The Doors will be performing. I start to ask if The Doors aren't the band we saw at the

Cheetah a couple of weeks ago. She frowns and shakes her head for me to shut up before I say too much.

I settle in to wait, not believing a band we saw here in Los Angeles is on the Ed Sullivan Show. We saw The Doors the Saturday after my freshman orientation; the Saturday after I first smoked pot at my sister's friend's house; the Saturday after Kathy and I became best friends.

I'd been to rock concerts before—only a month or so ago, my cousin and I went to a Herman and the Hermits concert. She embroidered her phone numbers inside a beret and I went right down to the front and tossed it on stage. But The Doors concert was different.

Even though it was three in the afternoon, the Cheetah Club was all dark, with swirling colored lights flashing behind the stage. And the singer—he was different than any one I'd seen before.

Ed Sullivan is introducing Yul Brenner. Muzzie sighs and I drift back to the concert in Santa Monica.

The singer is strutting up and down the stage, his leather pants so tight I can see his thing bulging. He's not really handsome, more pretty, like a girl with his wavy black hair all long and poofed out like a lion's mane. I look away, but Kathy tells me we have to get closer. She leads. I follow her all the way to the front. He's screaming into the mike, his eyes closed, the mike stand buried between his legs. Then he starts muttering something that sounds like poetry, but the words aren't clear, they're all disconnected and it sounds like he's just rambling.

The band behind him is so loud I can't hear myself think, the organ squealing, the guitar feedback whining along, and the drums pounding like a sick headache. I look up at the singer, he's clutching the mike in two hands and screaming at the top of his lungs about something I can't understand.

I want to go home, or at least outside.

The music blares even louder, the singer jumps high in the air, spins around, and lands on his knees, still holding the mike. The music cuts off and my ears are buzzing so loud the applause sounds all muffled. The singer doesn't bow or anything, just turns and leaves the stage.

Shirley slaps me on the arm. Wanna meet the band?

You're kidding? Kathy chirps. You know them?

Yeah. I used to go see them all the time up in Frisco. They played all the underground clubs.

Wow! Kathy's eyes are wide.

Come on. They're really cool dudes.

We trail behind Shirley out through the back door and around the side of the club. I stop dead in my tracks. The singer's sitting on the bumper of an old car kissing a girl in a psychedelic mini-skirt and thigh-high suede boots. He has his hand under her skirt—right there in front of everyone.

I turn around to leave. The singer says hi to my sister. I turn back around. Shirley's leaning on the bumper next to him, the girl in the mini-skirt on his other side kissing his neck.

So, can your man fix me up? We're leaving for the East Coast and I could use some good stash.

Sure. Whaddaya need? Shirley leans in closer, her hair falling over her shoulder. The singer picks up a handful and smells it.

I'll take some of that, he laughs and drapes an arm around Shirley.

She smiles and says, How much?

An ounce should be fine. And some crystal, not that powder shit he sold me last time.

How much?

Enough to last a week or so. But make sure he has the good stuff.

No problem. I'll give him a call. He'll have it here before your last show.

Groovy. The singer pulls Shirley in close and kisses her full on the lips, his other arm still around the mini-skirt chick.

I look away thinking what a jerk this guy is, all full of himself—like he's someone famous, not just some singer in a band doing an afternoon show in Santa Monica.

Hey, what's with the teeny-boppers?

My little sister and her friend, Shirley tells him. They wanted to meet you. Girls, this is Jim Morrison and The Doors, she tells us and we both nod at the singer and the other guys.

Yes, yes, yes. Fine young thangs, the singer grunts and detaches himself from the two older girls and takes a step towards us.

I back up; Kathy steps forward. I love your music, she coos. Really groovy.

Yeah, thanks, chickie, he tells her and looks around her at me. What's your problem, little love child?

I've forgotten about the psychedelic flowers painted on my face. I reach up and touch one and shake my head, but can't find my voice.

Nothing? he asks and looks over his shoulder at his band mates. Nothing wrong here, he tells them, then looks back at me. Then get your slinky ass over here, Little Miss Nothing.

I can't believe he's talking to me. Do I have a slinky ass? Do I have to do what he says? I look at Shirley, who's lighting a cigarette. She juts her chin towards Morrison and I take a step closer.

Yes, yes, yes. Now this is more what I like. Come on over here, darlin'. Come a little closer.

I take another step and try to pull my hip huggers up higher—they don't budge.

No, no. Don't change a thang. You look good enough to eat.

I stop and take a step backwards, feel tears well-up in my eyes.

Awww, now you gonna go ruin it all, he sighs and sits back on the car bumper. But ya gotta love the young thangs, all fresh and clean and innocent to the ways of the world ...

His voice gets all dreamy, like it was on stage. His words don't make any more sense out here than they did in there. He goes on and on about clouds and yellow skies and lizards and virgins and cold suns and withered rivers dried with bones. He's not even looking at us anymore, his eyes all glassy and unfocused.

I turn around and grab Kathy by the arm. No way! she tells me and pulls away. I'm staying.

I walk away and hear the singer almost crying, Stop the children! Stop the children fleeing the righteous kings of old ...

I turn the corner and wish I knew how to get back home on my own—don't want to wait around for Eric to bring whatever it is the singer wants—especially if it means I have to see him again.

Shirley and Kathy find me leaning against the wall in front of the Cheetah. Shirley calls Eric from the phone booth on the pier and talks in code. She hangs up and tells us Eric's meeting her at 5:30 at Muscle Beach, which is just down the beach a little ways from the Cheetah. We walk along the beach and just hang out, watching the weird people. We don't say much while we're eating burgers looking out over the sand at the waves and the surfers sitting on their boards just past the breakers.

Eric agrees to take Kathy and me home. Shirley stays for the late show and doesn't get home until one minute before midnight, her curfew. Dad's waiting. They don't say anything and I pretend to be asleep when she comes in the room. I don't know why I don't want to talk to her; but I don't. I don't want to remember the singer and his ranting; don't want to remember the day at all.

We wait through the entire hour-long show, through all the old songs and old performers, all the stupid jokes and long commercials. Refill our ice cream bowls and watch Dad scrape the glass on the inside of the aquarium with the long-handled razor blade during the commercials. Finally, just before the show is over, Ed Sullivan announces The Doors and the camera cuts to a colorful set—and there they are, the singer all shaggy and pouty, wearing the same black leather pants he wore at the Cheetah. He looks completely stoned, almost hanging on the mike stand and I wonder if he's on the stuff Shirley got for him. I don't dare look at Shirley, afraid I might give something away.

People are strange when you're a stranger, I haven't heard this song before and it really hits me that people *are* strange. I glance over my shoulder at Muzzie and Dad—think about all the teachers at school, most of the kids, definitely my folks—everyone I know is strange, everyone except Shirley and maybe Kathy. The singer's eyes are closed, his mouth so close to the microphone it looks like he's kissing it. He runs his tongue over his lips and I stop breathing. He looks much cuter than he did in Santa Monica. I look away, feeling all tingly inside and uncomfortable watching him in front of Muzzie and Dad.

I can hear all his words. They're so real and so deep. I look back at the TV. He's swaying and singing soft and clear—so unlike at the

Cheetah. He looks directly into the low camera, my heart skips a beat and I wish I'd stayed for the second show. I think about him saying I have a slinky ass—think I wouldn't walk away from those soft lips and dangerous hands, if I ever get a second chance.

They finish the song and the organ screeches out the beginning chords of *Light My Fire*. Shirley and I can't help but yelp and clap. Muzzie laughs. I don't look back at Dad, but know he's frowning again. He doesn't like long-hairs, let alone long-hairs who wear tight leather pants. Dad stands up and walks to the TV after the words, *girl we couldn't get much higher*. He keeps looking between the TV and us and I wish he would just sit down. I can't get into the music with him watching me.

When Morrison screams out *FIRE* he snaps the TV off and points at Shirley. I won't have this crap in my house. I don't care what you did in hippie-ville. You will not bring this drug-crazed music into *my* house.

Ed Sullivan's *your* friend, not mine! Shirley yells and jumps up off the floor. He's your good buddy. He's the one that had The Doors on his show. Talk to him about it. She takes off down the hall and slams the bedroom door. Dad is right behind her.

I crawl over to Muzzie and lay my head on her lap. She runs a hand down my hair, pats my shoulder. We don't say anything as Dad yells at Shirley to unlock the bedroom door. She doesn't so he screams through the locked door.

I don't want to hear what Dad's yelling about. Don't want to know about the men Shirley knew in San Francisco. Don't want to know why the McAdams made her leave their house. Don't want to know the terms under which she's allowed to live at home—but it doesn't matter what I want, even the neighbors can hear him yelling. We all know now.

Morrison's words come back to me and I wonder how he knows so much. I think about him on the TV, so different from everyone else, so wild, so full of fire—wonder if I could set the night on fire, set the whole fucking world on fire—decide right then that I should at least try, no matter how scary the world seems. Anything has got to be better than always being afraid.

Hall of Justice
September 1967

Suggested listening:
Single—*Patches*, Dickey Lee

Golden sunlight filters through the high windows of the courthouse. The marble floor glistens like a polished mirror. I reach for Kathy's hand. We walk the long hallway together. I don't know where we're going, or how we're going to find Tammy. Kathy does.

Spot tastes real good, Tammy says, her mouth full of burger. I look at my burger and ask, We're eating Spot? Yeah, she tells me and some of Spot drops out of her mouth and lands on the checkered tablecloth. She scoops him up and stuffs him back in her mouth. Only last month we climbed the wood fence out in the back to get into Spot's pasture—I thought he would be this cute little calf, but he was huge. I was scared to get close to him, but Tammy pulled me across the muddy field. Spot was so gentle and sweet. We washed him and fed him and petted him. I set my burger back on my plate; not hungry any more.

Tammy's dad comes in smelling like a dirty toilet. Burgers? I don't work all goddamn day just to get hamburger! Tammy's mom gets up and goes to the kitchen. Your steak's all ready. Damn well better be, he warns her and throws a long skinny leg over the top of the chair and sits down hard. I don't like him— his teeth are all stained brown, his hands are caked with black dirt that he never washes off, he cusses all the time and hits Tammy—tickles me real rough—kisses Tammy's older sister on the mouth and touches her big titties right in front of everyone.

Our shoes click on the sparkling floor and echo back at us. Here. Kathy stops and stands on tiptoe to look through the window of the wooden door. She's in here. We better wait over there.
I follow her to a low-backed bench on the other side of the hallway. I'm shivering.
Kathy takes my hand in hers.

Let's play "date," Tammy tells me. We're in her twin bed together. I'll be the boy. She hops up on her knees and straddles me. Before I know what's happening she's kissing me, sticking her tongue in my mouth. You're s'posed to slap me and tell me No, real mean, she tells me and kisses me again. I push at her for real and try to tell her NO! but her mouth is tight against mine and I can't say anything. Yeah, like that, she tells me then bounces down the bed and pulls up my nightgown and dives between my legs. I scramble to get away from her but she grabs my legs and laughs. That's right! You got it! She smiles and kisses me between the legs again and again. I stop struggling because it feels sorta good. Feels like something I shouldn't be doing.

You've played "date" before, Tammy accuses me from between my legs. I shake my head and tell her, No I haven't! Yes you have! She goes back to kissing me down there.

The door opens and Tammy's older sister walks out into the hall. A woman in a black pleated skirt with a matching shirt and man's tie has her by the arm. They pause for a moment while the woman makes sure the door closes behind them. Tammy's sister doesn't look up; her head's bowed, her chin on her chest. She's wearing all gray and her fluffy red hair is combed back and pinned in a tight bun at her neck, just like the woman's. They walk away without a word, the woman still holding the girl's arm. Even their shoes are silent. We watch them until they disappear.
Kathy let's go of my hand.

We sit in the dark room. I want to play "date" but Tammy says no. I even offer to be the boy. She climbs off the bed and sits in the corner, tells me she's never going to play "date" again. She won't tell me why. A door opens and slams closed down the hall. Tammy jumps up and locks her bedroom door then climbs over a pile of clothes and hides in her closet. Don't jus' sit there! Get in here, you idiot. I jump up and hide with her behind her dresses. He never looks in here, she tells me. Who? I ask. Him, she says and I hear her dad hacking up phlegm in the bathroom.

Tammy's mom comes out of the door and walks straight over to us. We stand up.

You can't believe anythin' that girl's been tellin' ya, she tells us. You can't believe the horrible things she's been sayin'.

I can't look at her because I do believe the horrible things Tammy's been saying; so does Kathy.

You don't know nothin', she spits at us. And if you say somthin' bad, then you gonna have'ta answer straight to her daddy! She looks us up and down. You don't know nothin'. She turns and walks away, her heels pounding hard.

Say you're wrong! Say it! Say it! Tammy and I are still at the dinner table, but her dad has her older sister pinned down in the recliner. The chair's leaned back so far it looks like it might break. I'm wrong, Tammy's sister yells at him. He let's go of her hair. She starts to turn her head away. He grabs her chin and twists her head back straight. What you doin', girl? Don't you look away from me! He scoots up in the recliner, tipping the chair even further back. He grabs another bunch of hair with one hand and pulls her head forward, pushes his crotch out, rubs her face on his dirty work pants. You look away again and you know what's gonna happen. He pulls her head back and she looks up at him and gives a little nod. You look away again and I'm gonna know you're askin' me to do it. She nods again and I see a tear edge out of the corner of her eye.

What's going to happen to Tammy? I ask Kathy. She shrugs. What are you going to say when they call you in there?

Nothin'.

I guess I shouldn't say anything, either. I mean, I didn't really see anything … I mean not really. I only know what she told me.

Kathy fiddles with the satin ribbons on her dress. I pull down the red paisley sleeves of mine.

I thought I was Tammy's only friend. But there are so many girls at Tammy's fourteenth birthday party, way more than were at mine. I turned fourteen almost four months ago and feel all grown up compared to the other girls.

After the gifts are opened, Tammy goes back in the house and spends the rest of the party talking with two girls I don't know. Both are blondes with really short dresses and already wearing makeup. I don't feel so grown up anymore. Tammy doesn't ask me to stay the night, so I leave before anyone else and walk home alone in the rain.

When she doesn't show up to school all the next week I go over to her house. Her mother tells me she's sick and that I can't come in. I sneak around the back and look in through her bedroom window. She's sitting on her bed drawing in a big sketch book, colored charcoal sticks scattered all around her. She doesn't look sick. She sees me and jumps off the bed and dashes to the window. Go away! Go away! she hisses at me, without opening the window. Are you okay? I ask, and then notice her split lip, a long purple-green bruise running up and down the side of her face, a jagged cut above her eyebrow. I'm fine … jus' go away. What happened? I stand on my tip-toes and try to see inside the whole room. Nothing! Go away before my daddy gets home, you idiot!

I saw it, Kathy tells me. On Tammy's birthday. He stunk of whiskey. Didn't even care I was right there in the room with her …

I know what Kathy means; know what happened to Tammy on her birthday. Tammy told me the next week, but I didn't know Kathy was the girl who stayed overnight after the party.

Will they put him in jail?

Not in your life. They'll lock Tammy up for ratting on him.

They can't do that!

Yeah they can.

Tammy's dressed all in gray, just like her sister. A woman has her by the arm as they walk out of the courtroom. She looks at us and asks the woman something. The woman nods and they walk over to our bench. We both stand up.

Thanks for comin' today. Tammy's voice is flat and hoarse.

Sure, we both tell her.

Sorry you came all the way down here and they didn't ask you about nothin'. She takes a big breath and looks back at the door as it opens. Her father walks out with two men in suits. His hair is slicked back and his hands are clean. He's wearing a dark blue suit, just like the other men. They're all smiling and her dad says something—their laughter echoes down the long hallway. Tammy looks back at us quickly and hunches up her shoulders.

There, there now, the woman tells her. Let's not have any trouble, shall we? We should be going anyway. Come on along now, Tammy. The woman turns to leave.

Tammy leans towards us. I had to say something, or he'd keep hurtin' us. They all hate me now; say I'm a slut and no good; that I caused all the trouble in the first place. But you know. You know I didn' do nothin' wrong.

That's enough! The woman barks. No more talking!

I reach for Tammy. When are you coming back to school?

Don't ... The woman has my wrist in her hand ... touch her!

I won't be coming back, Tammy says over her shoulder as the woman pulls her down the hall in the opposite direction her dad went.

I don't know what to do, what to say. Can't believe they're taking Tammy away when her dad did what he did to her.

Kathy breaks into tears and drops back to the bench. They always send them away ... always send them away. She buries her face in her hands and cries.

I remain standing—silent in the Hall of Justice.

Flying High
October 20, 1967

Suggested listening:
Album—Electric Music for the Mind and Body, Country Joe and the Fish

Another Friday night babysitting for Barbara. I'm looking forward to four more dollars in my pocket, which will make twenty I've saved, let alone at least another twenty I've spent on necessities for Kathy and me—movies, burgers, bus rides, uppers, downers. Once Shirley accepted that I was going to do drugs no matter what she said, she makes sure I get only the good stuff. I have to pay for pills, as she has to buy them from another dealer, but Eric buys pot by the key and gives us what we need for free. Shirley says he can afford it, what with all the money he makes selling four-finger lids for ten dollars each. I figured it out once and was blown away at how much he makes off a key. No wonder he drives a new car.

The clock on the wall shows 9:30. Barbara said she'd be back by ten so I get off the couch, turn off the TV and make the rounds; make sure everyone's dry, tucked in, and the apartment tidy. Kelly and Christopher are both sound asleep with their thumbs tucked in their mouths. I poke a finger inside Christopher's diaper—dry as a bone. I straighten Kelly's blanket, tuck it in around her feet and tip-toe back down the stairs.

I clean my dinner dishes, dry them and put them away. Wipe down the counters and table and sweep up crumbs from the kitchen floor. I feel very grown-up. I like Barbara's new apartment. Her old house didn't seem to fit her; this place does. It's modern—long and narrow and two stories, like nothing I've seen before. It's brand new and way cool; people living on either side of you, sharing the same walls.

A key clicks in the front door. I brush lint off my skirt and tank top, pull up my knee-high moccasins, which keep sliding down, and walk back into the living room. Barbara glides through the door followed by my sister's boyfriend, Eric. I stop in mid-step. Eric flashes me the peace sign and says, Wow, you watch Barb's kids?

I nod.

Cool.

You know each other? Barbara asks.

I don't say anything, try not to look at Eric. Yeah, Eric says and walks around us both and heads to the kitchen. She's Shirley's little sister, he tells her over his shoulder—all nonchalant.

Wow. How weird. Barbara looks me up and down, like she hasn't seen me before. Wow. Really? she calls to Eric, like I'm not even there.

Yeah, really, I tell her and go to get my coat out of the hall closet.

Wow. Cool. So we hang with the same people, Barbara says.

I don't turn around, knowing my face is bright red from catching Eric with another woman; a woman old enough to have two kids. I wonder if Shirley will be able to tell I know something bad when she sees me. I can never hide anything from her. I grab my pea coat and stuff my arms through the sleeves.

How'd it go?

Fine, I say to the open closet.

They give you any trouble?

No.

Hey. You okay? I feel a hand on my shoulder and know I have to face her.

Yeah, sure. I put on a smile and turn around.

Barbara's shorter than me, even with heels on. She's looking up at me, and I can tell she's concerned. Really? You don't look so good.

Eric walks back in with two beers. He takes one look at me and Barbara and says, Hey, it's all cool. Me 'n Barb 'n your sister. No hassles. It's all cool. Here have a beer.

Sure, it's all cool, Barbara assures me and takes one of the beers from Eric and hands it to me. You're off the clock. Have a drink. Want some smoke?

I take the beer. I have no place to be, except home, and that's no place to be. Kathy's away visiting relatives, and ever since Shirley moved out two weeks ago, I hardly see her. It's just me on my own on a Friday night. Sure, I say, but still can't look at Eric.

Barbara laughs and claps her hands together. Roll another one, brother. Your ladies need a slight respite from this dismal night.

At your command. Eric pulls a plastic baggie out of his pocket as he drops to the couch. Faster than I can imagine he dumps out a clump of pot on the glass-topped coffee table, whips out a pack of Zig-Zag papers, licks the gummed edge of one and attaches it to another, and starts rolling a nice fat one.

I keep my coat on, a bit concerned about the way both Barbara and Eric are acting; just a little too happy, or something. I can't put my finger on it and don't want to take my coat off just in case I need to leave in a hurry. I realize Barbara has to drive me home and get concerned when she takes the first hit off the joint, long and deep. I sniff the errant smoke. I've only been smoking a few months, but even I can tell this is high quality stash.

I take the joint from Barbara and suck on the already damp, flattened end. It's so smooth I can fill my lungs without coughing. I pass it to Eric, looking at him for the first time since he walked in.

Cool, he says and winks at me. It's all groovy, if you just let it be. He smiles and takes a big ol' hit.

We're all silent, not breathing, not moving, just being.

Bachelor number one. You show up for our first date and I answer the door in an old terrycloth bathrobe and my hair in curlers. What do you say? A high, whiney woman's voice floats through the living room wall from the television set in the next apartment.

We all burst out laughing and go straight into coughing fits. I try to drown the cough in beer, sniff some up my nose and start sneezing and coughing and laughing. Barbara takes the beer out of my hand and falls to the couch. The beer foams up and oozes out of the bottle. Eric licks the sides before it can hit the couch.

A tiny whimper silences us all. We wait, another whimper … a tiny call for mama.

Barbara climbs off the couch, putting a finger to her mouth to keep Eric and me quiet. Coming baby, she calls and hands me back the beer.

I don't move, just stand there with the beer in my hand. Eric pinches out the joint and slips it into his shirt pocket, packs up the weed and papers and stuffs them in his jean's back pocket and sits up straight.

Did you have a bad dream, we hear Barbara coo from upstairs. It's okay. Mama will sing all the bad dreams away. *Puff, the magic dragon lived by the sea.* The bedroom door creaks closed as Barbara continues, *And frolicked in the autumn mist in a land called Honnah-Lee …*

Wow, Eric sighs. She really loves those kids.

Yeah, I say and walk towards the front door. Guess I should go.

Why? Eric says, fishing the joint out of his pocket. She'll have Kelly back to sleep in time to finish off this doobie. Come on over and sit a spell. He cocks an eyebrow. I don't bite.

I shrug and walk back to the couch and sit at the far end. Eric chuckles, lights the joint and passes it over. I can't think of anything to say, Eric must not either. We sit in silence passing the joint back and forth across the expanse of orange and brown striped upholstery.

A door opens and then softly closes. Barbara descends. She takes the joint from Eric, whips a hairpin out of her puffed-up hairdo and snaps it across the remains. God, I need this, she says and takes a hard hit. The last of the joint flares and goes out. Eric hands her the new, slimmer one he just rolled. She crushes the ash in her fingers and snaps the hairpin around the new number.

Eric is suddenly standing next to her, lighting her up, his arm around her waist. All better now, he says and kisses her cheek.

I look away and wonder how I'm going to get home. I figure Muzzie might come get me if I tell her Barbara isn't feeling well. Can I use the phone? My voice sounds far off and croaky.

Sure, Barbara tells me. Why?

I blush and tell her I just think it's time to leave. She steps away from Eric and looks at him, like she didn't even know he was there. Eric chuckles again and flops back onto the couch.

Oh! Him? No. No. This is nothing. You can hang out awhile. Here. She hands me the joint. We're just tripping together. He got a new batch and thought we should give it a try before he deals it. Pretty sweet stuff. She looks over at Eric and back at me. You know …, she says. We're just tripping.

I shrug my shoulders. I've heard Shirley talking about tripping on LSD; heard my dad talking more about it; how it's killing our young people—making them crazy, insane—has them jumping off rooftops because they think they can fly. Sounds pretty interesting to me, but no one's offered me any. Actually, I haven't really tried to find any because I'm a bit freaky about taking something that could make me think I can fly.

You trip? she asks.

I shake my head.

She laughs. We have got to change that right now, she announces and then turns and snaps her fingers and holds her hand out to Eric.

For Christ sake, Barb, she's only fifteen, Eric tells her, and I feel my face coloring. Actually, I'm only fourteen, but if Eric thinks I'm older, I'm not going to correct him.

So what? Where better to take her first trip than here. She spreads her arms out encompassing the long, narrow room. She snaps her fingers again. Cough it up. It's only one hit. You've got a hundred more in that pocket of yours.

I don't have a hundred. And besides, she's a fucking kid.

I stand up and start to back towards the door. Now I'm certain they're talking about LSD, acid to those in the know, but I can't believe Barbara's actually thinking about turning me on, here—now—with them.

Come on. Barbara blows Eric a kiss. For me … please. It'll be cool. She should trip with *us* the first time. Who knows what could happen to her if someone slips it in her drink some night. It would totally freak her out. You know that shit happens all the time! She puts one hand on her hip and turns the other one palm up. Eric sighs and pulls a small white packet out of his coat pocket and tosses it to Barbara.

I stop—afraid this might be my only chance to try acid. I find myself wondering, Why not? Barbara's cool and Eric only deals good stuff. I take a step back towards the couch and wonder if I should wait and drop acid with Shirley for the first time. She's never offered, but then I don't think she's that into acid. I'd be one up on Kathy for a change, I think and take another step towards the couch.

Barbara dumps a few little whitish-blue pills out on her palm and looks up at me. Your mom expecting you home tonight?

I nod.

I better call her first. She pours the pills back in the packet and goes into the kitchen.

Eric shakes his head and sighs, Guess you're bound to trip at some point, and now's as good a time as any. He looks up at me. Think your sister'll be pissed at me if I get you off without telling her? I shrug my shoulders and sit on the far end of the couch. He sighs again and adds, Well, won't be the first time she's been pissed at me. Won't be the last. What the hell.

Mrs. Conrad? Barbara Woods here. No. No. Everything's fine. I'm just not feeling all that great and would like Donna to stay over tonight; take care of the kids if they wake up; get them ready in the morning and maybe even stay around to fix them lunch.

There's a long pause. Eric and I look at each other and he passes me another lit joint. I take a toke and wait what seems like an hour.

Thank you so much. I really owe you. No. Sure. I'll have her home just after lunchtime. What? Sure, just a second.

Barbara pokes her head from out of the kitchen, her hand covering the mouthpiece. Your mom wants to talk to you.

Not to worry, Eric says as I squeeze between him and the coffee table. Everything is cool and groovy, if you just let it be.

I smoke. I drink. I wait … and wait … and wait. Barbara and Eric do the same, watching me without trying to look like they're watching me. They make light conversation—laugh, roll joints, pop beers—watch me. We're all on the couch, listening to Lovin' Spoonful, Simon & Garfunkel, Buffalo Springfield.

Wait! I know just what we need, Eric says and jumps off the couch. He drops to the floor and flips through the albums leaning against the far wall, all hunched over and intent on what he's doing.

Barbara rests a long thin hand on my leg. How ya doin'? she asks. Her words are thick, heavy, hanging in the air above a lazy half smile on her lips. I stare at her lips; see the tiny cracks widen, their edges pale pink bleeding down to a deep scarlet at the center. I watch them run together, form tiny rivulets that empty into her mouth.

I blink and tear my eyes away, feeling I shouldn't be that close to Barbara's lips—wondering what it would be like to be even closer.

I look at Eric. He has an album in his hands, a big smile on his face. Now this will blow your mind, Country Joe and the Fish, he says and spins the jet-black disk on the tip of his finger, like I've seen the Harlem Globetrotters do with a basketball on TV. He leans over and flips the needle up, the album still spinning, serves it to the turntable like a pizza-pie in a cartoon, drops the needle part way through the album and steps back. *Section 43*, he announces and makes a deep bow.

Barbara laughs and pats my leg. Hang on, baby, she tells me and lets her arm go limp. Her hand drifts away.

Someone plucks a lone guitar string, real low. The floor vibrates and I look around to find who has the drum kit. A high-pitched keyboard squeals, backed by an electric guitar. The chord flattens me against the couch, dives into my chest, then pulls back, taking my breath with it. Eric sways with the impact and Barbara groans.

I think I'm tripping, someone says.

You are little sister, Barbara answers.

I give up trying to think and meld with the music—it surrounds me, consumes me. I rise and fall on whirling waves of color—crash against distant shores and become one with an endless sea of sound—soar into a starless night—plunge back to earth—collapse inward, shrink smaller and smaller—tighter—denser—so heavy I don't think I will ever be able to move again—then blaze like a sun flare—cool and solidify into one reverberating chord. Live a lifetime within *Section 43*.

I die sweetly, softly … Twang back to life, my heart racing along with the driving beat of the next song.

It's a bird. It's a plane. It's a man insane. It's my president LBJ.

I open my eyes, see Eric teetering on his toes, his hand pointing at the ceiling. I look up, but there's only the ceiling. Country Joe is shouting, *Send him back to Texas, make him work on his ranch …* I close my eyes, long to go back to where I was, wish the annoying song would go away.

A honky-tonk love song floats by. I open my eyes and the room settles around me. Warm, pulsating colors brush against my skin and dribble down into my fringed moccasins; form puddles around my feet. A burning stick appears between my fingers. I laugh and hear echoes all around me. Liquid fire fills my lungs. I push it down through my legs, send it flashing out through my soft leather soles. I float back up on rhythmic bass strings and brushed cymbals. Breathe out long, slow, and even; then breathe back in. Realize each breath is unique—each breath is identical—realize I'm tripping—really tripping.

Country Joe sighs and whispers in my ear: *Get so high this time that you know, oh, oh ... I'll never come down. I'll never come down ...*

Day Break
October 21, 1967

It isn't like I expected. Everything is the same. Muzzie's reading a magazine on the patio, blowing smoke in a long narrow stream that breaks apart by the time it reaches the lawn. Laddie's sleeping next to her, his head on her foot, his bushy tail covering his nose. I notice the sliding glass door hasn't been cleaned, big smudged fingerprints streak across Muzzie's head and blur the brick BBQ.

I tell myself to go say Hi, let her know I'm home, but I don't. I like the house all dark and quiet. Like being alone, for once. I stand and watch Muzzie's smoke shoot out and vanish, wonder why she always turns her head and blows the smoke to her left. Wonder why Laddie sleeps on her foot, he doesn't sleep on anyone else's foot. Wonder why my dad isn't home, it's Saturday, he should be watching baseball or basketball or football.

I stand in the kitchen and breathe in deep, smelling my home, smelling all those things that I live with every day and never notice, the cigarettes and talcum powder, the tacos and chicken 'n dumplings, the spaghetti and milk and Toll House cookies—they're all mixed up together—make this place smell like home. I turn away and walk to my bedroom—hope it doesn't smell like home. The long hallway feels narrow and cramped. The linen closet is open. I don't close it. My bedroom door is open, my bed covered with a new green bedspread.

Nothing has changed, not even me. I thought I would be

96

different, see everything different, be aware of each breath, aware of every color; that I would understand everything—just like I did last night. But nothing has changed. I'm still me and Muzzie is still smoking on the patio and Laddie is still sleeping on her foot and the sliding glass door still needs to be cleaned.

My world didn't change—it was all just a trick.

Trip the Light Fantastic
October 31, 1967

Suggested listening:
Album—Fresh Cream, Cream

Come, and trip it as ye go,
On the light fantastick toe.
And in thy right hand lead with thee,
The Mountain Nymph, sweet Liberty.
L'Allegro by John Milton

When I was little my world was wonderful, beautiful. My mom and dad loved me. My big brother protected me and my sister was my very best friend. I was adorable. I had big, brown, doe eyes and pale blonde hair my mom permed into golden ringlets.

As I grew older my hair grew darker—so did my world.

When I was nine, we moved from La Puente to Covina, bought a brand new three-bedroom, two-bath house with a swimming pool and a huge patio with a built-in brick Bar-B-Que. The first night we were there the neighbors called the police. The neighbors called the police many times during our first year on Nearglen Avenue. There would be a knock on the door, loud and persistent. My dad would stop yelling, push my mom into the back bedroom, close the door and warn us to stay in our rooms.

My dad was never arrested for beating my mom. He would flash his badge, have a quiet, reasonable talk with the officers out on the front porch; explain it was just a simple misunderstanding; explain that the neighbors were over-reacting—shake hands with the officers in a knowing way.

I was glad the police cared enough to come by and stop the fighting.

By the time I was ten I was beginning to wonder why my mom was almost always napping when I got home from school and getting the stomach flu so often. One day I came home and she was asleep on the couch—with nothing on. It wouldn't have been so bad if it hadn't been the first time my girlfriends decided to come to my house to play. The girls never came back. My sister found me crying in my room and told me Muzzie wasn't asleep—she was drunk.

By the time I was fourteen I knew more than I wanted to know—but couldn't do anything about anything.

Acid changed everything—and I couldn't wait to share it with Kathy.

How long does it take?

I shrug my shoulders.

My brother says he'd never take the stuff. Too weird.

I shrug my shoulders again.

Shouldn't I feel something? You feeling anything? I don't feel anything.

I lie back on the bed and watch the ceiling, not knowing what to tell Kathy. I've only taken acid once, last week with Barbara and Eric, so I don't know much.

Just don't say anything to Shirley, I warn her. She doesn't know we're on acid.

Yeah, I know. Kathy sits up and looks around. But why? I mean, I know you don't want her to know. But why? You got the stuff from her boyfriend.

I jolt upright. Don't you *dare* say a word about where I got it. I shake my head and wish I'd never told her where I got the acid. But I always tell Kathy everything, so it never occurred to me not to.

Kathy giggles and flops back on the bed, face down. I start tickling her—our little trick to get through the tough times. She flips back over and grabs me. I try to wiggle away while still tickling her.

What the hell are you guys on? Shirley's standing in the doorway looking at the two of us rolling on the bed, laughing hysterically and tickling each other. And just what the hell are you doing in my bedroom?

We try to pull ourselves together but can't quite manage it. Come on outta here. I got your costumes ready. We leave in half an hour, so get moving, Shirley informs us and closes the door as she leaves.

I go straight back to the tickle. Stop! Don't you dare! Kathy tries to squirm away. I aim for the rib-bone right under her arm, hit the mark. Kathy dissolves in a bundle of raucous laughter and slaps at me to stop.

Hitting the floor knocks the wind and the laughter, out of both of us. Kathy looks around the room. Wow! she says. Your sister's room is really big. I've never seen ceilings so high.

I turn over, having been the lucky one to land on top. Wow! They're way up there.

I've never seen anything so beautiful.

What? I ask.

Up there. All the colors … it's the most beautiful thing I've ever seen. She looks over at me, her eyes big black disks with only a thin circle of blue around the edges. Do we have to go out there? Can't we stay in here all night?

Get your butts out here now! Shirley yells from the front room.

Betcha the ceiling out there is even higher, Kathy says. We scramble off the floor trying to beat each other out the bedroom door.

Batman and Tweedle Dee, or is it Tweedle Dum, are dirty dancing to

Spoonful. My chair starts vibrating and I grab the arms, but it's only Kathy purring and rubbing up against me in her Cat Woman costume. How did Shirley know Kathy loves Cat Woman? I wonder.

I'm purrrrr-fect, Kathy mews, then hisses and bounces off after a mouse that's making off with her whip.

I cross my arms, my fingers pressing lightly against the silky black material and close my eyes; hope the acid will take me on a magical journey, just like it did last week. *I'm so glad, I'm so glad, I'm glad, I'm glad, I'm glad* blasts from the stereo speakers and I realize I *am* so glad to be here, now, tripping at a real party.

I open my eyes. A rhinoceros trots by followed by a lioness on her back legs. Four hyenas start shrieking on the far side of the room and a flock of swans take flight and soar out of the house through a slit in the ceiling. I lean back against my big chair and smile, content that everything is as it should be.

Hey. Wanna dance? I look over at a cowboy with an arrow piercing his head and coming out the other side.

I smile with my lips pressed tight together. Do you Tango? I ask.

Do I what?

Tango, Darling.

What the fuck? No!

Well then ... I don't dance. He walks away, the arrow drooping.

Hey, you look great. Told you you're a real stunner, a blue marbled bowling ball tells me and winks one of its holes at me. Can't believe Shirley got such a great dress so fast. You look the spitting image of Morticia Addams. Two arms snake around from behind the ball and lift the fringed edge of my sleeve. And your hair looks great with some waves in it. The ball rolls closer. Did she even dye it black? The top two holes blink and zoom in so close I lean back in the chair and almost tip over. The ball reaches out and saves me—if not my composure.

You okay?

I nod.

Really?

I nod again.

Then say something.

I can't think of anything to say. I nod again.

Shirley! the ball yelps. Get your ass over here!

A tall mop of wavy brown hair glides over to my chair and puts a gloved hand on top of the ball.

Cousin Itt, I sigh. How nice of you to come to my little party. I spread my arms out to take in the whole menagerie.

For fuck sake! The bowling ball slaps at Cousin Itt. What the fuck's she on?

Don't be so dense, Sandy. They dropped acid, Cousin Itt tells the bowling ball.

How do you know?

Kathy just told me.

Where'd they get it?

Where do ya think?

Eric! You fuckin' asshole! The bowling ball rolls away, picking up speed, looking good for a strike.

Hey, Punk. Itt touches my arm.

I look over and smile indulgently. Yes?

You know it's only a costume, don't you?

But of course, I tell Itt. A real rhinoceros couldn't possibly do the limbo so well.

Itt looks over at the dancers and back at me. Okay. You stay right here. Okay?

Why, where else would I be, my darling Itt?

Fred Astaire dances by with a chimpanzee in a tutu and I lean back against my chair, wondering where Gomez might be—glad Wednesday and Pugsley are both with Grandmamma at the graveyard.

She thinks she *is* Morticia Addams, I hear Itt telling Fred Astaire.

Sure looks like her, Mr. Astaire says to the bowling ball, who's rolled to a stop next to him.

What the fuck you give her? the bowling ball shouts.

Nothing. I swear.

Don't lie to me, you sack of shit. You gave her acid, you asshole. And Kathy? For fuck sake! They're only kids. Look at her! She's completely fucked up.

Looks pretty hot to me, Mr. Astaire says and leans in close to me.

I raise my hand for him to kiss. His mustache tickles.

Stop that! Itt slaps the back of his head and he drops my hand.

The bowling ball starts shouting, This one thinks she's Morticia fucking Addams and Kathy's out back in the yard trying to dig a hole to pee in and you don't thinks there's a fucking problem?

I wish it would quiet down. It's spoiling my wonderful party.

What? Mr. Astaire asks. Where? In the backyard? Oh, I have got to see this! he says and dances off leaving me with the bowling ball's black holes staring at me and Cousin Itt brushing back my hair.

But everything is just as it should be—except I am disappointed the baboon felt he needed to dress up like a rhinoceros for the party. His costume is not at all convincing now that he's taken the hood off to drink a beer … a beer of all things! I raise my goblet to my lips and sip the tart wine through swirling smoke.

Cousin Itt kisses my cheek and says, Ah fuck it. She's fine. She'll come down before morning. Come on! I have *got* to see Kathy trying to dig a hole! Is she still out back?

Cousin Itt rolls the bowling ball away and I settle back into my chair wishing Gomez would come tango with me.

Marion "Condie" Conrad, 1946

Helen "Muzzie" Conrad, 1946

Helen & Condie, 1944

Helen, gone fishing, 1942

Condie in Korea, 1951

Muzzie with Terry, me, and Shirley, 1955

Shirley (4th from left) and me (5th from left.
Dressing-up Day in Germany (1955).

Terry, me, and Shirley, 1960

TILLICUM
SCHOOL DAYS 1958-59

Halloween, 1965

Shirley's birthday, before the bust. That's me, second from the left, 1963.

Donna D. Conrad

A Night in Wonderland
Early December 1967

Suggested listening:
Album—Magical Mystery Tour, The Beatles

It's raining at Disneyland. It's a Magic Kingdom. It shouldn't be raining.

Dad holds the front seat forward and I climb out of the Galaxy 500 hoping he'll let Shirley and me head off on our own and not have to stick with him and Muzzie all night. It's the first General Telephone night since Shirley came home and we want to spend it together, not with the folks.

I've been to Disneyland bunches of times, but my favorite time is when only General Telephone employees and their families get the whole of Disneyland for the whole night. We don't even have to worry about using up all our "E" class tickets right off the bat and getting stuck with the crummy "A" and "B" tickets that only get us into the kids' rides at the end. Every ride is open to everyone, even Shirley's favorite, The Matterhorn. She always used to ride it with Terry because it scares me—but tonight I'm going to ride it even if it makes me scream.

I meet Shirley at the back of the car and roll my eyes as Dad tells us that we have to stick close together tonight. We follow him and Muzzie to the tram that's just pulling away from the stop. He sticks two fingers in his mouth and whistles really loud for the driver to wait, then tells us, Good timing. The man waves and stops the tram

108

and we all climb on.

The rain lightens up and Shirley squeezes my hand and smiles. But it's still cold and wet and the acid we took at home hasn't come on yet so I'm thinking we must have gotten burned. It's only my fifth acid trip, but I know enough to know it shoulda hit by now.

We climb off the tram at the front gate and Dad tells us to remember to meet under the clock at the end of Main Street if we get separated. Muzzie shows her General Telephone employee badge and tells the man at the gate that we're her family. The man tells us to enjoy our night in the Magic Kingdom and we join the other people crowding in front of the big map that has all the different Lands in bright colors—and I realize the acid has hit because the colors are flickering and running into each other and switching places and generally misbehaving; but no one else seems to notice.

I smile and ignore Dad as he tells us his strategy for getting from one Land to another in the most efficient way and wish again that he'd leave us alone for just one night. There's a light mist falling, soft and multi-colored and I raise my face to the sky and imagine I'm in a desert and that this is the first water I've seen for a month. I find I really like the rain.

Dad's voice snaps me back to the wet, cold, December night. He's telling us what to do again and I know I better listen or everyone will be in trouble. We'll head straight through Main Street to New Orleans Square and get in line for the new *Pirates of the Caribbean* attraction. He's talking fast and loud, like a drill sergeant or something. We can expect the line to be long and we might not get to all the other attractions tonight, but at least we'll get to …

My mind drifts off, following another family with three little kids who are laughing and chasing each other, even the mom and dad are laughing. I wonder if I'll scream on the Matterhorn and what the pirates ride will be like and if Shirley and I can still fit in the same car in the Utopia ride and if I even want to go on the submarine ride. It's so square with those really fake mermaids and everything.

Stop daydreaming, Punk. I open my eyes and see that everyone's moved away from the map and Dad is frowning at me with his hands on his hips. Shirley jerks her head and I can see in her eyes that she's peaking too and know that we have to keep it really cool in front of the folks so we don't get busted. I take a step towards them and my feet slip out from underneath me. Dad catches me by the arm and we all look down at my moccasins.

Must be the oil in the leather, Dad says. Just like the oil in the road when it first rains, leaches out and makes things slick. You better be careful, don't want you to break a leg. He turns away and then turns back real fast. Wait a minute! I thought I told you two not to wear those damned things out in public!

Muzzie touches his arm. Now, Condie. It's too late to change them, so let's just try to enjoy the night. Okay?

I don't like them looking like damned hippies out in public, he says. This is your employer for Christ's sake, and they're walking around in hippie shoes and likely to break their necks. Where would that put us?

All the young people are wearing moccasins these days, not just hippies. It'll be fine. Let's just go enjoy the new attractions and have a fun night. Okay? Muzzie says.

Dad snorts and takes off in the lead. Shirley and I kiss Muzzie on the cheek and link arms with her in the middle and follow him to New Orleans Square to see the pirates.

I don't think I can take the Matterhorn, but Shirley really, really wants to. Dad says he's too old for fast rides, so that decides it for me. I'll do anything to get away from him. My dad and acid are not a good combination. He's weirder than anything acid could come up with.

He started singing along in the pirates ride and saying, Aye, Matey, and A-vast ye landlubbers over and over again; and when I looked at him he turned into a real pirate with a patch and a big floppy hat and even talked like one until he turned into Abraham Lincoln and then Pluto and then Dumbo and then Jiminy Cricket so fast I couldn't keep up. But when he started singing, *I know you. I walked with you once upon a dream*, and turned into Sleeping Beauty, I really freaked out. Muzzie covered up and said I must have gotten too excited on the pirate ride and that they really should have warnings out front that it's so frightening, especially for young girls.

She walked us over to the emergency aid station and gave us a lecture about taking whatever it was we took and that she didn't want to know but we'd better snap out of it fast. She gave us an hour to straighten up and said she'd tell Dad she'd left us at the aid station to rest. She walked away and shook a warning finger at us, telling us to be under the clock at 11:30 sharp. We headed straight back to the pirates ride and totally lost it the second time through—goading the pirates on and yelling that they should share some of their wine with us.

We were told not to come back to the ride again by the man who helped us out of the boat. Two times was enough so we didn't really care and headed off in search of other weird rides. We had to hold each other up to keep from sliding around on the wet walkways in our moccasins, but as soon as we got the hang of it we started pretending we were roller skating and got around much faster than if we were just walking; though we did skate into a few folks who yelled at us. We got chased by some boys, but lost them in Frontier Land.

We made it to Mr. Toad's Wild Ride and Utopia and were still able to get back to the clock by 11:30. Dad said he was glad I was feeling better and Muzzie gave me a warning look and said I'd better take it easy the rest of the night. Dad said we all got to choose one last ride before the fireworks at midnight. We picked the Matterhorn and they picked It's a Small World. He decided it was okay if we split up for just the one ride, but told us to meet them in front of Sleeping Beauty's castle in time for the fireworks. We skated off without a backwards glance, heading straight for the Matterhorn.

I look up at the mountain hovering above us and won't get in the bobsled. Your turn, Miss, the man tells me and takes my arm. I resist and Shirley yells, Get in, you jerk! real loud and I let the man guide me down into the sled.

For fuck sake! Don't make a fucking scene, Shirley whispers and the man raises an eyebrow. We both keep quiet until the car pulls away from the platform. We're in the front. I'm too scared to turn and see who's behind us.

I can't do this! I tell her and try to push up the bar that's tight across our laps.

Oh stop it! She slaps my hand and leans in close, kisses my cheek. Nobody's died ... yet.

I scream the entire ride. I'm all shaky and have no voice left when we climb out of the sled and have to pantomime that I want to do it again. We're gonna be in so much trouble with the old man, Shirley laughs and hugs me.

We rush back and get in the now short line for one last ride as fireworks explode over the Matterhorn.

Dionysius at the Shrine
December 22, 1967

Suggested listening:
Album—Strange Days, The Doors

The others love him, think he's some kind of god. I still think he's a fool. Though, wearing tight, black leather pants, his hands stroking the slender metal rod thrust between his legs, he looks like he could be the god of Love.

Shirley, Sandy, and Kathy are pushing through the crowd, swimming upstream to be closer to the great Jim Morrison. I follow as usual and wonder why Shirley didn't get backstage passes. She knows the guy. Her boyfriend deals whatever the band needs when they're in L.A.

He's better than I remember him at the Cheetah a few months ago—or at least the sound's better at the Shrine. He's still pouty and pretty and prancing, but something's different about him. He's more sure of himself. Who wouldn't be after they'd been on the Ed Sullivan show? He looks like he's just playing with the three thousand kids in the audience—pulling them in—pushing them away—making each one feel like he's there just for them. I look around and see hundreds of glassy eyes longing to be close to him—hands reaching to touch him.

I look up at Morrison, screaming into the mike the pent up frustration inside all of us—screaming out our need to be heard. He jumps high in the air, spins around and lands on his feet, lurches back to the mike, screams again, and then collapses on the floor. The band crashes out the end of the song.

The crowd explodes. Morrison climbs to his feet and turns his back on us all. The drummer starts a Latin beat, joined by the organ and guitar. Morrison storms the mike, cradles it and tells us, *You know the day destroys the night, night divides the day. Try to run try to hide, break on through to the other side.* I look around and can't find Shirley or Kathy or anyone I know. *We chased our pleasures here, dug our treasures there.* The crowd screams and shouts and starts bouncing up and down almost as one. His words crash against my resolve to hate him, to see him as just another guy who thinks he's better than anyone else; a guy who thinks he can have any chick he wants; that to him, I'm only another chick to score with.

Can't you still recall the time we tried to break on through to the other side, break on through to the other side. I look up at him, realize I've made my own way down to the front. He's screaming again, but this time I can dig it—want to break on through with him—screaming and yelling all the way through to the other side. And it's not enough to set the night on fire any more, I need to break on through—break on through.

He closes his eyes and the band keeps playing the same driving beat over and over and over and my mind is close to something real, close to some barrier that can be broken down.

God, he is so stoned. I want what he has, Kathy shouts in my ear.

What? I shake my head and look at her. The spell is broken—Morrison's shouting annoying, like at the Cheetah.

Morrison, she shouts. He's totally fucked up. I want what he has.

You're on it, I shout back.

What?

He's probably doing the same White Lightening that Eric's dealing. You're on it.

Cool, Kathy coos and starts shaking her head like a shaggy dog, her hands held high over her head, clapping in time.

That's the problem with acid, I think. Anything can bring you down so fast. I snap my fingers. Just like that. I snap them again and again and again, tripping on how they can make such a loud noise by just sliding against each other, wonder if everyone else can hear my snapping over the music—don't know how they can't; the crisp clean snap is so loud and clear.

Arms wrap around my waist and lips kiss the back of my shoulder. I try to whip around but Shirley keeps hold of me. Hey there, wild thang! Chill. It's all cool. She nods at the stage. Groovy, huh?

I nod and start swaying in Shirley's arms to the funky song about whiskey and women and dying. We bump together and crack up laughing. Kathy and Sandy pull us apart and join in. We start spinning in a circle, our arms on each other's shoulders. Spinning faster and faster and faster. Others join us, making the circle bigger and bigger until I trip on something and crash into the stage and three or four others follow me down. We're all in a big pile, all singing along and crying for more whiskey.

Rough hands are pulling us off the ground and shoving us back away from the stage. The music stops and Morrison is saying something into the mike and I realize the pigs are rousting us. One has me around my waist and I kick at him, but he just picks me up and tosses me away from the stage.

Fucking pigs! Fucking pigs! Fucking pigs, we all start shouting. Morrison looks down, his eyes all dreamy and distant. He raises the mike above his head and drops it to his other hand on the drum beat. The music starts and we forget about the pigs, forget everything but the music and Morrison's voice calling us to join him in finding a new way to be, a free way to be, a way to be that the pigs can't touch, that the pigs can't control—a way to be in our minds that can't be tamed or caged or denied.

The lights pulse and change colors in time with the music. Everyone is dancing and singing and everything is music and light— everything is pulsating and moving—everything is connected to everything.

This is the end ... the words dig deep, echo and ring back out, fill the auditorium and it is The End. The music is no more, only kids screaming and whistling and clapping and stomping their feet, wanting more and more and more. But there's only silence from the stage and bright lights that show the trash on the floor and girls with smeared makeup and tangled hair and guys looking around like they're lost.

I reach in the front pocket of my black leather hip-huggers and pull out two more tabs and stick one in Kathy's mouth and one in mine. She swallows and starts dancing even though there isn't any music. The pigs start moving out from the stage and we're pushed back towards the lobby.

Shirley's right in front of us. She waves some wads of paper and shouts something, but I can't hear her words over the music that's still pounding in my head. The pigs hesitate and she pulls me through their line and I pull Kathy behind me.

Bright green lights streak by trailing long red and yellow banners. I watch them flash and spin and dive and disappear. I reach in my pocket for another tab, find my pocket empty and wonder what happened to the two extra tabs I brought along just in case. Some guy I don't know is looking at me and mouthing something. He seems concerned, so I pat his face and tell him it's all cool, all groovy. He dissolves in pools of warm orange and yellow light that work their way up my body and dissolve me—make me one with all the colors in the rainbow and all the colors between the colors in the rainbow.

A door opens and the room is muted shades of blue and violet and I hear voices telling me to come in and enjoy myself; come in through the doors of perception. I laugh and think that's pretty lame, to be quoting some dead English poet. They should be quoting Ginsberg or Ferlinghetti, someone who speaks for us—the freaks.

The thought freezes in my mind when I see him slumped in a chair, one long leg thrown over the padded arm. I stop and look around, wonder how I got to this place, where this place is. I don't see Shirley or Kathy or Sandy anywhere in the room, but there are more doors leading to somewhere else I don't know. I giggle, the Doors have many doors, I hear my voice echoing like I'm in some empty cavern. I take a step towards him. A girl with reddish-blonde hair leans over and kisses him.

I want to be that girl, all thin and pale and kissing him. He reaches up and pulls her closer. She does a smart little turn around the chair arm and falls into his lap and I stop—watching them kiss—wanting him to beg for one last kiss from me, like he does in the song. Lights dart in and out of focus, grow bright and dim again and I wait for him to stop kissing her. Wait for my chance at him.

She laughs. He runs his hand up her leg and back down. She laughs again and climbs out of the chair. He tells her to get him some whiskey and slaps her hard on the bottom, tells her she's a good girl, and suddenly he's not the god Jim Morrison I saw on stage—he's the pouty singer sitting on the bumper of the car in the parking lot in Santa Monica and she's the girl in the mini-skirt. I blink and look around, but Shirley and Kathy aren't there. There's no parking lot, just this room and Morrison leaning back against the chair, his eyes closed.

He opens his eyes, looks at me and nods and says something about my being fine, about my being ripe and tasty and I think he's crude and tasteless and crass just like he was in the parking lot—and I want him to want me—and for me not to want him. I look at him leaning back in the chair, just waiting, and realize we look like twins, both in low cut black leather pants and wide silver Concho belts and black boots; and a part of me wonders if that's why I stole these pants—to look like him.

I reach behind and pull the string on my halter top and take another step towards him. Two guys back away and say something that the acid turns into nonsense. Morrison licks his lips and holds out his hands to me. I drop the halter on the floor and move closer; stand right in front of him.

Alright now, he says and licks his lips again. Alright now … come

Donna D. Conrad

a little closer. I stand my ground, my head starts to spin and the lights start flashing colors that aren't real colors, were never real colors.

It's my birthday. I hear my voice echoing in the big room and wonder why I'm telling him that.

Well come get a nice birthday present, he says and holds out his hands, fingers twitching and grabbing the air.

Can I have your autograph? I ask.

He laughs and slaps the leg of one of the guys standing there. Get a pen and paper he tells them.

You don't need paper, I tell him and brush my hair back over my shoulder and don't even blush when it uncovers my tit. I never show my little tits to anyone; am too embarrassed about how small they are next to Kathy's. Wonder what it is about him that makes it seem right to show him my tits.

Alright now. Bring that over here, he tells me. A pen appears in his hand. I drape myself across his lap like the girl who just left. Drop my left arm back over my head. There's laughter and lights and someone holds a joint to my lips and I suck in the fine, fine stash that I recognize as Eric's top grade Mexican.

The pen slides along, tracing his name on my flesh and I realize it's not possible to deny him anything—resign myself to do whatever he wants me to do no matter who's watching or who's wanting me to do anything else.

I raise my head and see Morrison's shaggy mane of black hair with pinpricks of light blinking on and off in its depths and realize his lips are on my tit. His tongue is like fire and ice all at once, his hand sliding its way down my belly, heading for the low black leather—and I surrender myself there in the drizzling acid rain—forgetting that he's just a singer in the band; that he doesn't mean a thing to me.

What the fuck? The voice sounds familiar. Hey, hey, hey! I'm yanked away and fall to the floor. Morrison's out of the chair and swinging on a guy I can't see for all the people scattering to get out of the way.

I get a glimpse of the guy and it's like having ice water poured over me. Eric! I shout and scramble off the floor, grab for my halter and pull my hair back in front, covering my tits.

Morrison stops short and looks at me. You know him? Then at Eric. You know her?

Yeah, she's Shirley's little sister. What the fuck's she doing here? She's like not even fifteen for fuck sake.

Morrison falls back into the chair, laughing. The strawberry blonde hands him a bottle of whiskey and looks me up and down. Shirley's little sister? He nods knowingly and tosses back a big swallow. Thought I'd seen you before. You're the teeny bopper who doesn't like singers. He licks his lips and adds, Guess you changed your mind, huh?

Eric grabs me by the wrist and pulls me away. Put your fucking top on! Jesus Christ. How the hell did you even get here? Where the fuck's Shirley? Put your fucking top on ... now!

That's right, baby girl. Run on home to your mama and daddy. Run away. Run away from the wicked man. Run away. Run away. Morrison tells me, and the mini-skirt chick takes my place on his lap. His lips are kissing her now and all the lights go pale white and there's no color anywhere—just Eric pulling my halter-top over my head and spinning me around and tying it too tight and dragging me out of the room—rambling all the time about his bad luck and young girls and blah, blah, blah.

But it doesn't matter where Eric is taking me—I remain behind—in the room of many doors.

Cheap Thrills
December 23, 1967

Suggested listening:
Album—Easy Rider, various artists

The house is silent. Kathy's father is out cold on the couch, Chris and his friends are long gone. We tiptoe past the living room and burst out laughing the minute the bedroom door clicks closed. Dawn is creeping in through the windows and we collapse on the bed. I tell Kathy again about being in the room with Morrison.

I can't fucking believe you were fucking with him! I mean I was right behind you and then you were gone and I was stuck with your sister and Sandy, who were all freaked out and making me nuts. I can't fucking believe you were with Jim Morrison! You bitch! She swings playfully at me and I hit her in the face with a pillow.

You are so lucky we hung around the Shrine, she says, tossing the pillow on the bed. I bet Eric is still catching hell from your sister.

Yeah.

I don't get why she's mad at him. He's the one that found you and drove you back to the Shrine. You're the one that should be pissed at Eric, not your fucking sister.

Yeah, I know. I pick up another pillow and hug it tight—glad Eric found me, afraid of what might have happened if he hadn't.

You got Jim Morrison and all I got was your fucking sister. She sticks out her lower lip and pouts all dramatic like.

I cuddle close and wrap my arms around her. He's a jerk, I assure

120

her.

I'd fuck him, she sighs and rolls back over. He's bitchen! Good God, he kissed your tit! She pushes up on her elbows. Let me see where he wrote his name.

I lift my t-shirt, which doubles for pajamas.

Kathy leans in close and I drop my shirt. What? I have to get close, it's all smeared. God, Jim Morrison signed your tit. She falls back on the bed and kicks her feet.

I shrug and climb out of bed. He's still a jerk.

I'd fuck him in a second, Kathy moans.

I laugh. Probably all the longer he could go. He's so strung out on speed.

What the fuck do you know? You never fuck anyone.

I turn and walk to the window. I can't think of anything to say. Kathy's right, I don't fuck. I dig in my pocket and pull out a dull red capsule, a holdover from the concert. I always have a downer with me in case things start going bad. I stuff it back in my pocket for another time.

We spend the day talking and listening to music, still buzzing from all the uppers we took right after Shirley and Sandy dropped us off at Kathy's house. Kathy's dad doesn't even check on us, never does. We hear him coughing and slamming doors on his way to work.

We meet up with Shirley at our house before dark and wake up Muzzie, who showers and puts on a bright pink dress with tiny red flowers, red high heels, and a matching red purse. I don't bother to change my leather pants, but throw a sweater over my halter top in deference to Muzzie. She shakes her head and tells me the least I could do is run a brush through my hair. I shrug and walk out of the house ahead of her.

We all pile into our red Galaxy 500 and hit the freeway. Muzzie treats us to dinner at her favorite restaurant in Chinatown for my birthday. She's still sore that we saw the Doors on my birthday instead of being with her, but a few drinks at Hop Sing Tong's Canton Bar make her feel a little better. A few joints and another hit of acid make Shirley, Kathy and me feel better. We haven't slept in close to thirty-six hours, so we add a few whites for good measure. The mix puts us in a mood to party.

The night's warm, the car windows are down, and the lights of the city flash by as we speed down the main boulevard that runs through Los Angeles. Someone in the car gets the bright idea that we should head up to San Francisco and see Big Brother and the Holding Company—I think it might be me.

Muzzie says, I love the way that girl belts out a tune. Let's go!

We head home to pack a few things, pick up our stash and a few guys, including my new boyfriend, Jesse. We make a fast pass through the house, grabbing cans of soda, handfuls of beef jerky and big bags of potato chips. Shirley stuffs jeans and tank tops into a duffle bag for both of us. Muzzie writes a note for Dad saying I got sick and she had to take me out to the Air Force base.

That should throw him off our track, she says and flips off the note.

When it rains, it pours, especially in southern California. The sky opens up just as we hit the junction of the 10 and 101 freeways. Buckets of water pound the windshield. Fuck! Shirley screams and smacks the steering wheel with her palm.

Just a little water, Muzzie says. Want me to drive?

I lean forward to stop her if Shirley agrees. As stoned as I am, I know Muzzie's too drunk to drive. No! I don't want you to fuckin' drive! Fuck no! Shirley yells at her. I lean back into Jesse's arms as Muzzie curls into a ball with her head propped against the window and says, You're doing fine. I'll just take a little nap so I can drive when you get tired.

I watch the rain on the window streak into liquid fire. Red and yellow and orange fingers try to hold on to the glass, get whipped away by the wind. Whole fists of fire slam into the window and I move closer, wanting their warmth and light.

Fucking truckers! Shirley shouts and hits the steering wheel again. I sit up and look out the front windshield. A huge wave crests and breaks against the glass. Shirley's knuckles are glowing white and look like they're part of the steering wheel. The car shimmies and slides to the right, then back again, all the time the wave is still cresting over the car.

I thought we were goin' to Frisco? Kathy asks. Whadda we doin' at the beach?

Shut the fuck up, Kathy, Shirley screams and Muzzie snuffles and sinks lower in the seat. Everyone shut the fuck up!

Fuck you! Shirley screams as another wave crashes into the windshield.

Pull off at the truck stop, Jesse says and taps Shirley on the shoulder. The rain has to let up pretty soon.

Brilliant, asshole. We're in the middle of fucking nowhere. Do you see any fucking truck stops?

Yeah. Right there. He points out the front windshield at a carnival of colored lights.

Stop it! You're gonna get us kicked out of here, Shirley warns. Jesse ignores her and gives the ashtray a push. It skids along the long table and comes to rest right on the edge.

Alright! he yells and pumps his arm in the air above his head.

Shut the fuck up! Shirley grabs the ashtray and pounds out her cigarette. Here she comes, don't do anything!

A tiny wrinkled woman walks up to the table carrying our food. She has plates stacked two high all up and down her left arm and two in her right hand. French toast with scrambled, she announces and sets one of the two plates in her right hand down in front of Jesse. French toast with sunny side up and bacon. She hands the other plate to Jesse who passes it along.

Yeeeww, that's gross, Kathy chimes in as she hands the plate to me and I pass it on to Robert. The two eggs stare at me, all slimy white and pale yellow. Drew grabs a piece of toast before his plate hits the table.

Side'a toast with butter, she says and hands the plate to me. I take it and look at the neat triangles glistening in the harsh diner lights. They look so perfect, no crumbs scattered around the plate, the butter soaking into every little chink in the bread, the patterns of the toast evenly spaced, nice and light brown, the crust a perfect sharp line of dark brown outlining the sides, the cut down the center, clean and even.

The waitress walks away and I look up. Everyone is shoveling food in their mouths like they haven't eaten in a year. Shirley and Muzzie are both taking hits off their cigarettes between bites and sipping on steaming black coffee.

The toast is too pretty to eat. I rearrange it on the plate, stacking the halves so the points stick out at odd angles. Re-stack them so they form a set of stairs, then circular stairs, then bridges that span the plate, then an escalator, then a house with a front door that can swing out ...

Stop it! Shirley smacks my hand and the house collapses. Eat the fucking food. Stop playing with it.

I look around and everyone's slowing down. All the breakfast plates have been cleared away and the guys all have small plates with the remains of dessert disappearing. I look over at Muzzie and she's dozing off, her head resting against the back of the booth. Her cigarette's smoldering in the ash tray. I snatch it and take a big hit before Shirley grabs it out of my hand.

You wanna get us busted? she hisses, then flags down the waitress for the check. The rain's stopped, she tells everyone. Let's hit the road!

Jessie and I splash across the wide parking lot hand-in-hand. The lot is a giant pond of colors and cars with submerged tires and flashing lights. By the time we get to the car Muzzie is already crashed in the backseat behind Shirley so Jesse and I claim shotgun. Kathy and Robert and Andrew pile in the back. Jesse slumps against my shoulder and is out before we hit the interstate. The Galaxy 500 skims along the wet road, purring softly, rocking me to sleep.

Someone taps my leg and I jerk awake. Everything's dark and stuffy and has an eerie blue cast. The car's still sailing along the road, Jesse's still asleep against my shoulder. You were moaning, Shirley tells me. Having a bad dream?

No. No, I'm fine. I rub my eyes and try to focus on the road through the rain-streaked windshield. Jesse feels heavy against me. I push him off and he flops against the window.

Where are we?

About an hour outta Frisco. Go back to sleep.

No. No, I'll keep you company.

Shirley puts her arm around my shoulder and pulls me close, steering with one hand. She holds her lit cigarette close and I take a hit and blow smoke rings into the blue night.

She laughs and wiggles her fingers. I take the cigarette and hold it for her. She blows a big, perfectly round smoke ring.

You have to teach me how to do that, I tell her.

It's all in the way you pucker, she tells me. You should be good at that!

Yeah ... since kissing is all I do.

Keep it like that. Don't let them, she nods at Jesse sleeping, push you into doing anything you don't want to do.

I don't know. I think I kinda want to ... Kathy says it's great.

Kathy is no one to listen to when it comes to sex. Christ, she doesn't have any discretion. You're better than that. She pulls me in close and kisses the top of my head. Besides, you just turned fifteen. You got time.

There's a pause and then a long silence. I know she wants to ask me about last night. I have no idea what Eric told her, but I don't want to tell her what almost happened.

What you tripping on? she asks.

Same as you.

Naw, I didn't take any acid. Stuck it in my pocket since I was driving. Want it?

I shake my head and snuggle closer. I'm cool.

Then alright. It's still night. Sleep tight.

I just might. I drift off happy that we're rhyming, like when we were kids and couldn't fall asleep.

The hallways twist and turn and I feel like a mouse in a maze. I follow the back in front of me, not caring any more where we are or why we're here—only want to fall into a bed and sleep off the day with its grey skies and the motel's greenish-yellow flickering lights and too many voices and bodies.

Muzzie struggles with the key, trying to fit it into the lock on a door. Drew takes the key and says, We got it Mrs. Conrad. We're fine. All the guys pile up behind Drew. Jesse doesn't even try to kiss me when I stumble past.

All I want is to strip off my clothes and stand in a hot shower—wash away the last two days and sleep through this one. I head straight for the shower once we're in our room. The water is warm and soft. I just stand there under the spray until Kathy tells me I'm holding everyone up. I lather up the wash cloth and scrub all over until my skin is pink and tingly.

I climb out and Kathy hands me a towel then shrieks, You washed it off? You fucking washed it off?

I look down at my tit and realize I scrubbed Jim Morrison away. Oh fuck! I yell, which brings Shirley flying into the small bathroom.

What's the problem?

Kathy points at me and cries, She washed it off! I can't believe she washed it off!

Washed what off?

And I know for sure Eric didn't tell Shirley .

I cover myself with the skimpy towel. Nothing … I sound lame even to me.

Nothing? Shirley puts her hands on her narrow hips and cocks one. Nothing?

Shit! Kathy looks back and forth between us. Sorry. I ... I ... I'm gonna go to bed. She starts to duck out of the bathroom and Shirley grabs her by the arm.

Not quite yet, little miss big mouth. What did she wash off?

I know I'm busted. I've learned it never helps to lie to Muzzie or Shirley. I fess up. At the ... after the ... you know ... the ...

The concert? When you disappeared for two fucking hours! You mean then? Shirley's hands are back on her hips.

Yeah. I can't look at her, talk to the floor. Uh ... well ...

Just get to it!

Yeah, you gotta tell her, Kathy adds and we both glare at her. Fine, I'm outta here. She makes a break for the door and Shirley doesn't try to stop her.

So? Shirley juts her chin at me and I can't find my voice. Hey, it's okay. What happened? Did he hurt you?

I shake my head. No. Eric stopped things from getting ... you know ... outta hand.

Well I'm glad he did something right.

He's really great. You shouldn't be so hard on him. He's really great.

Yeah, yeah. Great. So go on. What happened?

He gave me his autograph.

And?

That's all.

She taps her foot and cocks a hip.

He was kissing me where he wrote his name, when Eric broke things up. I look at her really quick and back down at the floor, wish I was braver, wonder why I'm so afraid to tell her what happened.

Where he wrote his name? Where the fuck did he write his name?

I drop the towel a little, keeping my nipple covered and point to the outside of my tit.

He autographed your tit? You have got to be kidding me!

I shake my head.

Lemme see!

I just washed it off.

You washed it off? she nearly shouts. You fucking washed it off?

Told you, Kathy yells from the other room. Whadda idiot.

You stay outta this, Shirley yells back, then turns back to me. You washed it off? Are you insane? She pulls the towel down and looks real close at my tit. Good god. You really scrubbed that off ... wait a minute ... no ... there's something there.

Where? Kathy yelps and runs back in the bathroom.

They're both looking at my tit as I back up against the tub.

Hey, hold still, Shirley tells me and moves a little to the side to let Kathy in closer.

There! There! It looks like a J. And there's the big M and some squiggly lines other here. Shirley lifts my tit a little to get better light and I slap her hand.

What? You let Morrison sign your tit and all of a sudden I can't touch you? For fuck sake.

Kathy steps back. You can't tell what it is. It could be anything. Fuck! We shoulda taken a picture of it last night! I pull the towel back up and shuffle my feet, not sure if I'm in trouble for letting him do it, or for washing it off.

Fuck! Shirley shakes her head and takes a drag off her cigarette.

I feel tears welling up. I didn't mean to ... I was trippin' and he was acting like a jerk ... and I thought ...

Shirley grabs me and hugs me and kisses the top of my head. You are too much! Good god, you actually had Morrison sign your tit? She pushes me a little away and looks in my eyes.

I nod and smile, a little pleased with myself and say, Yeah.

Damn. Wish I'd seen it.

Someone bangs open the door and starts whooping and hollering that it's party time. I pull my head out from under the pillow and see

Muzzie dancing to no music with a group of young guys I've never seen before, trailing behind her. I pull up the sheets and wonder how I'm gonna get outta bed with all these kids flooding into the room. I left my clothes on the bathroom floor. Shirley comes to the rescue and tosses me some jeans and a new tank top from the duffle bag.

I stuff my legs through the jeans and slip the top over my head under the covers and resurface to find at least ten guys scattered around the room. Jesse and Drew and Robert all have beers and are leaning back on the dresser checking out the new guys. I hope they're not going to pick a fight.

Beer cans are popped open and joints start circulating. I try to ignore all the guys, wonder where Muzzie found them, but don't care enough to ask. Shirley, Kathy and I start flipping through the newspaper Muzzie brought back, looking for the concert ads.

Here we go, Shirley tells us and sits up cross-legged and folds back the paper, then folds it in half and lays it back down on the bed. We all scan the columns looking for Big Brother—don't find them.

Can't be, Shirley says and flips the paper over. They have to be here. They're always playing at the Fillmore or the Matrix, or somewhere.

Who? a stocky guy with a bright orange shirt and red slacks asks.

Big Brother and the Holding Company, we all say at once.

Don't think they're in town. Hey, Davy. Are the Holding Company in town?

Naw. Not tonight. Think they're outta state somewhere.

What? Shirley booms and Muzzie turns around with a beer in one hand and her other arm around a bearded freak with long hair and tie-dyed clothes. Hey, keep it down. Don't want the manager banging on the door.

Shirley just stares at Muzzie with her mouth open.

Be cool, Muzzie tells her.

The band isn't playing, she hisses. They're not even in town.

So find someone else to go see, Muzzie suggests.

I don't want to see anyone else! We drove all the way up here to see Big Brother and the fucking Holding Company! Shirley's voice gets louder with each word. Now all the guys are looking over at our bed and a couple are stubbing out their cigarettes and turning for the door.

Keep your voice down, Muzzie warns. The freak ducks out from under her arm and heads for the door. You don't want the manager in here with these kids and all the beer.

I didn't fucking invite them, Shirley yells. In fact … she bounces up to her knees and points at the door. Get the fuck out! All of you! NOW!

Everyone makes a dash for the door, even our guys. Jesse, Drew, Robert, she shouts. Get your shit together. We're outta here in ten minutes!

You too, she smacks Kathy on the leg and nods at me.

I don't know why you're acting like this, Muzzie says and opens another beer. Why can't we see another band? Why'd you make all those nice young boys leave? I just don't understand you sometimes. She shakes her head sadly.

Someone has to act like an adult! Shirley fires back. And it sure the fuck isn't you.

Don't use that language with me, young lady.

Oh go fuck yourself, you drunken old bitch.

Muzzie sets her beer down on the window sill and just stares at Shirley.

Even I'm shocked and try to calm Shirley down. Hey, it's cool. There's nothing fucked.

Shut the fuck up and get packed. We're going home. She looks at me and Kathy and yells, NOW!

We start scavenging around the room, grabbing clothes and stuffing them in the duffle bag. Shirley sits cross-legged on the bed and lights a cigarette. Her hands are shaking. Muzzie doesn't move so I pack her clothes too and wish we'd never come to San Francisco. Wish I'd never had a birthday.

The ride home is long and lonely. No one talks. No one sings along to the radio. When we stop for gas it's no different. We grab snacks and drinks and head back to the car while Muzzie puts it all on the gas card. Halfway home Muzzie takes over and Shirley curls up against the passenger window.

It isn't raining, but it's cold and dark outside. I take the tab of acid out of my pocket and look at it, put it back; don't want to be the only one tripping, especially in this dismal car.

We drop the guys and Kathy off at their homes and pull into the driveway at 6:30 in the morning. It isn't even light out yet. Dad's car's there and the porch light's on.

Let me handle your father, Muzzie tells us and turns off the car.

He's standing in the doorway and starts yelling before we even make it to the porch. Don't bother lying to me about where you were! I called the damned base and you weren't there! And you do know it's Christmas morning and we have people coming for supper at noon?

We all stop and look at each other. Muzzie bursts out laughing and Dad takes a step back. I don't think this is a laughing matter, Helen, he tells her and I close my eyes, afraid he's going to hit her.

Oh for Christ's sake, Condie, she laughs. What else can you do but laugh? She reaches over and pats Shirley's arm. We better get going if we're gonna pull this one out of the hamper.

Dad shakes his head and turns away. It's your damn family coming over, he tells her. I won't have anything to do with it.

As if you ever do, Muzzie says under her breath, and smiles at us. Let's get going girls. Lots to do!

1968 in the news

- ❖ The population of the United States is 200.71 million
- ❖ The national debt is $347.6 billion
- ❖ Average income per year is $5,572
- ❖ Minimum wage is $1.60 per hour
- ❖ Average cost of a new house is $26,600
- ❖ Average monthly rent is $130
- ❖ A gallon of gas costs $0.34
- ❖ First class postage is $0.06
- ❖ A movie ticket costs $1.50
- ❖ *In the Heat of the Night* wins Best Picture
- ❖ *Up-Up and Away* wins Best Song
- ❖ *Sgt. Pepper's Lonely Hearts Club Band* wins Best Album
- ❖ The musical *Hair* officially opens on Broadway
- ❖ Movies released: *2001: A Space Odyssey*; *Bullitt*; *Rosemary's Baby*; *The Green Berets*; and *The Planet of the Apes*
- ❖ The following TV shows debut: *Rowan and Martin's Laugh-In*; *Mister Rogers' Neighborhood*; *Adam 12*; *The Doris Day Show*; *Mod Squad*; *60 Minutes*; *Hawaii Five-0*
- ❖ President Johnson announces he will not seek or accept the nomination of his party for the Presidency
- ❖ The Rev. Dr. Martin Luther King, Jr. is shot and killed in Memphis
- ❖ Sen. Robert F. Kennedy is shot and killed in Los Angeles after winning the California Presidential Primary

- ❖ North Korea seizes the USS Pueblo, claiming the ship violated its territorial waters while spying and holds the crew captive for 11 months

- ❖ United States Army soldiers of "Charlie" Company murder between 347 and 504 unarmed civilians in the South Vietnam village of My Lai. The victims were women, children, infants, and elderly people

- ❖ The Republican National Convention nominates Richard Nixon

- ❖ The Democratic National Convention nominates Hubert Humphrey while outside thousands of peaceful anti-war protesters are met with violence when the Chicago police riot

- ❖ Integrated Electronics Corporation (Intel) is founded by Robert Noyce and Gordon Moore

- ❖ Virginia Slims cigarettes are marketed to women; the "Slims" is to remind them that smoking is non-fattening

- ❖ 911 emergency telephone number is instituted in 600 cities

Stone Free
February 10, 1968

Suggested listening:
Album—Are You Experienced, The Jimi Hendrix Experience

Your dad believed you?

Yeah, why not?

Because you never go to church, to start, and there aren't any bible camps this time of year. Is he dense?

No. I'm just good at making up stories.

Spending the weekend at a bible camp, in February, when you don't even belong to a church, isn't a good story! Your dad is so lame. I thought he was some kinda Narc.

He is.

Then he can't be that dense.

Doesn't matter. How's this look? I turn around and try not to slouch. I shoplifted the red and yellow paisley outfit yesterday, wasn't sure if it would fit. I didn't know the hip-huggers were cut so low, the halter-top so skimpy.

Man! I wish I were tall and skinny, Peggy sighs.

I'm not skinny. Geesh, look at this! I pinch a bit of skin on my belly and look down in disgust. I hate seeing any bulges or curves, means I'm still fat and ugly. I sigh, I'll never get thin.

Oh shut up! Look at this. Peggy pulls her t-shirt up and grabs a couple fingers width of fat on her belly. Now *this* is fat. *That* is skinny. She drops her t-shirt and falls back on her bed.

So your Mom really knows Jimi Hendrix? I ask for the tenth time.

Yep.

How?

She shakes her head. Don't know. But she has tickets to the concert *and* back stage passes. I saw them.

And she's gonna take us?

Peggy nods.

Why?

'Cause she's cool and we're cool. And she doesn't know any adults around here who even know who Jimi Hendrix is. This town is so square!

Yeah. I know.

Peggy's new in town; started Charter Oak in September. I like her. Kathy doesn't so much. But we hang out with her sometimes. I was really surprised when she asked me if I wanted to see Hendrix. I really dig his music, but I could never afford two concerts so close together. I didn't tell Kathy 'cause she'd be pissed if she knew I ditched her for Peggy. Having two friends can get complicated.

So Whadda ya think? It has a matching head band. I lay the thick strap of material against my forehead, flip my hair up and tie it low against the back my neck.

Groovy. Definitely groovy.

Halfway through the concert I'm wondering if I'll ever be able to hear again. Jimi Hendrix's blasting the crowd with guitar licks I can't even imagine. His fingers race up and down the frets, his other hand plucking like a mad man. He turns to face the giant wall of amplifiers, runs his guitar up and down, in and out. The amplifiers screech and moan and scream.

He's fucking the amp! Peggy yells in my ear, then yells at the stage, Yeah, man, fuck'um Jimi!

I feel my face flush and look away. I hadn't thought about his playing like that, but now I can't think of anything else. I glance back and see his hips humping and grinding against the amplifiers and look away. I pull my pants up and my halter down, but neither one moves much. I wrap my arms around my waist feeling almost naked.

The song screeches to a finish. The crowd explodes! I plug my ears and think I really won't be able to ever hear again. He starts right in with another song.

Peggy's pulling on my arm, pointing to her mom with her other hand. Her mom's standing on the stairs to the stage and I feel my face flush again. She doesn't have her blouse on. Her tits are enormous, bouncing up and down in time with the music. She's waving at us. Peggy drags me by the arm through the dancing, shouting crowd towards her mom.

We finally make it to the stage and Peggy's mom yells, Lose the tops girls. Flash 'em!

Foxy Lady. Here I come, coming to get you! Hendrix coos seductively into the mike and breaks into another wild guitar lick.

Peggy pulls her tank top off over her head. She's almost as big as her mother, though her tits don't bounce as much. I keep my halter top on, feeling absolutely flat next to the two of them.

Her mom flashes me the peace sign and then gives me the thumbs up and pantomimes taking my halter off. I shake my head no and look away.

The auditorium is packed with people, thick puffs of smoke float across the rabble. I smell pot and hash and something else I don't know. Peggy hands me a joint. The end is sucked flat and sticky. I look at it a minute, not knowing who sucked it before me. Peggy slaps my arm and motions for me to take a hit. I close my eyes and try not to think about all the other mouths.

It's good weed, goes right to my head without a single cough, tickles the edges of an acid rush I've been waiting for, pushes me into the haze.

Purple Haze all in my mind ...

I look up at Hendrix, not believing what he's saying. He looks over and for an instant our eyes meet.

Acting funny and I don't know why ...

I look away and wonder if he's talking to me, wonder why he's not singing. *Excuse me while I kiss the sky.* His guitar whines and the band joins him. I blink and look around. Everyone is dancing, waving their hands in the air, some are singing along and I wonder how they know the words, thought Jimi was talking to me.

Way out! Peggy shouts in my ear. Way far out!!! I see her mom being lead backstage by a burly, tattooed dude that looks like a biker. Peggy smacks her hands together and follows up the stairs. I take a last look, try to figure out if I could make it back through the crowd on my own, then realize we're going backstage with Jimi Hendrix. I take another hit and hand the joint to the biker dude and pass behind the curtains—pass into a cool, almost silent world of electrical cords and amps and guys that all look the same, sitting on steamer trunks playing cards, drinking whisky and smoking.

They slap Peggy's mom on the butt as she walks past, do the same to Peggy. I swerve out of reach. They laugh almost silently at me and I wonder how it can be so quiet here when on the other side of the curtain the sound is deafening.

Peggy's mom is buttoning up her sleeveless red blouse. Peggy grabs her tank top from where she stuffed it under her belt and pulls it back on. We're lead down more stairs and piled into a limo already filled with girls. I step in and the door closes, pushing me head first across Peggy and her mother's laps.

Let the party begin, Peggy's mom whoops and all the other girls take up the cry. The limo lurches forward and I fall on the floor. There's a wide space between the seats and I think about staying put, but hands are grabbing at me, pulling me off the floor, stuffing me between Peggy and the door.

There's a loud pop and I jump. Chill, dude, Peggy tells me and points to a girl holding a foaming bottle of champagne across from us. She starts pouring the golden liquid into tall thin glasses held by another girl. A third starts passing the filled glasses around the Limo. *Purple Haze* blasts from the stereo and all the girls start singing along.

Donna D. Conrad

I shake my head at Peggy who's offering me a glass of champagne.

Don't be a downer, she shouts over the music and the shrill sing along.

I'm not. I just don't like the stuff.

Hey, got any beers in there? Peggy kicks at the girl across from her and I notice there's a sunken box directly across from me. The girl lifts the lid and pulls out an amber bottle, pops the top and hands it to me.

Ask and ye shall receive! Peggy tells me and downs her champagne. A bottle floats across the divide and fills her glass.

The acid starts peaking and I scoot onto one hip and look out the window, try to ignore the raucous choir inside, single out Hendrix's voice from the stereo, watch the streets flashing by through the darkened windows.

I down the beer and suddenly it's full again and the bottle has changed color and shape. I giggle and take a big drink. It tastes like apples and cinnamon. I'm game for anything, have learned to take whatever acid hands me and go with it. You know you're going to trip—may even stub a toe or two—but you'll never fall ... never fall down.

The houses vanish, so do the streetlights and then the curbs. I pull my head back away from the window and wonder if everything outside the car is being dissolved. Peggy kisses my bare back and gives it a little scratch.

You tripping? She asks.

I nod my head and look back out the window. We're climbing now. There are houses every once in a while, nestled in shadow, their yellow sunburst lights glowing and dimming, trying to keep up with the limo, not able to for very long.

We make a hard left and all the girls are thrown together. I hang on tight to the leather strap above the door, keep to myself, don't want to be one of the chickies clucking and chirping over champagne. I look over at Peggy and her mom. They both have their tops off again. Peggy's mom is holding her tit in her hands, twisting it so the other girls can see a wavy blue black line. I realize it's a tattoo. I let go and slide over. I've never seen a real tattoo up close.

A dolphin leaps from the whitecaps and clears the mound, dives back under on the other side. I blink and look away. I look again just as the dolphin breaks the surface, soars, and dives back underwater.

How does it do that? I ask Peggy's mom.

Do what?

Jump like that and land on the other side.

I hate acidheads, she says. An ice cold wave hits me in the face and I scoot back against the door.

Fucking acidheads.

Hey be cool, she's my friend, Peggy tells her.

Then you need new friends. The bitch won't even take her top off. Not that she's got any reason too! Flat as a board and never been nailed. Peggy's mom bursts out cackling like a witch out of Shakespeare. I click a button in my mind and a window rises between us, shuts her and her laugh out—leaves me alone with the passing shadows and light.

I'm the last out of the limo. Follow the herd through enormous doors into a foyer as big as my whole house. Music is blaring, people are laughing and screaming and racing around, some without any clothes on.

I grab Peggy's arm. Where are we?

She hands me a joint. Mom says it's Peter Torc's house and he's always having a party.

Who?

Peter Torc. You know the Monkee.

Peggy's mom dances past leaving a trail of clothes on the floor.

A Monkee? No way.

Yeah. Pretty cool, huh?

This can't be a Monkee's pad. They're so fucking square.

That's what she said. Peggy takes the joint and walks off sucking

Donna D. Conrad

hard. She waves for me to follow.

I can't find a place to light. Every time I stop someone hands me a joint and tries to get me to take my top off, tries to get me to get naked. I never get naked except to shower, I tell them and they take the joint away. One guy offers to show me the shower. He's plenty cute, but old, probably at least twenty-five. It's all disgusting, all the naked bodies, couples having sex right in front of everyone. One woman has her mouth around a guy's dick and is pumping up and down. She's in the pool, he's sitting with his legs in the water. I turn away and walk back into the house.

It's not much better there. I find a corner in the big front room and sit crossed-legged on the floor. I can't give in to the acid, don't trust anyone around me, don't want a bad trip. So I ignore the flying Monkees and bright yellow halos that float by, ignore the pounding music and the tits and dicks that flap past me, ignore the butts and hairy legs and shrieks and howls and moans.

I'm fine where I am. I only hope Peggy finds me when it's time to leave. I don't count on it though. The last I saw, she was standing naked in a second story window taking dares to dive into the crowded pool. I didn't know she wasn't a natural redhead.

I decide it would be best if I were invisible. The air flickers around me, the music and the lights dim, and everyone looks hazy and distant. They pass by without even seeing me. I relax my guard, play with the light show that surrounds people. Think, I'm in a Monkee's house. This could be my best trip yet.

Young thang.

The words are the first I've heard since I became invisible.

Young thang, there.

I look over and see a black man with giant hair and greenish-gold lights flashing all around him.

You do not belong in this house with these men, he says to me from his high-backed chair, only an arm's length away.

He looks over his shoulder, snaps his fingers, and says, Allen. Take her out of here. Keep her safe.

A tall, terribly thin man reaches for me. There are the most beautiful amber and lavender lights flashing all around him. I trust him for some reason—take his hand. I stand up and look down at the black man, realize it's Jimi Hendrix—almost lose my footing. Allen holds me up as the room swirls.

It's cool, he tells me and leads me out a side door, away from Hendrix.

You tripping?

I nod.

Where you from?

I shrug not able to find my voice after being invisible for so long.

How'd you get here?

We're walking along a long driveway and I nod at the jet-black limo.

Fuck. They brought you here? How old are you?

My legs give out and I drop to the ground. He hauls me up and half drags me to a metal bench. Hey be cool. Don't cry. It's all cool.

I hadn't realized I was crying, but now I can feel hot tears running down my face. Is my eyeliner running? My voice sounds squeaky.

It's fine, he laughs. Glad you can talk. Had me worried for a minute there.

I'll take it Allen, a voice comes out of nowhere. I jump and feel the tears rolling again.

Sure, boss. She's cool. Allen steps aside and there's Jimi Hendrix standing right in front of me.

You came in the limo? Hendrix asks and his voice is so smooth, so calm that I know I can trust him.

I nod.

You don't belong here. He sits next to me and I scoot all the way over, nearly fall off the end of the bench.

I don't bite.

I look at him from under my lowered eyelashes. He's smiling. His face is pitted and faintly yellow. I chance it and look at his eyes. They're kind and soft and not at all like the other men in the house.

You tripping?

I nod.

Is it a good trip?

I smile and nod again.

Do you know where you live?

I blink and wonder why he wants to know.

Do you?

I nod.

I'll have someone safe take you home.

I back up on the bench, not wanting to leave; not wanting to go home when I'm tripping.

He grabs me just as I'm about to fall.

Hey, hey there. It's all groovy. You're too young to be here is all. You should go home.

I want to tell him that Peggy's my age and she's jumping out of a window into the pool, naked. But I can't find the words.

If she's doing that, then she's not as young as you are, he says, and I wonder if he can read minds.

No, he says. It's all cool. But I wouldn't mind some of what you're on. He looks back at the house. All this going down and you're having a groovy trip. Now that has to be some *fine* acid.

He stands and looks down at me.

Don't go getting in any more cars unless you know the dudes, and even then you still got to be careful.

I smile up at him and nod, but can't find my voice.

And don't go tryin' to grow up too fast. You don't need to be like that friend of yours. Just be yourself. He turns and walks back toward the house, stops next to Allen and says, Find out where she lives and get her home. No messin'round now ...

Not a problem, Boss. She's too young for me. I like my women seasoned.

That's why I keep you close Allen, Hendrix says and smiles at me. Before opening the front door, he adds, Get Stone Free over there home safe and come pick me up around dawn. I'll be down by then.

Glory Train
March 1968

Suggested listening:
Single—*Respect*, Aretha Franklin

It's like stickin' your dick in tapioca. You gotta go try it, man. It's totally weird.

The words float down the hallway and out into the living room on a cloud of pot. I don't recognize the guy's voice, probably a friend of a friend of someone. When my dad's away on week-long assignments the house is always full of freaks. I'm not really sure how they all know to show up, I never tell anyone when my dad's gonna be gone. Don't really know all that many people to tell, besides Kathy.

You fucked her? You gotta be kiddin'!

The voices float closer, and I think they must be talking about Kathy, she's always fucking someone. But I can't believe she'd fuck someone in my bed without asking me.

I swing my head around and see Kathy on the floor with a longhair's hand down her pants and wonder who else would be fucking in my room. My sister and Sandy are out in the backyard. I've never fucked anyone. That doesn't leave anyone else I know.

I light another joint, take a couple of tokes and hand it to the guy lying on my lap. I think I like him but can't remember his name. Then it comes to me, Jesse. He asked me to go steady last night, gave me his St. Christopher medal.

Fuck man, her tits are huge. They hang down on her belly ... I look around and see some other guys I don't know coming out of the long hallway, one zipping up his pants.

I turned her over and fucked her up the ass.

Fuck no, you didn't.

Fuckin' A I did.

You are fucked up, dude.

They slap each other on the back and flop onto the floor next to me.

I don't ask, 'cause I don't want to know who's using my bed to pull a train. Don't want to even think about the mess that's gonna be left when everyone leaves.

Two more guys head down the hallway. I lean back against the couch and watch them walk past my dad's room, stop at the closed door opposite my bedroom, the door to Muzzie's room. I push Jesse off my lap and stand up. The first shot of panic claws it way up into my throat at the thought of someone fucking in Muzzie's bed. She'll know for sure when she gets back from work.

I turn in a circle and can't figure out how to make them stop before we all get busted. I suddenly want my sister to come inside, want her to make these people get the hell outta our house. Muzzie is cool, let's us do most things we want, but a bunch of kids fucking in her bed? She'd freak out and ground me for a month.

Jesse climbs to his feet, stretches, and then heads down the hall. Hey Jesse, one of the guys on the floor yells to him. Check out the old broad in the back room. She's pulling a train!

The room spins and I think I'm going to heave. They can't mean Muzzie ... she's at work, I tell myself.

Then I remember she isn't at work, that she called in sick. Said she had the flu and went to bed early this afternoon. I knew she was just drunk again, had been since the night before dad went out on his case ... since he beat the crap out of her because I hadn't ironed his shirts or cleaned the house the way he liked.

I stumble into the kitchen and take another red out of my jean pocket, pop it in my mouth, down it with a beer, but that doesn't stop my mind from screaming, they can't mean Muzzie … it can't be her …

I can't stand the thoughts all scrambled in my head, can't stand all the freaks leaning against the walls, sitting around the dining room table, the music blaring so loud I can't think of what to do.

Kathy wanders in and I scream, Get them the fuck outta here.

Why?

Get them out!

Ok, be cool.

Her brother's sitting at the table with a girl tucked under his arm. Kathy waves him over to the sink where we're standing.

She wants everyone out, Kathy tells him.

Now! I scream.

Fuck you, Chris answers. You on the rag or something?

I yell, Get out! and shove him.

He backhands me across the mouth and yells, Fuck you, bitch!

I feel hot tears stinging my eyes and run to the sliding door, shove it open looking for Shirley, but can't see her for all the freaks outside, crowded under the covered patio to stay out of the drizzling rain. I push my way back through the living room and head down the hall.

I bump into a guy coming out of Muzzie's bedroom. I shove him out of the way, push open the bedroom door. I back up and shake my head—can't believe what I'm seeing.

Muzzie's naked, sprawled on top of the covers, slobbering drunk, and nearly unconscious from *Old Grand Dad*, the cheap whiskey she hides in her underwear drawer and thinks I don't know about.

My new boyfriend, is fucking her.

I can't move, feel like my feet are glued to the carpet. I want to close my eyes, to stop seeing Jesse's butt rising and falling. Want to block out Muzzie's groans and Jesse's panting. Want to be anywhere but here.

I scream, Get off her, you fucking pig! Jesse keeps on pumping, breathing even louder.

I back out of the doorway and don't know where to go, what to do. I've never felt so alone, so sick to my stomach. I stumble back down the hallway and lock myself inside the bathroom. I crumble to the floor telling myself this isn't happening, that it's just a bad trip.

I can't stop crying; it's getting harder to breathe. I hear a loud crash from the living room and know it's real. The freaks, the house being trashed, Muzzie ... all of it.

I dig in my pocket and find four reds. I pull myself up to the sink and down the pills, swallowing handfuls of water between sobs. She can't do this to me ... Muzzie can't do this ... I tell myself over and over and, for the first time ever, wish I were dead.

I fall back onto the soft, rose-pink carpet and sing to myself—sing to block out all the noise—sing to block out everything—sing *Penny Lane* and pretend I'm in London with all the cool people—sing while I wait for the reds to sweep away everybody and everything I want to forget, forever.

The next morning, I wake up in my bed. I don't remember how I got the split lip or the bruise along my jaw. Figure I must have tripped and fallen. I swallow an errant red I find lying on my nightstand because my jaw really hurts. I realize my dad won't be home for another couple of days. Think it would be cool to have some freaks over for a party.

On the Corner of Nowhere and Nothing
April 1968

Suggested listening:
Single—*Season of the Witch*, Donovan

Dull gray door staring in.

White tiles peering up.

Shiny silver walls at arm's length, standing straight and tall.

My feet balanced atop a shimmering white rim, hovering high above the tiles, my body caved in on itself.

A bell rings. Voices fade away.

I can't remember how I found my way here. Or where here might be.

But I'm safe and I'm not moving.

We drive on the sidewalk surrounding the Shrine Auditorium before dawn. Shirley says we can, Eric says we can't. So we all pile into the Galaxy 500 and drive the thirty miles, bump up over the curb and do one lap around the Shrine ... an offering to the gods of folly. Jesse is in the back seat with me and Kathy and two other freaks I don't know. I have his Saint Christopher's medal, which means we're going steady. That I'm his girl. He thinks that gives him the right to put his hand down my hip-huggers. I don't mind his hand.

A door groans.

A slight breeze carries the scent of stale cigarette smoke.

I hold my breath and curl into a smaller ball on my perch.

Shoes click against tiles, moving closer.

Somehow I know it's a teacher. Know I'm in a bathroom stall.

Know she'll bend low and look under each door, one by one.

Know she won't see me because I'm not really here.

I wake up in my father's twin bed. The speckled white ceiling is watching me. I turn and find a boy I don't know next to me. I reach beneath the covers and feel for my jeans and take a deep breath. I touch my t-shirt. I have my clothes on, he doesn't. My hair is wet and a dream of being held upright in the shower, clothes and all, floats just below the ceiling. I touch my jeans. They're wet, so are the sheets, so is the boy.

The teacher stops in front of my stall.

Her brown shoes and pearl necklace show beneath my door.

I want to kick the door open. Smash it into her face.

But if I'm seen I'll vanish.

They say that fucking is love and to love you have to fuck, but I don't believe them. They just want to fuck. I hold the Saint Christopher medal in my hand and break the chain. Jesse is no better than the rest. When I won't put out, he pulls out, he and his friend, but first they break into my dad's bedroom and steal his gun.

The footsteps retreat.

A door groans open, then slams closed.

My vault remains sealed.

The white tiles breathe a sigh of relief.

When Jesse and his friend get busted, they tell the pigs I asked them to kill my father. Me and my sister. The pigs call and my dad takes us down to the station. They separate me and my sister. A pig asks me if I want my dad dead. My dad's standing next to me and I don't want him dead. But I'm not telling the pig that. So I pop my gum and roll my eyes and will myself not to cry. You're a tough cookie, the pig says. But this is conspiracy to commit murder and you won't be so tough after serving twenty years … Cookie. My dad turns his back and looks out the window and I wish I'd told the pig I didn't want my dad dead. But it's too late to say it now and so I say nothing.

The white tiles pull at my feet and I drop them.

I sit on the toilet rim and curl forward, holding my head in my hands.

I know I have to leave this shelter.

Know I must return to books and papers and bells.

Return to nowhere I am known.

To nothing I care for.

Chance to Dance
May – June 1968

Suggested listening:
Single—*Oh Death*, by Kaleidoscope
Album—Little Wheel Spin and Spin, Buffy Sainte-Marie

I twitch one long finger to the opening twang of guitar and banjo; nothing more. Wait for the song to take off.

O, Death. O, Death. O, Death. Won't you spare me over 'til another year?

Snaking out arms and legs from a tangled lump in the center of the gymnasium, I rise … slowly. The black scarves attached to the sleeves of my black leotard float and billow as I twirl, my arms stretched high above my head.

Well I am Death, none can excel. I'll open the door to Heaven or Hell.

I stop twirling, reach for a fellow student. She cries out and backs away. I don't reach out to the others as I had rehearsed. I twirl instead—jump high in the air and land softly, drift back and forth across the gym floor, my arms and scarves far in front of me, then trailing behind, high in the air, tight against my sides. I make one last leap, then slide slowly to the ground into the splits, my arms above my head all the way down. I wait four beats then start to slowly tuck my legs and arms back in around me. End as I began—a black smudge on the gym floor.

No clapping. No talking … nothing. I raise my painted face and see the entire dance class, including the teacher, Miss Warren, staring at me. I untangle myself and stand up, not sure what to do. I expected something other than silence after my mid-term dance performance. I was prepared for giggles and raised eyebrows from the more experienced dancers—after all, this is my first modern dance class and I know I need to practice more. But silence was never a consideration.

Yeah! Kathy yells and puts her fingers to her mouth and whistles like she's at a ball game. Everyone covers their ears, including the teacher. I make a swishy exit. Sit cross-legged on the floor next to Kathy.

Uh ... yes ... well, the teacher begins, pauses, clears her throat. Very original, Miss Conrad. Though I do question the choice of songs, the dance itself was well choreographed and did clarify the intention of the ... uh ... the lyrics. She sputters to a stop.

Thank you, I say to the floor in front of me. My voice cracks and I know my face is bright red.

Yes ... well ... yes ... She stops again and I look up. She isn't usually one to hesitate. She's looking across the gym and seems a bit distracted. Yes ... well ... she taps her clipboard and says, Who's next. She looks at her list of dancers. Audrey, you're up. She nods at a senior who's taken modern dance for four years now.

Audrey leaps up. Kathy and I stifle a laugh too late.

That will be enough, Miss Conrad, Miss Weston.

We try not to look at the pudgy fairy in purple tights as it skips to the center of the gym, its large wings lying limp at its back. But the first notes of the song have us laughing out loud. The teacher shoots a killer look at us and we sober up fast. But, *The Dance of the Sugar Plum Fairies* is hard to take seriously, even if we were straight; and as always before a big event like mid-terms, we dropped a handful of uppers at dawn and split a tab of orange sunshine at lunch. I'd figured the acid wouldn't come on until after my performance. This time it was a close call. I decide not to cut it so close from now on. Decide to wait until after dance class to drop. Not taking the uppers isn't even an option.

The not so little fairy dances nicely, with perfect form and excellent timing. But she doesn't look like she's having any fun, even though she's supposed to be a fairy. Her dance ends and everyone but Kathy and me claps, even the teacher—and I wonder why no one clapped for me.

They're a buncha assholes, that's why, Kathy whispers, and I realize I said something out loud again when I thought I was only thinking it. Tell myself I have to stop doing that.

I bite my bottom lip to keep quiet and try to ignore the lines on the basketball court when they swirl around the next dancer and follow her back to her seat.

I'm more nervous than the last time; not only because this dance is the final exam for modern dance, but because I let Kathy talk me into doing the dance with her. We've practiced in front of Shirley and Sandy, in front of Shirley and David, in front of Shirley and Muzzie. But, we always seem to mess something up and have to start over. We can't do that today and I'm worried.

Very interesting, Miss Warren says, and taps her clipboard. She looks over at me. Miss Conrad *and* Miss Weston will be performing a duet today.

We both nod.

I believe this is the first duet in my class. I look forward to your performance. She taps her clipboard again and nods for us to start.

I walk across the gym floor and hand the album to Audrey, who's standing next to the record player. First song, please, I tell her.

Audrey looks at the label and says, *Little Wheel Spin and Spin?* She giggles and whispers, This is going to be even worse than your last one, especially with *her.* She juts her round chin at Kathy.

I don't say anything back, just turn and walk out to the center of the floor and raise my eyebrows at Kathy. What did she say? Kathy asks.

Nothing, I lie. Go get in place.

Before she even takes a step, Audrey sets the needle down hard and the song starts.

Audrey! Miss Warren yells above the guitar intro.

Sorry, Miss Warren. Audrey snatches the needle off the record and I know she's scratched it on purpose.

Be more careful, Audrey, Miss Warren tells her. That's not your property. If you've scratched it, you'll have to buy Miss Conrad a new album.

Audrey's face turns bright red. She waits until I give her the signal to start and this time sets the needle down nice and easy.

My back's to Kathy's and I just hope she's ready. The guitar picks through a complicated series of notes. I raise my arms above my head, bring them back down slowly and Kathy and I turn and face each other exactly right, just as Buffy Sainte-Marie starts singing, *Little wheel spin and spin. Big wheel turn around, round.*

Kathy's in a red leotard with black tights, I'm in red tights and a black leotard. It was Muzzie's idea. I wonder how we look, Kathy short and round, me tall with sharp angles. But there's no more time to think as we close on each other. Kathy starts twirling slowly in large circles around me, her arms waving up down as she turns. I spin on the balls of my feet, my arms tight against my side, staying in one place.

Kathy keeps turning as I break out of the spin and reach to the ceiling, then drop to the floor as the music takes over all my thoughts and leaves me just dancing. Nothing else exists, not dad's yelling or Muzzie's drinking, or Shirley moving out. I don't even think about Kathy and everything we rehearsed. I know she's feeling the music too; know she'll be there when we meet up for the third verse.

Blame the Angels, Blame the fates, Blame the Jews or your sister Kate.

Kathy's right there in front of me. I push her away and she drops to the floor and really looks like she's crying for just a second, then jumps up and starts turning around me again in a big circle for the chorus.

We both leap into the air at exactly the same time and drop to the ground "*when the world explodes,*" then spin and turn like the earth and the moon in orbit.

Swing your girl fiddler say - Later on the piper pay - Do see do, swing and sway - Dead will dance on judgment day.

We take each other's hands and do a nice imitation of a square dance, like Miss Warren taught us. I drop into a tight tuck on the balls of my feet and Kathy takes my outstretched hands and spins me real fast. I keep one point on the far wall in sight and actually stay upright, spinning all on my own. I can only hope Kathy is turning again. She's back right on target for the next round and spins me again and again as the song dies away. My last spin winds down and Kathy stops turning just as I stop spinning. We reach out for each other, then drop our hands and heads on the last pluck of the guitar string.

There's a moment of absolute silence, and I don't know what to do to get un-tucked and off the balls of my feet. I see Kathy's black-toed feet and look up. She has her hand out to me. I take it and stand. The class bursts into applause, including Miss Warren, and I think my legs are going to give way. Kathy wraps an arm around my waist and without it even looking like she's helping me, she walks me over to our seat and lets go.

I've danced for real this time and can't imagine a time when I would ever not dance—not ever.

Tryst without Consent
August 24, 1968

Suggested listening:
Album—In-A-Gadda-Da-Vida, Iron Butterfly

Our dresses are short, but mine not short enough. My legs are long; I want everyone to know it. Kathy jabs straight pins through the hem of the slick black satin, but she's too stoned to thread a needle, so the pins will have to hold for tonight.

Her brother drops us off at my sister's new apartment, glad to be rid of two fifteen-year-old girls that cause him nothing but grief. My sister and her best friend Sandy's new apartment is on the ground floor of a huge complex, new to the likes of Covina.

Parking spaces veer off a long circular drive that has a name as if it were a real street. Chris stops and we jump out of the back seat. He takes off, leaving us in the parking lot unsure where to go. We turn down one walkway, *In-A-Gadda-Da-Vida* calls to us, and we know we're hot on the trail.

The door is unlocked. We walk into a haze of smoke and Iron Butterfly. Everyone is smoking pot and drinking beer. Kathy says, All right now! and heads straight for a guy smoking a fat joint.

I wander through the living room looking for my sister or Sandy. My head starts to throb and I want to pull the pins out of the hem of my dress. I drift into the kitchen and see Shirley leaning against the stove.

Fuck! You're so skinny! she shouts and hugs me, a joint in her

156

hand. She passes it off to me.

I take a deep toke, close my eyes and hold it in. The throbbing in my head spikes, vanishes, and I open my eyes. Shirley's hair is wild and frizzy and filled with light from the overhead fixtures. She used to curl her hair with enormous plastic rollers to straighten it. I used to curl mine with tiny ones to make it wavy. We both let that go when it became cool to be "natural." I still use black liner on my eyes and curve it out into ends that split. Shirley doesn't wear any makeup; she doesn't even wear a bra.

Whadda ya think? she asks.

Cool, very cool, I say, sucking in another toke. Where's Sandy? I ask holding my breath.

Shirley looks around and shrugs her shoulders. Don't know. Where do the folks think you are?

Dad's out on some campus case and Muzzie's working a split. I have until midnight to be home.

Cool. Shirley takes the joint and points to a tub of ice filled with beer on the sink. Help yourself. Someone calls her and she turns in a complete circle puffing hard on the joint, starts coughing, then laughing as she hurries away.

I snag a Brew 102 and head back to the living room.

You wanna score some pot? Kathy plunks down on the couch next to me and hands me a lit joint.

I've been watching something on the silent TV and listening to Steppenwolf pounding out of the waist-high speakers. I don't understand all the references, but the lyrics are heavy and mean a lot to me alone on the couch with an apartment full of college freaks I don't know.

With who? I ask, sucking in the harsh smoke. This stuff sucks! I hiss. Sandy needs a new dealer. Ever since Shirley broke up with Eric, their stash is crap, I add and take another hit.

She nods at two guys near the door. One has shaggy shoulder-length brown hair and his leg draped over the arm of the chair, the other is leaning back in his chair, looking directly at me with the most piercing blue eyes I've ever seen.

Who are they?

Just some guys. They're cool. Come on! She tugs at my arm. I don't budge. You're starting to be a real bummer, you know. You never want to have any fun. Everyone says so.

Who's everyone? I hand her back the joint and arch my eyebrow.

This party sucks. And you just said we need better weed. She puffs on the joint and winces. This is shit! She smiles at the guys and gives them the high sign. Besides, they're cute! she coos.

I didn't say I'd go.

Fine. I'll go without you.

I grab her arm and take a deep breath. I'll go. Let me tell Shirley we're taking off.

Can't. She left with Sandy to score some speed way out in Laurel Canyon. We'll be back way before they are. She tugs on my wrist and I climb from the couch, pulling my boots up and my dress down. One of the straight pins jabs my finger. I suck on the blood as we walk across the room.

The guys are standing by the door. The tall, lanky one with jet black hair and blue eyes curls his top lip and says, Glad you decided to join us. I blush and walk under his arm when he holds the door open.

Guess you're mine, Blondie, the shaggy one tells Kathy as the door closes on the party.

The night is sultry. A slight breeze caresses my face and bare arms. I gather my hair into a ponytail, whip it around and pull the end through the loop and sigh. It won't stay bound for long, my hair is too thin to hold, but the breeze feels good on the back of my neck.

Blue Eyes catches up with me and places a hand on the small of my back. I swerve away and he laughs. So it's like that, huh? I ignore him. Kathy already has her arm around the other guy's waist and is rubbing against him with her tits.

Over here, Blue Eyes says, and points to a two-door, jet-black T-Bird, sleek and shiny and slick. I've never been in a sports car. He opens the driver's side and Kathy dives in the back seat with the shaggy guy following her, a big grin on his face. Blue Eyes walks around the car, unlocks and opens the passenger door for me. I sink into the wide leather bucket seat and rest my head against the smooth back.

The reds I took at the party are still with me, making me mellow and loving the feel of leather against my skin, and the thought of speeding through the night with a cute guy in a fast car. My sister is going to be so pissed she missed riding in a T-Bird. I smile and give a short laugh.

A hand is on my bare leg, rough and warm. I open my eyes. Another guy, in jeans and a brown corduroy jacket, is leaning in the door.

Move over, chickie. He slaps my leg and I cock my hip up and onto the center console between the seats. There are buttons and dials and knobs near the dashboard, so I pull my legs close and lean against the thin rise at the back of the console, but there's nothing else to rest on. I hug my knees to my chest and hope I can stay upright.

You can share my seat, chickie. The new guy pats his lap.

I'm fine, I say.

Blue Eyes puts his arm around my waist. I'll keep you safe, chickie.

Let's hit it! the guy in the back with Kathy yells. The engine roars. I can feel the new guy's eyes on my legs and wish I had more skirt to pull down.

Moans drift from the back seat and I pray Kathy isn't doing what I know she's doing. Blue Eyes takes his arm from behind me and I almost tumble into the backseat. He grabs my knees and steadies me.

Sorry. Just want to turn up the sound, he apologizes and twists the knob on the radio. *Jumping Jack Flash* blasts through the speeding car and Blue Eyes' arm is back in place, keeping me from falling.

Frank will be mad I kissed that guy. We're going steady you know. Kathy pulls a class ring from between her breasts and dangles it in front of me on a thin gold chain.

I didn't know.

We're sitting alone in the car on a steep driveway of some house on some hill somewhere I've never been. The three guys from the party are leaning on the trunk with three other grungy looking guys talking and laughing. They scare me. I want to go back to the party.

Guess I shouldn't let him feel me down again on the way back, Kathy continues in her sweet voice, as if we were sitting in her bedroom talking about some guys we actually know. I like it though when they touch me there. Frank doesn't like doing anything like that. He just likes to screw. I promised him I wouldn't do anything with other guys. She looks at me. Don't tell him about kissing that guy, okay? Or the touching part.

I shake my head. Not a word, I assure her.

I keep an eye on the guys through the rear window as Kathy chatters on about Frank and how much she loves him. I see money and plastic bags filled with pot exchange hands. The guy with the corduroy jacket from the party takes off down the driveway. I let out my breath not realizing I had been holding it. Now we'll go back to the party and I'll never do something stupid like this again, I silently swear.

Blue Eyes pulls open the driver side door and flips the seat forward. He points a finger at me and says, You're in the back with me, chickie. He flips his thumb at Kathy and says, Out Blondie, you're up front.

Kathy climbs out and I squeeze between the bucket seats into the back. Blue Eyes is already waiting. Where's your friend going? I ask, pointing at the guy walking down the road.

He has something else to do. Anyway there isn't enough room for him.

I wonder what he means, there's plenty of room. Just then the passenger seat flips forward and one of the dealers climbs in and sits next to me.

The other dealer slams the seat back and flings himself in. He reaches back and runs a skinny hand up my leg above my boot. Nice piece! He winks at Blue Eyes.

And I know we're not headed back to the party.

I throw myself against the front seat, trying to get out. Blue Eyes grabs my arm and pulls me back down hard. Calm down, chickie. No place to go. His lip is curled, like at the party.

Kathy straddles the console, her butt in the air, her hands on the dealer's legs. Her underwear peeks out from under her short skirt. The shaggy guy from the party climbs in on the passenger side and crowds the dealer in the front seat.

Hey Blondie, he chirps, and pats his lap. Kathy giggles and crawls over to sit on his lap, her bare legs draped across the dealer in the middle and her feet on the center console. The dealer starts stroking Kathy's legs. She giggles some more.

The third dealer slides into the driver's seat. He coasts back down the driveway and swings the silent car around facing downhill. The engine roars to life and I'm thrown back against the seat as he hits the gas.

Tires screech and Blue Eyes slams the back of the driver's seat. Fuck off, Asshole! You fuck my car and I'll fuck you up so bad your mother won't recognize you! He slams his palms against the seat again.

The car slows.

I try to think clearly, but the reds and pot are making my mind sluggish. But they don't stop the panic; they only fog my brain, keep me from figuring out what to do.

Kathy giggles. I see the dealer's hand up her skirt while she's kissing Shaggy and I know she's already forgotten her promise to Frank.

The dealer in the back seat keeps touching my legs. I keep pushing his hand away. Kathy giggles louder and he digs his hand deep between my legs, saying, Hey now, be cool. Be like your friend. All we want is a good time.

The car makes a sharp turn onto a road that climbs and I'm thrown against Blue Eyes who's staring down at me. It's as though he's looking right through me—as if I don't exist. The dealer's hand is pawing its way up my leg again. I manage to curl up on the seat and kick out at him with both boots. I make contact but recoil back against Blue Eyes who wraps his arms around me, pinning mine to my side.

You fucking cunt! the dealer yells and grabs one of my flailing legs.

Razor, be cool, Blue Eyes says, holding me tight. Chickie here just doesn't like your action.

The bitch kicked me!

The car takes another tight curve and throws everyone to the left. Razor falls on top of me. Kathy ends up half on the driver's lap and half in the back seat.

Asshole! Blue Eyes yells and kicks the back of the seat. Pull over!

We're almost there, the driver yells back. He takes the next turn nice and slow and pulls onto a road that has no street lights.

He kills the lights. The T-Bird rolls to a stop. Kathy laughs. I scream.

Blue Eyes has me pinned and Razor is pulling at my boot, trying to get it off while I'm kicking at him. He grabs one leg, yanks the boot off and throws it out the open window.

Kathy laughs and shouts, Hey, cut it out, I'm going steady with a guy!

I look over and see the driver has opened his door and is stretching Kathy's legs out across the driver's seat. The other unzips his pants outside the passenger door. Shaggy's already on top of her and between the break in the seats I see him holding his dick with one hand and ripping Kathy's panties off with the other. Kathy laughs or maybe shrieks when his dick disappears between her legs.

I start kicking wildly. Somebody's skin piles up under my nails and I hear wild screaming coming from somewhere—realize it's me.

Get that cunt outta here! the driver screams and throws the front seat forward over Kathy and Shaggy's legs.

Blue Eyes climbs out of the car and I kick Razor square in the face and use the impetus to hurl myself out of the car. I stumble then start running. The street is so dark I can't see it clearly. I half run, half hop on the bootless foot. But I know I'm free now and will find my way …

The asphalt slams into my face and knees. The air's knocked from my lungs and I can't breathe, can't even move because of a weight on my back. I suck in a little air and scream, a thin sick cry that sounds more like a whimper.

Blue Eyes flips me over onto my back, straddling me with his knees, and clamps a hand over my mouth. Now this can go easy or tough. Your choice, chickie. If you're a good girl, you won't get hurt.

I hesitate, and then nod. He removes his hand from my mouth and stands. I take his outstretched hand and allow him to pull me up. As soon as I'm on my feet I start to run again.

This road has to lead somewhere, I tell myself. My mind clears for a moment and I realize it's a dead end. Where are the fucking cops when I need them? I silently scream.

My head is yanked back hard and I know he has me by my hair. I stop. He pulls me back up the road. I stumble backwards, each step making me sob louder and louder. He spins me around, one arm tight around me. He slaps me across the face and points back to the car with his free hand. Easy or tough, your choice.

I can see a naked butt through the rear window humping wildly, Razor is standing on the passenger side with his pants down and his hips pushed way inside the car, his head arching back. A third has his dick out and is screaming, Fucking finish already, asshole! The driver is casually leaning against the back bumper. He's looking at me, smoking a joint.

Blue Eyes spins me around, holds me tight. He tilts my chin up

Donna D. Conrad

and I close my eyes so I don't have to look into the blue devils that lured me to this desolate place.

Now we go down into that gully nice and quiet and I keep the other guys off you. He brushes back my hair. I wanna keep you all to myself. Anyway, your girlfriend doesn't seem to have a problem taking care of them.

I feel my stomach churn at the thought of Kathy with four guys fucking her in that car. I know she does guys, but not like this, not ever like this! I lurch forward and throw up the beer from the party and pray that my sister will notice I'm not there. That she knows this place and these guys. That she finds me.

Blue Eyes slaps me on the back. You better get it together, chickie, or you're headed back to the car. And that would definitely not be a fun time for you. I choke back tears and take a second to look around. There are no lights, no houses, no signs—nothing—not even curbs.

I hear Kathy scream, Enough, you fucking dicks!

One of them yells back, Yeah, dicks and more dicks and you love 'um. Here suck mine, cunt!

Blue Eyes holds out his hand. I take it.

That's a good chickie. He leads me down the side of the embankment and catches me when I start to fall. He reaches down and takes my other boot off and tosses it back up to the roadway. I follow him, no longer hoping to get away, no longer trying. He takes his jacket off and lays it on the rough ground.

Please don't do this, I beg. Please, I'll do anything, just please not this! He pauses for a moment and looks at me, a question in his eyes he doesn't ask.

His chin juts out at the coat, Easy or tough, your choice. I burst into tears. He grabs my arm and drags me to the ground. He unzips his pants and kneels in front of me. He pulls my underwear off and pries open my legs, shoves deep inside. I scream and he covers my mouth. He pushes hard into me, ripping me apart. I struggle and writhe against the pain and he smiles and says, That's more like it.

164

My shoulders are pinned to the ground. I try to kick free. He smiles and throws his head back. He pushes deeper and pain surges into my stomach and I bite my lip and whimper. He stops moving but the pain keeps growing, burning through me and I whimper again, beg him to stop. He thrusts again.

I can't fight him anymore. I silently cry … not like this, not like this. He collapses on top of me, pushing me into the dirt. Pebbles cut into my butt and legs, but they don't matter; the burning inside hurts worse.

Blue Eyes climbs off me. He shakes his dick, stuffs it back in his pants and yanks up his zipper. When he offers me his hand I turn my head away and pull my dress down over my nakedness.

Come on, the others are waiting, he says and pulls his jacket out from under my back and head. He yanks me off the ground and I grab him around the neck. Don't let the others … I can't say the words. I just hold him and cry. I did what you said. I didn't cause you any trouble. Please. Don't let them …

He takes my face in his hands. I got nothing to do with them, chickie. You're on your own. You made your choice to go easy with me and I made it easy on you. Now be a good girl and get your ass back up to the car. He grabs my underwear from the ground and tosses them at me and heads up the hill.

I look around and wonder how far I could run before they catch me.

Come on, chickie, he calls. There's nowhere to go but right here. You don't want them to chase you down in the brush, trust me.

I step through the leg holes in my underwear and pull them up, wincing when they touch my crotch. He holds out his hand and I begin to climb the embankment. He takes me by the wrist and pulls me up to the road and the waiting T-Bird. Kathy is laughing from the front seat. Shaggy and the driver are leaning against the trunk smoking. The driver dangles my boots at arm's length, but pulls them away when I reach for them.

Hand 'um over, Blue Eyes tells him. The driver drops them on the

Donna D. Conrad

ground and I snatch them from in front of him and stuff my torn feet and legs inside. They push off the trunk and walk to the front of the car. I follow a few steps behind.

You're in the back with me, the driver smiles and kicks at the guy still on top of Kathy. Move it, asshole.

The guy scoots in further and backs Kathy up against the passenger side window. He pushes me into the back and climbs in after me. I move to the far side. Kathy winks at me over the seat. I start to sob again and curl up in a tight ball. A door slams.

Where the fuck is Alex, Blue Eyes asks from behind the wheel of the car.

He had enough and took off, one of the guys says.

Fuck it if I'm stopping to pick him up. The engine roars and we lurch onto the road. I'm alone in the back with the former driver, Kathy crammed in front with the other three.

Don't worry, chickie, he coos. I'm not gonna hurt you. We'll just have a nice quite ride back. Just stop crying and come over here to me.

I believe him. I need to be close to someone who won't hurt me anymore. I uncurl my legs and move closer, still crying, my insides burning.

There now, isn't this better? The road flashes by. He kisses my neck. I start crying again. Just touch it, he whispers.

No, I tell him.

Just touch it. I want you to touch it.

How's she doing, Blue Eyes asks from the driver's seat.

Just fine, just fine.

If I touch it, you won't make me do anything else? I sob.

Nothing else. He smiles.

He lies.

I think of other times, other places; of concerts, parties, late night movies on TV as he shoves himself inside. I think of times when I was scared and my sister would hold me. I pretend this is her, just holding me; that the panting is Laddie; that I'm safe in my bed with

166

bad cramps. It works for a time. I forget the pain. I forget leaving the party with these men.

He pulls out and the pain rushes back—I shriek.

Shut the fuck up, he snarls and slaps me across the face. Fucking cunt! He pushes me away and moves to the far side of the car. I pull my underwear back on and curl up in the opposite corner, keeping absolutely still, praying the other two won't remember I'm here.

They drop us off in the alley next to the apartment building. Kathy laughs and waves goodbye as they drive off. I limp through the hallway and into the apartment. My sister looks up from a line of speed, sees the cuts and blood on my legs and hands, my bloody nose and split lip, launches off the couch. Who did that to you? Where are they? I'll kill the fuckin' bastards. She runs for the front door, leaving me in the apartment. I can't look at anyone.

Simon & Garfunkel are singing *Silent Night*. People are crashed on the floor, the air hazy with pot and cigarette smoke. I head for the bathroom with Kathy on my heels. I hurt in places I've never paid attention to before. I drop my white cotton underwear and sit on the toilet; pick the few remaining straight pins out of my hem; try to ignore the pain that feels like it's splitting me in half; try to pee but can't.

Kathy leans against the sink and looks down at the splotches of blood staining my panties and says, Shit, I didn't know you were a virgin. Damn. That's heavy.

She pauses a moment then adds, They were kinda cute though, weren't they?

Poker Night
September 7, 1968

Suggested listening:
Single—*Sympathy for the Devil*, The Rolling Stones

I hate poker nights. My dad's old war buddies show up at the house and smoke and drink and talk too loud and, when I'm stuck at home, make my life hell because I'm a girl. And that means I have to make drinks and serve snacks and empty ashtrays and all the while try to keep out of trouble and try not to listen to what they're saying— because what they say makes me sick to my stomach.

Muzzie always seems to be working a split-shift on Poker Night and gets to leave at five and not come home until after midnight. I wish she didn't have to work tonight. I even asked her to stay home, but she said she couldn't, that she'd missed too much work already. It isn't my fault she's been drinking again and doesn't go to work most days. It pisses me off that she picked tonight to stay sober.

Tonight is going to be even worse than other poker nights. I can't stand the sound of men's voices; not after what happened two Saturdays ago. I set out all the booze and mixers and nuts and sandwiches and extra ashtrays and the cards and poker chips before anyone gets here; before my dad even gets up from his nap.

I know I can't go to my room, not before I'm told I can, so I sit on the couch and wait for my dad to wake up, for the men to show up, for the night to be over. I can't believe I got grounded because of the party at Shirley's and what happened to me and Kathy.

Shirley drops me off a few minutes after midnight. We both freeze when we see Dad's car in the driveway. He always works late on Saturday nights, unless it's a poker night, which it isn't.

It's okay, Shirley tells me. The lights are off. He's probably asleep. Just be quiet when you go in. Don't change clothes or anything. It'll make too much noise.

She's wrong. He's waiting for me.

A minute's as good as an hour! he shouts when I try to explain I'm only a few minutes late. When I say midnight, I god damned well mean midnight! And look at you! You look like a tramp with all that makeup on and your hair a mess.

The extra makeup Shirley put on me covers the bruises on my cheek and my split lip—but just barely. I'm thankful only the hall light's on and that it's not very bright.

I'm glad I thought to put my slacks back on under my dress or he would kill me. As it is, he grounds me for two whole weeks. And not just any two weeks. The last week of summer vacation and the first week of school. And the last Saturday night is poker night. It couldn't be worse.

My dad starts coughing and blows his nose—he's up. I pick up a book and pretend to be reading. He goes straight to the bathroom and I set the book back down on the couch, straighten my slacks and matching blouse, the outfit I always wear for straights and relatives. I try to keep my mind from flipping back to the college guys and the T-bird. But it's no use. I dig my nails into my palm and tell myself I can't cry, not in front of all the old men. They'd only say it was all my fault if they knew what happened.

Hey, Punk. I jump and knock my book off the couch at the sound of my dad's voice so close; thought he was still in the bathroom. What the hell's got into you? He doesn't wait for an answer, and I don't even think about giving him one. Come in here, he tells me and walks toward the dining room.

My heart sinks, dreading a lecture or worse about how I set up the drinks and all.

I guess grounding you is the best way to get you to do some work around here, he says. I try to keep my face all smooth and not wrinkle my nose or do anything that he can yell at me for. It looks good. He leans over to kiss my cheek and it takes all my willpower not to shy away.

The doorbell rings. Well, don't stop now, he tells me. Go get the door.

I didn't think the night could get any worse, but it just did.

Mr. Randall, Mr. McCullough, Mr. Sanders, and Mr. Whitlock: I've known these men all my life and know enough to have scrubbed my face clean and my hair braided into a long tail in the back that I curled around and pinned tight against my head—know enough to try to look and act like the good kid they all think I am.

I take their coats and hats and smile at their stupid straight jokes about my dad having a live-in maid, and how they wish their daughters were so helpful. They slap my dad on the back one by one and then head for the high breakfast bar that runs between the kitchen and dining room, where all the booze is waiting.

I want to dump all their coats and hats on the floor, stomp on them, and walk straight out the front door. I don't. I hang up the coats in the hall closet and set all the hats on the shelf above the coats and try to remember whose hat is whose and hope I'm asleep way before they leave and I'd have to remember.

Come on in here, Donna, Mr. Randall shouts from the dining room. No reason to hide out there in the hall. He's the nicest of them all, but still a Narc, like my dad, only he works deep cover, which means he has to keep a beard and let his hair grow kind of shaggy— but not at all like a real long-hair. The other men always kid him about being a damned hippie and that he should use the back door to come and go.

He drapes an arm around my shoulder and I can't help but cringe. They all notice. Don't mind her, my dad tells them. I grounded her.

They all nod knowingly, and Mr. Randall leans around and looks closely at my face. I duck my head, but it's too late.

What happened? he asks.

I let my dad tell them the story I made up to explain the bruises and split lip. She was out walking the dog the day after I grounded her and he took off after some stray cat and dragged her half way down the street, cut up her legs and arms too.

Laddie? Didn't think he was that strong, Mr. Randall says and I'm worried he's going to ask more questions.

He's a big dog, my dad tells them. But I think she wasn't paying attention; off daydreaming or pouting over being grounded.

Mr. Randall takes another look at my face and nods. You should be more careful there, Donna, he tells me and gives my shoulder a tight squeeze. Well, never mind the fall or being grounded, you put out a great spread here tonight. Just want you to know we appreciate it. You keep this up and you won't end up an old maid. They all laugh and I know my face is bright red.

If you have everything, may I go to my room now? I chance a quick look at my dad, knowing he won't scream at me in front of his friends; not unless I really fuck up.

Ah, come on, Condie, Mr. Randall, chides my dad. Give the kid a break. At least let her watch some TV after doing all this. The other men agree and I'm afraid my dad's going to say okay and I'll be trapped in the living room all night.

Why the hell not? my dad says. Go on and watch something, but keep the sound down so we don't have to yell over it to hear each other.

I blink back a tear and thank Mr. Randall, who tells me I deserve to watch some TV. I don't think I've done anything to deserve having to stay in the living room and listen to them all night.

So the little bastard shoves his girlfriend out the front door and I nearly shoot her instead 'cause I can't tell the difference, his hair's so damned long he looks like a girl. Mr. Randall laughs and the other men join him.

I scoot closer to the TV, wishing I could turn it up enough to drown them out.

Little bastard, tryin' to make a girl take the heat, Mr. Sanders adds.

Yeah. By the way he ran I think he knew I meant business this time.

Either that or he finally figured out who you really were and wanted to make a run for it before you could bust him, Mr. McCullough says, then adds, The kitty's light. Who didn't ante?

There's a clink of a chip as Mr. Randall says, You might be right, Mac, that was a consideration. But, in any case, if the chicken shit hadn't pushed his girl in front of me I might have taken him in. But when he did that I thought, I'll be damned if I'm gonna drag him in just so some judge can cut him loose over some damn technicality. I'm not about to blow my cover for some punk. No way. Anyway, the way I see it, we lost one deadbeat but we saved the girl. After what she saw she'll go straight. Least-wise I don't 'spect to see her hanging around anymore dealers. One-for-one. Mr. Randall crows like a rooster and my blood freezes.

They've been talking about their cases all night. About the hippies and druggies and draft dodgers they bust every fucking day. They're so proud of themselves. Sitting around drinking bourbon and trying to one-up each other. All of them hating kids like me who only want to get high and not get killed over in Viet Nam. We've never done anything to them for them to hate us so much.

Sometimes you just gotta do what's right, Mr. Whitlock says. Like the time Condie and me were working for Ridgeway in Korea …

Ridgeway was a real soldier, my dad adds under his breath.

We all know how you feel about MacArthur, Con. But anyway, we were playing good cop-bad cop with this slope-head commie kid; couldn'a been more than seventeen, eighteen, maybe. Condie fakes like he's puttin' a live round in a chamber—so th' kid thinks th' gun's loaded—spins th' barrel and holds it to th' kid's head. I'm practically on my knees pleading for Condie not to do it—I always had to play the good cop 'cause Condie's so damn good at palming the bullet. So, when the guy cracks and we knew we weren't gonna get nothin' more from him, I take the gun from Condie and finish th' job. Had to be done, Mr. Whitlock adds, matter-of-factly.

Had to be done, my dad repeats. Ante-up! He says and taps the table.

Mr. Whitlock gives me the creeps. His pure black hair's always slicked way back and his eyes are almost as black as his hair. He usually doesn't say much, which makes him even creepier. He's my dad's oldest buddy. They served together in Germany and Korea. They sometimes talk in what sounds like code about what they did behind German lines—things they don't even share with the others.

You been awfully quiet tonight, Condie, Mr. Sanders says, changing the subject.

Don't like sharing my business when it's this close to home, my dad says in a flat, low voice.

I scoot over on the couch, closer to the dining room, hoping to hear something about what he's working on now. If he's working close to home that would explain why he was home early and caught me sneaking in after curfew; why I'm stuck here listening to them talk about their busts.

You're on the college detail, aren't you? Mr. Sanders asks, and it takes a long time for an answer.

Out at Cal Poly the last coupla weeks. Still can't believe those Ag kids are dealing drugs and dodging the draft. But I learned different. Ante-up, you slackers! he barks, then adds, Most of 'em farm kids. I'd have thought their parents woulda raised them better.

Not easy raising kids anymore, Mr. McAdams says. You're lucky Terry's safe over in Korea and your youngest is such a good kid. I'd hate to think of them involved in all this mess going on at the colleges.

You're right about that, Mac, Mr. Randall interrupts. Why last week I followed a group of clean-cut looking kids bringing in a carload of pot. Looked like Lettermen or Frat boys. Lost 'em when they hit L.A. But I'll find the bastards. They always surface to spend the money.

If I had that kind of money I'd play it real cool, Mr. McCullough says. Keep my head down until I got to South America.

Well then, we're lucky we're not tracking you, Mac, my dad says, then taps the table twice and announces, Five card stud. Nothing wild but the dealer.

Unrequited Lust
September 1968

Suggested listening:
Album—Over Under Sideways Down, The Yardbirds

If you need a fix, you go to the Brady Brothers. It's that simple.
They're the only game in town and they always have heroin. I stay
away from them, though it isn't easy because they're Chris' friends
and hang out at Kathy's house when they're not dealing from their
sapphire blue Buick Wildcat. Luckily, when they happen to be at
Kathy's house, they pay little attention to two girls who giggle and
lock themselves in their room for hours on end.

When school starts I walk over to Kathy's house each morning,
smoke a joint and drop some reds or whites depending on whether
I've slept the night before. Some mornings we split a tab of acid and
walk the short block that ends at the front lawn of Charter Oak High.

When I walk into class that fall my teachers don't notice anything
different. I'm still too tall, too thin, too *hard-ass* for Covina. My very
presence is a bad influence—just like my sister. I don't acknowledge
them and they ignore me except to send me to the Principal's office
when my skirt's too short.

It's been a month since the party at my sister's. I don't talk about
the rape, not with Kathy, not with my sister, not with anyone. I
refuse to think about it. Not even acid brings back the memories. But
a car door slamming in the night makes me jump, and I threw up
when a black T-Bird and a red Corvette raced along the main drag

while Kathy and I were walking home from a movie.

I spend parties on acid, sitting in a corner watching the crowd and digging on the music. I don't dance, I don't drink, and I don't mix. I sit and watch, and ignore any guy who tries to hit on me. Kathy doesn't try to set me up with anyone anymore.

One morning a few weeks after school starts, Kathy and I pop a couple of reds on our lunch break at Kathy's house. She eats while I drink a Double Cola. I still don't like food and it doesn't much care for me. We head back to the campus feeling much better.

The reds come on harder than usual and I keep dozing off in Social Studies. When the bell rings we decide to head over to my house and take a nap. We know her brother and his friends will probably be at her place soon. Neither of us wants any more noise. The teacher's tirade for sleeping in his class is enough yelling for the day.

We walk quickly through the oak trees that form a small, clean forest on the rim of the campus and duck around the front of a house next to school. We slow down, knowing we've cleared the one teacher on patrol. We cross in the middle of Covina Boulevard and decide not to chance walking through the junior high campus that sits directly behind the backyard of my house.

That means a long walk up Covina Boulevard, across Bend, and back down the six blocks to my cul-de-sac. It's hot, we're stoned, we're tired, we need sleep. I want a joint and another Double Cola. Kathy wants some of my mom's chocolate chip cookies. All reasons to accept Jeff's offer for a ride when the Brady brothers pull alongside.

I hesitate. Kathy hops in and yells, I'm too tired to walk, so get the fuck in the car!

I climb in the back seat. Jeff closes the door behind me. Ray turns in the driver's seat, Where to? Your place? he nods at Kathy.

No, hers, she tells him.

And that might be where? he asks looking at me.

I can't find my voice, or my breath. His face is pitted and pale, his hair slicked back and greasy, his hands dirty where they rest on the steering wheel. Ray is older and no longer in school. Jeff's a senior and the better looking of the two. They both have the same green eyes and black hair and thin, tight lips that I never see smile.

Hey, Stone Free, he says to me in a bit louder voice. Where do I go?

Kathy answers, Around Cloverdale, behind the school.

Thank you so very much, Ray says and pulls away from the curb.

He turns right and I grab Kathy's leg and dig my nails in, still unable to speak. She slaps my hand away and taps on the front seat. Hey, you're going the wrong way. You need to go up Covina.

We have to make a drop first, Jeff says without turning around.

I feel tears forming and take tiny gasps of air, trying to be quiet. The car moves slowly past the elementary school and turns right down a side street. I close my eyes and can't hold back the tears.

What the fuck's her problem? Ray asks.

Nothing, Kathy says and pinches my leg hard. I don't open my eyes until I feel a bump and the engine stop. We're parked in the driveway of a track home, one of ten thousand with the garage in front, a narrow cement sidewalk leading to a screen shielded front door with a kitchen window looking out over the small, concrete porch—so 'Mom' can see who's at the door from her station at the sink.

But Mom isn't home.

I don't get out when the guys do. Jeff flips the front seat forward. We'll be a few minutes, might as well come in.

I close my eyes and silently sing, Cancel my subscription to the Resurrection. Send my credentials to the House of Detention I got some friends inside ...

He pulls me out of the car and along the sidewalk up to the front door. I pull away and walk fast back down the sidewalk.

Jeff is suddenly in front of me. What's your problem? he asks.

I don't want to go in there, I tell him.

He takes my arm. Come on. We'll just be a few minutes. You can trust me. Hell, you're Kathy's friend. What do you think is gonna happen? Christ. He leans in close and looks into my eyes. You stoned?

I look away. He pulls me back up the sidewalk and into the house.

Two other guys are in the kitchen with Ray. Small waxed paper packets are being counted and separated on the breakfast bar. I take a breath and let Jeff lead me into the living room. Kathy is sitting on the couch toking on a joint.

Jesus, she says to me, here, have a hit and chill, dude. You look like shit.

I take the joint and stand in the center of the room, looking for all the doors without trying to be obvious. The weed is good quality. My head clears and my heart slows. The pounding in my ears dies away. I take another hit and hand it back to Kathy.

Jeff pats the couch. I shake my head and he grabs my wrist and pulls me down.

Kathy laughs. Chill. You are way over done!

Jeff leans over and kisses my cheek just as Ray and the other guys come in from the kitchen. I stop breathing.

Ray grabs Kathy's wrist and they head off down the narrow hallway.

The other two guys check me out and I pull down my dress, thankful for dress codes that make me wear dresses down to my knees. Jeff shakes his head and drapes an arm over my shoulder. One guy shrugs and leaves through the front door. The other one follows Kathy and Ray down the hall.

Jeff stands and offers his hand. I shake my head over and over, my hair flying, covering my face, covering my tears. He pulls me to my feet and down the hall to a bedroom.

I hear Kathy laughing.

Jeff closes the door behind us and juts his sharp chin towards the bed. I close my eyes and sink inward, telling myself I'm not here. Telling myself this is a bad acid trip. That I'm at home, in my room. I open my eyes when I hit the bed. Jeff's on top of me, pulling my dress up, jabbing his hand up under my panties.

I hear myself screaming but don't feel anything, not in my throat, not between my legs, not when I dig my fingers deep into Jeff's scalp and twist as hard as I can. I hear him cuss and clamp a hand over my mouth—I bite down hard—taste blood and know it must be his, but I'm not turning him loose.

He grabs my pubic hair and digs deep. I feel heat clawing at me and dig my nails deeper into his head.

I'll fucking rip you apart, bitch! He hisses, but doesn't take his hand from my mouth. I feel blood and skin under my nails and a deep satisfaction cools the heat from below.

He slides his hand lower, grabs between my legs and digs in. I stop biting and he takes his hand from my mouth. Now stop it, or I'll hurt you bad.

I shriek with all my might. He thrust his hand inside me and squeezes hard with his thumb on my pube. I tear at his face with my other hand, which he pins to the bed.

My hair covers my face and I realize I'm tossing my head back and forth in time with the shrieking.

Stop it! he yells. Stop it! He slaps me across the face and I stop screaming, but neither of us let go. You are psycho, bitch, he says, as a thin rivulet of blood inches down his forehead. I dig my nails deeper and he squeezes harder.

I cry out in pain this time.

There! Now you listen to me, bitch.

I quiet down.

You let go and I'll let go and we'll both just back off. I get it. This isn't a good idea.

I nod, somehow believing him, though a part of me screams that I shouldn't. I tell that part to shut the fuck up. I let go of his hair. He lets go of me and falls over onto the bed next to me. His breathing's as rough as mine.

Psycho bitch, he says and rolls over onto his knees. I see that his jeans are unzipped and his dick is bouncing around like a sprung Jack in the Box. I scream again and roll off the bed. He grabs at me and we both fall on the floor.

He's on top with his hand over my mouth. Shut the fuck up! I'm not doing nothing to you for fuck sake! Just shut the fuck up!

I lay there and he stands up and stuffs his dick back in his pants and zips them. He pulls me off the floor and throws me on the bed and pins me there. He has me by the wrists, with my hands above my head and his knees pressed into my legs so I can't kick.

You lay there nice and quiet and listen to me or I will hurt you more than you can imagine.

I have a good imagination and know he's a hard core pusher that takes people down when they don't pay up. I nod and look away.

I gasp and Jeff tightens his grip. Now you and me are gonna go out there and you're gonna look like you just got fucked and that you liked it. You do that and I let you go unfucked. Got it?

I nod.

Good. He twists off the bed so that he's clear of my hands and legs before I can strike out. But I hurt too much to even move. My belly cramps and I think I might throw up.

You hurl 'n I'll beat the shit outta you!

I suck in my breath and take his offered hand. I start to stand and drop to the floor in pain.

Serves you right, he says wiping the blood from his forehead and patting the top of his head gently with a white handkerchief that spots red.

I struggle to my feet holding onto the bed and pull my dress down and try to stand up straight. He yanks my wrist and drags me to the door. We stop and my breathing stops. He pulls another handkerchief from his jeans and hands it to me. Wipe your face, you look a wreck. And fix your hair. You're supposed to look fucked, not fucked-up!

I dab my eyes and cheeks and run my shaking hands through my hair and pull it back behind my ears. He opens the bedroom door and takes me by the hand.

We get to the empty living room and he pulls me to the couch and pushes me down. He stands for a moment looking down on me. You are one fucked-up bitch! He turns and points to the hall. You look happy and well-fucked when they come out, or I'll find you when nobody can hear you screaming and then we'll replay this little scene my way. Got it?

I nod.

A door slams against a wall and Ray comes out of the hallway looking disgusted, the other guy and Kathy in his wake. He has blood on his hand and goes in the kitchen.

Kathy's explaining, I told you I was on the rag!

Jeff drapes his arm across my shoulder and laughs. Ray looks around the corner and nods at me. Jeff pulls out the end of his handkerchief spotted with blood and shakes his head. But we had a sweet time anyway, didn't we? Jeff says and kisses me on my neck.

I cringe and feel his fingers dig into my arm. I smile sweetly at Ray and snuggle closer to Jeff, my skin crawling and a scream rising. I stuff it back down, knowing I have to get out of this house—that Jeff is my ticket home.

So, Stone Free puts out after all? Ray asks. I heard she didn't.

You heard wrong. Let's get the fuck outta here, the place stinks like a rag factory. He stands and pulls me with him. I lean against him out through the door and down the sidewalk; the pain in my belly so intense I'm not sure I could walk without him. He puts me in the backseat with Kathy and climbs behind the wheel.

What the fuck, Ray asks, coming up to the driver side.

You're shotgun. I'm taking this load of jailbait back to school.

Fuck you, Ray says and flips Jeff the bird as he climbs into the front seat. He turns and drapes an arm over the seat. Stone Free puts out, huh?

Cool it Ray, Jeff says and throws the car in reverse and screeches out of the driveway, spinning the car on the street ending up facing the wrong way.

I shrink inside and wrap myself around the pain and silently sing:

Raindrops on roses and whiskers on kittens. Bright copper kettles and warm woolen mittens.

Jeff hits the gas. We fly through the streets and stop right in front of Charter Oak. Kathy and I climb out and blend in with the crowd of kids leaving school for the day.

The hall is nearly empty, the second bell having already rung. I reach in the back of my locker and pull out my science book. *She's only thirteen, and she knows how to nasty*, hisses in my ear and I spin around. Jeff pins me to the lockers, his whole body pressing against mine.

You're still mine, Stone Free. Look around when you're all alone—I'll be there waiting for you. He smiles, then pushes off and walks away.

I slump to the ground, my back against the lockers, the combo locks banging me as I drop.

I sneak off campus, hardly breathing, my heart beating so fast I think it's going to explode. I wait until no cars are on the street and run all the way through the Jr. High fields and the back gate, slowing only when I reach the quiet of my house. Muzzie's at work and Dad's sleeping, like he always does after he's been out on an all-night case.

Late in the afternoon, Kathy calls, wants to know why I didn't come back to school. Wants to know why I ditched without telling her.

That guy totally freaked me out today.

What guy?

That . . . that guy, I stutter, afraid to say his name.

Who? Kathy demands.

The drug-dealer guy and his brother … you know … the Brady guys.

Ray and Jeff?

Yeah, them. I try to calm my breathing. Jeff trapped me between classes. He's freaking me out. He said he'd find me when no one was around and ... and . . .

Just ignore him. He's pissed you wouldn't fuck him, that's all. Guys get like that.

Did he say something about me? I ask, starting to tremble.

Not really.

Not really! What did he say? When? What?

Chill out! Christ! No wonder he thinks you're psycho.

He told you I'm psycho?

Yeah. Kathy bites into something crunchy and chews and talks at the same time. He and Chris and some other guys were talking and all and Ray said something about you putting out and everyone laughed 'cause they know you don't and Ray said Jeff got something off you but nobody believed him. So they asked Jeff and he said you were psycho and besides we were both on the rag, so no, he didn't get nothing off you ...

When? I cut into her story.

When what?

When did he say that?

A day or two after they took us to that house.

I'm dead, I say and lean back against the pillows. He's never going to stop, Kathy. He'll find me no matter where I am. He's gonna kill me ... I know it ... or worse.

You going psycho again? Kathy asks.

He's gonna kill me. One night, he'll find me all alone and kill me and no one will ever know.

Stop it! Kathy yells. Her tone snaps me out of the vision of my dead body with Jeff standing over it.

You are way over done! Jeff isn't gonna do nothing to you. He's messing with you is all. Just tell him to back off.

Back off! I shout, and then remember my dad's sleeping in the next room. Back off, I whisper. Jeff's not some dealer selling pot. He's a hard core pusher. He sells heroin for fuck sake. He kills people! He's not gonna back off because I tell him to!

Oh, chill. He doesn't kill anyone. Christ, you are way over done. I'll ask my brother to talk to him …

Don't you dare! Don't you dare tell Chris anything about this. Jeff'll kill me if I say anything to anyone.

What? Hey, you're really losing it! Got anything to calm you down? If not I'll bring you something. You need to sleep for a day or two. You're way over the top.

I know I'm doomed. Know nobody can help me. Know the next time Jeff slides up beside me may be the last time. Nothing seems to matter anymore, nothing except Kathy knowing who did it, when they find me dead.

Yeah, you're right, I sniff. Thanks. It'll be fine. I'll get some sleep. Thanks.

You okay? she asks.

Yeah. You helped a lot. Thanks. Gotta go, my dad's home.

Wanna see a movie tomorrow?

Sure.

Call me.

Okay.

She hangs up. I leave the phone to my ear, not able to move. I hear a second click, then the dial tone. Great move, idiot! I think, knowing my dad must have been on the extension. Just what I need. I'm busted for sure this time. I hang up the phone and grab my stash of drugs and high-tail it into the back bathroom. I lock the door and flush all the pills and blotter paper down the toilet along with the tinfoil wrappers and small squares of waxed paper.

I wait a few minutes, not wanting to face him, trying to figure out how to get out of this one. I hear a door slam and then his car start. I climb into the empty tub and slide the window open a crack, find the driveway empty.

I tell myself he didn't hear; tell myself the only thing to be scared of is Jeff.

That night we eat dinner together, me, Muzzie and Dad. It's taco night. I watch Dad through my lowered eyelashes, waiting for him to start yelling. He doesn't say a thing ... nothing, not all through dinner. He goes into the living room and turns on the TV. Muzzie clears the table. I head to my room and count my blessings. My dad must not have been on the extension after all. I'm home free.

I ditch school all the next week, but have to go back 'cause Muzzie's working the late shift the following week. I stay within the crowds of kids walking to and from classes until lunch and then duck inside the F head.

A blonde with teased hair is leaning against the sink, a cigarette hanging out of her mouth. I stop mid-step because I know she's Jeff's girlfriend. I want to run back outside, but *he* might be there, especially with his girlfriend inside.

Shit! she says without taking the cigarette out of her mouth. What's your problem? Look at her, she says to another girl leaning against the far wall, she's gonna pee her pants. The other girl laughs, I feel tears welling up in my eyes.

Oh for fuck sake, don't cry.

What's her problem? the other girl asks the blonde.

Jeff's fucking with her.

Fucking her? The other girl is off the wall and moving towards me.

The blonde grabs her arm and pulls her back. Fucking *with* her, you idiot. Playing with her mind ... you know, like he does everyone.

He's such a jerk!

Yeah. Hey come here. She waves to me.

I don't move.

Come here! I won't hurt you.

Shit, she's not a senior, the other girl says. What you doing in here, creep?

Ah, leave her alone, Janet. She's just scared. You know how Jeff can be.

She walks over to me. With her high heels on, we're the same height. She looks me in the eye and leans close, whispers, Don't let him get to you. He don't mean nothin'. He's just messing with you.

I nod and blink back tears.

I'll keep him away from you, sweetie. She lifts my chin and I can see in her eyes that she means it.

Someone bangs on the door and I hear Jeff yelling, Get your ass out here, Dory.

I duck behind her and bump into her friend. Watch it, asshole, she warns and pushes me out of the way. Let's go, Dory.

Yeah, sure. She winks at me.

We pass in the crowded hall between classes. One arm around Dory's shoulder, Jeff flips me the peace-sign. I look down.

Don't look away, bitch, he says and I look up. He's standing with Dory tight at his side in the middle of the open hallway. Everyone walks around us, as far around as they can.

Don't think Dory could stop me if I wanted to mess with you. I just got tired of your skinny ass. He flips me off and turns away, adding, Don't let me see your face around Chris' or I might change my mind.

Dory winks at me and walks away with her man.

I stay the hell away from Kathy's house.

A week later I'm stuck having dinner with my folks again; wish I were anywhere else.

My dad asks if I know the Brady brothers, Raymond and Jeffery.

I glance up at him and quickly back at my food. He's staring right at me.

No, I lie.

Well, not to worry, he says. They won't be bothering anybody for a long time. No sir, not for a good long time.

I chance another glance at my dad. He's still looking right at me but his eyes have softened a bit.

You can thank Mr. Randall next time you see him, he says and takes a bite of food.

Romeo and Juliet
October 1968

Suggested listening:
Album—Wildflowers, Judy Collins

We never stay in the car—that would be too square. If we want to see the movie, we sit on the hood and leave the speaker on its stand. If we don't care about the movie, which we usually don't, we walk around, hang out at the snack bar, meet up with friends, smoke joints in the back row by the tall fence where kids who want to make out park.

Tonight we're in the first row, on the hood with both speakers, ours and the space next to ours, at full blast. Our homework assignment is due on Monday and the Covina Drive-In has just saved us from getting an F.

Chris leaves before the movie starts, but warns us that we'd better not scratch the hood, so we take our boots off in the car and throw a blanket under us. He's in the back row in his girlfriend's car. We had to pay him five dollars to drive us here, plus the movie for him and his girlfriend.

We blame our teacher for the cost.

This is so lame, Kathy says for the tenth time. Why are they talking like that? And the guys look so dorky.

It's Shakespeare, stupid. I tell her. They always talk like that in Shakespeare.

How do you know?

I don't say anything. Don't want Kathy to know that I've seen a bunch of plays with Muzzie at the Carousel Theater ... that some of them were even Shakespeare.

I can't tell them all apart. Can you?

Sure. Those guys on the left are the Montagues and they hate the other guys, the Capulets.

Why?

How should I know! They just hate them 'cause they're a different family.

Why are they all wearing tights and talking so funny?

I already told you, it's Shakespeare and they always talk like that! Geesh.

But we have to know what they're doing! How'm I gonna write 500 words on this? I don't get it at all.

For fuck sake, Kathy. Just watch the movie. You don't have to know what they're saying to figure out what they're doing.

By the time Romeo and Juliet are secretly married, Kathy and I are totally into the movie. And when we see them naked in bed after they've spent the night together, we're both glued to the screen. Juliet looks so happy asleep with Romeo next to her. That's how it should be, I think. And when they wake up, Juliet wants him to stay, but he can't. I look away from the screen and blink back tears, wishing it was really like that with guys—but it's not.

We stay on the hood of the car all through the credits and a little longer. We don't say anything for a few minutes, just watch people walk past headed for the snack bar.

Wow, Kathy finally breaks our silence. Wouldn't it be great to have someone kill themselves because they love you so much they can't live without you?

Yeah.

I can't do it. I can't keep my eyes open another minute, Kathy tells me as her head droops slowly to the table.

I slap her arm. C'mon. We're almost done. Here, have another white. I got three left, we'll split them. I dig in my pants pocket and pull out the small tinfoil roll and peal it apart.

Kathy looks up from the table. I can't do anymore. I'd rather flunk the class than write another fucking word.

C'mon. We got to. I can't fail the class or I'll be grounded for the rest of my life!

She opens her mouth and I pop two of the three whites in. She struggles to sit up and I offer her my Double Cola. She shakes her head and swallows them without anything. Where are we?

Romeo just killed the Capulet dude and is running away.

I'd rather flunk, she moans.

I can't!

So you write it.

I am! But you have to write yours.

I'd rather flunk …

Here are your papers back, class. I must say I'm very disappointed in some of you. Mrs. Andrews starts walking up and down the aisles placing papers on the corner of the desks. I'm in the last row on the right—she always hands out papers starting on the left.

I crane my neck to see the papers. Most have lots of red marks all over them and writing in the margins. I sit back in my chair, sure mine won't have any marks except an *A* on the top. Maybe even an *A*+. She only asked for five hundred words, which is all I wrote for Kathy, but I went all out on my paper and wrote almost nine hundred words—every one of them perfect. I told her all about the different uniforms and colorful clothes and allegiances and betrayals and about the morning after Romeo and Juliet's secret marriage and how at least they were able to make love before they died. I put everything from the movie in the paper and just know it will get at least an *A*.

Mrs. Andrews pauses next to me, holding my paper in her hand.

And you, Miss Conrad … I smile up at her. You truly disappoint me. I stop smiling. You should know better. She tuts at me and lays the paper face down on the desk and I can see all the red marks and writing in the margins through the paper.

The next Friday night, Chris drops us off at the far side of the snack bar and drives off towards the back row of the drive in, like always.

I can't believe she gave me a fucking *F*!

Yeah. Welcome to the crowd.

What the fuck do you mean? You got a *D*, not an *F*. At least you passed!

Yeah, I know. Kathy laughs. And you wrote both papers. She lights up and hands me the pack. I struggle with the long cigarettes, trying to get one out of the pack without tearing it. Here! Let me. She taps the bottom of the pack and one slides out far enough for me to grab it by the filter.

Fucking bitch! I spit. Kathy lights my cigarette and we walk away from the snack bar towards the far side of the drive-in. We look up at Romeo and Juliet on the balcony, professing their love.

Fucking movie! I snap. Who the fuck makes a movie that doesn't follow the fucking play?

Yeah! I hate this fucking movie.

I hate Mrs. Andrews. The bitch! There's no way I deserved an *F*. I did the damned assignment.

No you didn't. Kathy spits out a loose piece of tobacco and looks at her cigarette.

Yes I did! I insist. I even did yours!

You … *we* were supposed to read the fucking play and write about *it* … not watch a fucking movie and write shit that was wrong.

She did it on purpose. I flick my unfinished cigarette onto the pavement. She knew the movie was coming out and that we'd all go see it. The fucking bitch set us up. I hate her!

Kathy's looking over my shoulder at something. I turn and see a group of guys heading our way. Oh great, just what I fucking need! I sigh

Exactly what I *fucking* need, she says and fluffs her short hair.

So you live around here?

Yeah.

I take it you've seen the movie before.

Yeah.

Did you like it?

No.

You don't talk much do you?

I don't bother to answer him.

I like that.

Do you?

Yeah.

Why won't you go back to their car? Kathy's putting on more lipstick, puckering and throwing kisses to the mirror.

They're too old. They're all in college.

So? The one with the beard and wavy red hair is really cute. She looks over at me. I think he likes you.

So?

So, we should go back to their car. You don't have to do anything, just watch the movie.

I hate this fucking movie.

It's almost over. You can watch the next one. She looks back in the mirror. If you don't like the one with the beard, I'll take him.

No you won't! I don't know why I care. I don't want anything more to do with guys. All they want to do is screw. But I don't want Kathy to have someone who might like me.

She smiles at me through the mirror. So you like him?

He's okay.

I think he's cute.

His beard tickles. I try not to laugh, but can't help it. He rubs his face against mine and kisses me again. You'll get to like it, he tells me.

I think I might.

I turn my head back towards the screen.

Hey. I thought you didn't like this movie, he says and turns my head back, kisses me again. We don't have to do anything else, he tells me between kisses. This is fine with me.

I believe him.

He drives me home from the movie and walks me to the porch and kisses me goodnight, sweetly, and waits till I go inside and close the door behind me. I run to the kitchen and watch him walk down the driveway and get in his car—a cool looking tan sporty car with bucket seats and a great eight-track player.

I dance down the hall and throw myself into bed, clothes and all.

Ken KEN **Kenneth** *Kenny* Ken Ken Ken.

Stop writing on my walls! Kathy warns. My dad's gonna kill me. Besides, I thought you didn't really like him all that much.

I spin around and drop to the bed next to Kathy, still holding the pen. That was before last night, I sigh. He kisses so good.

Donna and Kenny sitting in a tree, k-i-s-s-i-n-g, Kathy coos. You're totally fucked up over this guy, aren't you?

I smile and nod my head.

Did he ask you out again?

I nod. Next Friday. We're gonna go to get pizza and then go to a real movie, in a real theater instead of a drive-in.

God. He must be serious. How old is he?

I don't know. I think he has a job and all. How else could he pay for dinner and a movie? And did you see his car? I bounce up on my knees.

Yeah. I was in the back seat with that big guy, whassis name … Bear. Remember?

It's a Cougar. A brand new Cougar! I sink back on my heels. He's got to be loaded to have a car like that. I wonder what he does.

Think he's married?

What?

I mean, he's old enough and has money and drives a fast car and doesn't hassle you about fucking. He might be married already or at least engaged or something.

Fuck you! I grab a pillow and hit Kathy in the face with it. She dives at me and starts tickling.

Kathy's dad is gone for the weekend. We sneak under the fence at the drive-in, hoping they'll be there. They are, in Bear's old car, not Ken's Cougar. We invite them over to Kathy's after the movie. Kathy's already pulled out the davenport in the living room. I blush when Ken walks in and looks at the double bed with two pillows where the couch should be.

Kathy's dad's gone for the night, so I'm staying here, I tell him.

He smiles. No problem. He walks over to the upholstered arm chair and holds out his hand to me. I sit on his lap and he wraps me in his arms.

Bear comes out of Kathy's room in a little while and tells Ken it's time to go. Ken tells him he's staying awhile longer, that he'll hitch later.

We go back to kissing. Somehow we make it over to the davenport. He says I don't have to do anything I don't want to.

We kiss until we fall asleep in each other's arms—just like Romeo and Juliet.

194

Rotta Run
November 1968

Suggested listening:
Album—Buffalo Springfield Again, Buffalo Springfield

I don't know what I'm doing here. I thought it was going to be just Ken and me. He didn't mention the other guys when he asked me to go on a Rotta Run. Not that I know what a Rotta Run is.

I thought we were just stopping by his friend's house to pick up a tent. I thought they were just walking us out to the car. But when they got in the backseat I froze. Ken didn't know anything about me getting raped or about the Brady brothers. He tried to reason with me, tried to figure out why I didn't want to go anymore. He thought I didn't want to share him with his friends. I thought he wanted to share me with his friends.

I finally reasoned that I knew Bear and Mike; that Ken had already told me I didn't have to do anything I didn't want to do. We'd even slept together, without *sleeping* together, like that. I figured I could trust him and the other two. Besides, Kathy and her family are gone for the weekend so I can't go to her house, and I can't go home when I'm supposed to be at the Baptist Youth Camp for the weekend.

But now … I don't know where we are, just that we've been driving for almost an hour and the road keeps getting darker and narrower and more winding and I'm hardly able to breathe.

It's the next right, Bear says from the backseat.

Is this Rotta? I ask real quiet so just Ken can hear me.

No. We're just picking up a couple other guys.

I gasp and it sounds so loud I hold my breath.

Hey, you okay? Ken touches my bare leg and I shrink into the seat. I can't answer him, don't even trust myself to take another breath. Hey. He slows down and leans over trying to see me in the dark.

Watch it! Mike shouts, and Ken swerves back to his side of the road.

If you can't keep your fucking hands off Spider Chickie, let me drive! Bear shouts over the seat.

Cut it out, both of you, Mike tells them. Turn right again here.

Suddenly there are street lights and curbs and houses all in neat rows, with lawns and lights in the windows. I let out my breath and take another one, feeling safer, like I'm back in my own neighborhood—only the houses are a lot bigger, all of them two stories with fences around the front yards and flashy cars in the driveways.

I'll get 'um, Mike says and dives out of the car, pushing Ken's seat forward.

I'm out, too, Bear says, and bangs against my seat to let him out. I scoot forward and he pushes the seat so far forward I'm squeezed against the dashboard.

Watch it! Ken yells and slams my seat back, catching Bear's foot. He almost falls but doesn't, flips Ken the bird and leaves the door open. Sorry 'bout him, Ken tells me and rubs the back of his hand along my cheek. He's just pissed I brought you. It's always been just us guys making the run.

I don't have to go, I offer, hoping he'll just take me back home.

He leans over and kisses me softly on the lips. I'm not letting you go now that I've got you here. He smiles and my stomach flips and I think I might be sick. I notice his eyes are blue and I start to cry.

Hey. Hey. Hey. It's all okay. Really. What's wrong?

I ... I ... The words won't come, but I'm screaming in my head, I don't want to do this! I don't want to …

Move it, Spider Chickie, Bear tells me and shoves the front seat forward, smashing me against the dashboard again. He's followed by his brother, Mike, and two other guys. One of them, Andy, takes my seat and I scoot into the space between the bucket seats.

We head out of the rolling hills and catch the highway heading north. The guys are all laughing and talking like regular guys, about sports, and music, and girls they know. Ken has his arm around my shoulder and tells me I'm in charge of the eight-track, but I'm too scared to do anything. When the tape runs out Bear tells me to put on something else, but all I can think about is trying to get out of the car.

Andy sorts through a box of tapes on the floor and pops out the old one, puts in another one I've never heard. I realize these guys aren't into acid rock, and I wonder if they even take acid. All the music is kinda corny.

Those are great boots. Suede? Andy asks and reaches out a hand to touch my boots.

I snatch my leg away as far as I can, which isn't very far. I bump Ken's arm and the car swerves a little then rights itself.

Hey, what ya think you're doing? Ken shouts over the song that's blaring from the speakers. I told you guys no rough-housing while I'm driving. Now cut it out, Andy.

We start to climb a steep hill leading away from the ocean. The rain has stopped, but the headlights reflect off the wet road. It's black beyond their reach. Andy puts on the Rolling Stones and turns the sound up loud. All the guys start singing, *Hey, Hey, you, you, get off of my cloud* …

I try to reason with myself, tell myself I'm safe. I look over at the guy in the passenger seat, Andy. He's looking at my legs and I'm scared.

Hey, pull over up there, Bear shouts over the Stones. The car slows and pulls into a paved area off the main road.

I can't breathe, can't even cry. I want to be brave, fight my way free, run off into the woods. But I know I won't.

I pull my legs in tight as the guys pile out, saying Yeah. Me, too. They follow Bear into the bushes. I don't even bother to slide over into the passenger seat.

Don't mind them, Ken says, and rubs his hand along my leg. I close my eyes and try to pretend I'm somewhere else. But he doesn't do anything else, just rubs my leg.

Stop it asshole, someone shouts outside the car. I open my eyes and see one of the guys kicking water out of a puddle at Bear. The other's join in and Bear dives at them, grabs one. The others jump him and try to bring him down.

Ken rolls down the power window and yells across me. Cut it out! We're never gonna get to San Luis! Get in the damned car!

Bear ruffles his brother's hair. Andy jumps in the air and smacks Bear on the top of his head. Bear turns and grabs Andy and spins him around a couple of times and they all head back to the car, laughing and slapping at each other.

Never mind them, Ken tells me. They're always like that.

I close my eyes and pray that they'll just get in the car and not touch me.

The farm house sits all alone on a wide stretch of land, far from the main road, which isn't much of a road, two lanes with no lights and no shoulder. Everyone piles out of the Cougar. Ken waits a minute then asks, You okay?

I scoot up onto the passenger seat and tell him I don't want to go in the house.

Why? They're cool. You'll like Suzanne, she's really cool.

Suzanne? I ask.

Yeah. This is her and Tim's place. Tim's Bear's older brother.

I smile at him and begin to hope that this time won't be like the other times.

Let's go in. Okay? he leans over and hesitates. I lean forward and kiss him quickly on the lips. He smiles and pats my leg. Let's go.

Everyone is sitting around on low couches, bean bags, and broken down chairs with torn upholstery. I don't see Suzanne, only a big group of guys. I recognize a few, from the Cougar. The others look older and my breath catches again. I try to stop the thoughts, try to convince myself that I can trust Ken, trust these men—but I can't. I sink down on a pile of pillows and sit cross-legged and put my hands in my lap and push my skirt down to cover the gap, so no one can see up it.

Ken disappears. No one says anything to me. I study my hands in my lap, wonder where San Luis is—where I am. Ken comes back with a couple of beers and Bear passes him a joint as soon as he sits down next to me.

All right! he says. This is more like it. He takes a big hit and holds it to my lips.

It's not very good, or strong, but I smile and hold in the smoke longer than he does; realize he doesn't have much experience with pot; wonder again if he trips; look at him closely and realize he doesn't.

Where's Suzanne? I whisper to Ken.

Hey, Tim! he shouts over the music. Where's Suzanne?

She's out with some friends. Figured this is a guys' night in, so she'd have a girls' night out. She'll be back around midnight or so.

I feel a little better knowing Suzanne really exists, and take another hit off the joint. One of the older guys passes around a Playboy magazine. Ken hands the magazine to Bear without looking at it and takes my hand.

We should head off, he tells me. Bear looks up from the centerfold, and chuckles. Go to hell, Ken tells him, but doesn't sound mad. He takes me by the hand and leads me outside.

Just us? I ask him.

Yeah. I don't want those guys around. He kisses me on the lips and adds, Let's grab our sleeping bags and head out over there, under those trees.

I stand on my tiptoes and kiss him back.

It isn't much. Doesn't really hurt. Doesn't really feel like anything. It's over real fast and I try not to lie in the wet puddle on my side of the spread-out sleeping bag, but Ken's on the other side so I try and ignore it, tell myself it'll dry soon. Ken kicks his jeans off the rest of the way and falls asleep; leaves me with my skirt still on, my underwear around my ankles.

I look at the stars and wonder what all the fuss is about. So far sex hasn't been anything great. I don't think I even want to do it again—it's too messy.

The Cougar climbs a long, steep hill on the interstate and drops down fast into a huge valley covered with low trees and farms, turns off the interstate and climbs again along a dirt road and stops in a tree-covered parking lot with a damp, dimly lit building in the shape of a wine barrel. Rotta turns out to be a little winery tucked in behind some hills north of San Luis Obispo.

I can't believe the wrinkled old woman who owns the place is actually pouring wine in a small plastic cup for me. But she's pouring for all of us, anything we want. The gold one, please, I ask and offer her my empty cup.

The Muscatel? she asks and I nod, not sure which is which anymore.

I take a sip and think I've found heaven on earth. It's sweet and smooth and thick and so pretty.

Why do all the girls like Muscatel? Bear asks. The guys ignore him, crowding in to have their cups refilled. Here, he takes my empty cup and hands it to the old woman. Give her some Zinfandel. The woman pours and Bear hands me the cup. Now this is a real wine.

I hesitate.

Take it, for Christ's sake! What's wrong with you? Here! he pushes the cup at me.

I take a sip, almost spit it out it's so sour. But I don't. I swallow it and when Bear laughs and tells the guys that I'm just another girl who can't take real wine, I down it all and hand the empty cup back to Bear.

I've had better, I tell him and everyone busts up laughing. Ken smiles at me and takes the cup from Bear, who's just standing there, not saying anything for a change.

Another Muscatel, please, Ken tells the old woman.

She chuckles and fills the cup nearly to the top.

I feel obliged to down it, too; realize too late that I've had too much.

Hey, it's okay, Ken tells me as he holds my hair back so I don't puke all over it. I've barfed my share of times up here. It's one of my favorite places to heave.

I chance a look at him. His eyes are looking out over the valley we drove through. It's so peaceful here. He sighs and looks over at me.

I wipe the back of my hand across my mouth and hope there's no barf on it.

He smiles. Feel better?

I nod and take my hair from him and try to breathe slow and easy through my mouth so I don't smell the mess I made.

Come on. Let's get going. We've got a long drive back to L.A.

We're not staying the night?

No. Bear has to be at work at four in the morning.

Oh, I say, trying to figure out what to do. It's just that I thought we were staying and I … sorta … I don't have any place to go since I told my dad I'd be gone all weekend.

Where'd you get the idea we'd be gone all weekend? He helps me down the small hill and I'm feeling sick all over again.

I thought you said the weekend.

No. Rotta runs are always just an overnighter.

But my dad thinks I'm gone for the weekend. I can't just walk back in a day early. I try to keep my voice calm, thinking all the while that I'll never be able to leave overnight again if I get busted.

Stay with Kathy.

She's not home.

I don't know then. Maybe with your sister?

I stop in my tracks. With Shirley! You're a genius, I tell Ken.

It wasn't that hard to figure out, he says and shrugs his shoulders.

The ride back to the farm is so quiet I can hear the gallon bottles of Rotta clanging against each other in the trunk. Everyone stumbles around grabbing their gear and stuffing it in the trunk around the cases of wine. There's not enough room so everyone in the back seat has stuff piled on their laps. Up front I wish I had something to lean back against and try to get comfortable.

Come on over here, Ken tells me and holds up his arm for me.

I settle in the open space between the seats with my legs tucked under me, my butt pressed against the passenger seat, my head in Ken's lap. The Cougar purrs along the winding road and I drift off into a dream of sailing on a calm ocean.

We stop in Santa Barbara for gas. I stumble into the head and don't even bother to look in the mirror; know I have to look as bad as I feel. I splash cold water on my face, but it doesn't help clear my mind. My head's throbbing and I wish I could throw up again, think it would help. But I hate throwing up and so take a pee and splash my face again, dig some whites out of my purse and pop them, run my fingers through my hair and twist it up into a high ponytail and tie it off with a rubber band.

I hazard a look at myself. My makeup is rubbed off and my eyes are red and swollen. I keep looking at myself and wonder why Muzzie drinks so much when it makes you feel so bad. Wonder if I'm going to turn out to be just like her, drunk all the time and miserable.

I study my face—it's long and narrow, not round at all like Muzzie's. My eyes are dark brown with no hint of Muzzie's deep green flecks. My skin is white and clear and almost shining, no hint of Muzzie's dull, pasty pallor.

I splash water on my face again and wipe my hands on my jeans and dash for the door. Home doesn't seem so bad now that I have a boyfriend who's nice to me; a boyfriend who protects me.

I kinda run-skip to the Cougar and throw my arms around Ken's neck and kiss him on the lips. He picks me up and swings me around while we're kissing and sets me down with my back against the car and keeps kissing me. I can hear the guys hooting and laughing, but I don't care—they won't hurt me now that I'm Ken's girlfriend.

I'm safe and I'm not worried any more.

Code of Conduct
December 1968

Suggested listening:
Album—Beggar's Banquet, The Rolling Stones

I hate our English teacher, Mrs. Andrews. I nickname her Julie. I figure everyone in dumbbell English can make that connection. Most don't. But Kathy and I sing, *So long, farewell, Auf Wiedersehen, goodnight*, walking down the hall to third period English.

I'm still pissed that I got busted for the Romeo and Juliette assignment in October. She assigned that fucking play on purpose, I tell Kathy for the fiftieth time.

God, are you still freaking about that? You need to chill out or something.

I shrug and walk in ahead of her and go to the back of the class. I haven't turned in any homework since the Romeo and Juliette disaster, even though we've had two assignments. I lean back in my chair and pop my gum and look everywhere except up front.

I hate her.

She drones on and on about something to do with plays again, with Shakespeare and some old guy who sells his soul to be young.

Wouldn't you love to be young, I say under my breath. Kathy and some trailer park dude next to me laugh.

Please, Miss Conrad. Share your insights with the class. Mrs. Andrews is standing in front of her desk holding a thick book open half-way, looking right at me.

How the hell does she always catch me? I didn't say that loud enough for her to hear. I look at her and wonder if she put microphones under each desk. Have to stop myself from looking, remind myself to look when class is over.

We're waiting, Miss Conrad, she says louder and taps a foot.

I said you'd love to be young, that's why you're reading that moldy old play. Everyone laughs.

I meet Mrs. Andrew's eyes for an instant and can see how hurt she is. I smile and don't look away, glad that for once I could make her feel as bad as she makes me feel all the time.

Kathy and I take off at lunch and head to my house. The wind is ice cold and cuts at my face. It takes four matches to light my cigarette and I almost give up, but Kathy keeps trying and lights hers off mine once it's going good.

I can't believe that old bitch actually expects us to read another fucking play! Kathy says into the wind that's whipping our hair and pushing smoke back into our faces. And now we fucking have to because of the fucking movie mess-up. It isn't fair that we have to read two plays!

I nod and want to button up my pea coat, but want to look cool and like nothing bothers me, so I leave it open. My legs are freezing and I can only keep one hand in my pocket. The walk home has never seemed so long.

Hey. Slow down, Miss long legs, Kathy shouts and grabs my free arm.

I'm freezing, I tell her, but slow down anyway.

Button your fucking coat, dumb-shit. She flicks her cigarette into the bushes and digs her hands deep inside her coat pockets.

I follow her lead and flick my half-smoked cigarette into the bushes and button my coat to the top button and bury my hands in the slit pockets, and thank Shirley again for snagging the pea coat for me.

I'm freezing, Kathy moans. It's not fair that guys get to wear pants to school and we have to wear skirts. Fucking dress code! I'm freezing! Why didn't we go to my house? It's so much closer.

Cause your dad's home sick.

Oh. Yeah. I forgot. I'm freezing.

Let's run! I take off running slower than I can so Kathy can keep up.

I fucking hate running, she pants.

Yeah, but at least we're warmer. I laugh and keep trotting up the sidewalk, feeling somehow free and light and not angry anymore at Mrs. Andrews.

We walk the last few blocks with the wind at our backs. The street's quiet and empty, everyone at work or school or staying inside. I turn over the second rock from the door in the little atrium on the porch and wipe the key on my pea coat.

I turn to Kathy. It's always here, if you need to get in sometime and I'm not home.

Why'd I want to get in your house if you're not here?

I don't know. You just might want to. I fit the key in the lock and find the door's unlocked. For a minute I freak and turn around looking to see if my dad's car is in the driveway.

What? Kathy jumps back and looks around.

Shit! I thought for a minute my dad might be home.

We just walked up the driveway, dude. You would have had to walk around his car if he was home. You okay? She turns back to me and leans in close, looking at my eyes.

I'm fine. It's just that the door's unlocked and it's always locked.

Can we go in? I'm freezing. Kathy stamps her feet and digs her hands back in her pockets.

Sure. Yeah. I look around wondering why I'm spooked all of a sudden, think maybe I shouldn't have taken so many whites this morning.

Shirley's in the living room listening to the radio. She looks up from her magazine. You look half frozen. I lit a fire. She nods towards the fireplace and Kathy and I almost trip over each other getting to it. The power went off at the plant so I got the day off. I came over here thinking you might'a ditched with the weather so bad. Want some lunch?

I'm starving, Kathy says, stripping off her coat and bumping me aside to get closer to the fire.

Baloney and cheese?

Yes please! Kathy coos and moves aside to give me a chance at the fire.

Nothing for me, I tell Shirley.

No way! You're eating something.

I'm not hungry.

You would be if you'd stop popping whites all the time. I found two wrappers in the trash. How many you taking now? She sets her magazine on the table and stands up, stretching like a big cat.

Not many. I tell her and scoot further behind Kathy even though my legs are burning up.

Don't bullshit me. She turns and heads for the kitchen. You're eating whether you're hungry or not. Got it?

I nod and then shake my head. The thought of food makes my stomach turn.

I'll eat yours if you don't want it, Kathy whispers.

Thanks.

We sit cross-legged on the floor in a semi-circle on a yellow and white checkered table cloth in front of the fireplace with our sandwiches, potato chips, and the no-name cokes dad gets at the army base. Joan Baez is singing about Queen Jane dying. She sounds so much better on the big stereo than on the little record player in our room. We rarely get to hear her out here, but dad's out on another week-long case and so we're not worried about him walking in.

Shirley moved back home when she and Sandy couldn't pay the

rent on their apartment. It's great to have her home, though she does boss me around a lot. She and dad don't fight as much as before. They try to avoid each other, which means Shirley stays at friend's whenever she can. I don't mind too much. It makes the times she's home more special.

You guys going back? Shirley asks and lights a cigarette.

No way! It's too cold out there, I say and look at Kathy.

It's not fair that we can't wear pants when it's so cold. Dress codes suck!

You guys should protest, Shirley says and offers Kathy a cigarette. I reach for one. Not 'til you eat that, she says pointing to my plate, which is still full. You're skinny enough, for fuck-sake. Terry won't even recognize you.

When's he coming home, Kathy asks.

In March sometime, I tell her. We won't be able to do this when he's home, I sigh.

Why not? Shirley asks. He won't care.

I laugh, Sure. He'll just let us ditch school and have parties here and not say anything.

Shirley takes a long hit off her cigarette. We won't be able to have the parties, that's for sure. But he won't care if you ditch school when it's this cold out.

Sure. I huff and take a bite out of my sandwich.

You don't even know him, so don't act like you know what he'll do when he gets home. He wouldn't care.

He never ditched, or threw parties, or did pot or anything. I take another bite and think I might throw up if I have to eat anymore.

Is he gonna move in here? Kathy asks.

Probably. Shirley stubs out her cigarette and looks around. Wonder where the old man's gonna sleep. Muzzie won't let him sleep in her room.

She won't have a choice, I mumble and push my plate towards Kathy. She grabs the second half of my sandwich and gobbles it down while Shirley's staring off into space.

She pushes the plate back in front of me just as Shirley starts dumping her cigarettes out on the table cloth. The last cigarette out is hand rolled and we both smile. She lights it and passes it to me without saying anything, still looking at nothing, her eyes glassy and turning red.

We finish the joint as Joan Baez sings about four little girls that were killed in Birmingham.

Wow, that's a real bummer, Kathy sighs. They all died?

Shirley and I both nod and I feel the tears welling up in my eyes.

Who killed them?

The Man, Shirley says. It's always the Man. Shirley gets up and puts on another album, Country Joe and the Fish.

She and I sing along, and it's one, two, three, four, what are we fightin' for?

Kathy taps me on the arm. Your brother's in the army isn't he?

Yeah. So what. He's not in Vietnam.

Be the first one on your block to have your boy sent home in a box.

It's just creepy, all those guys going off to Nam. Quinn's older brother just got drafted. Chris said he's a dead man.

We stop singing.

Let's clean up, Shirley tells us and starts picking up dishes. Kathy and I help and I'm glad she doesn't say anything about the food left on my plate. Kathy eats all the chips on the way into the kitchen and grabs what's left of my sandwich before she dumps the plate in the sink. We turn to leave.

Hey, hey. I cooked. You two clean.

We turn back, resigned to do the dishes. It wasn't that great of meal, Kathy whispers.

I laugh and hand her the gloves. You wash, I'll dry.

The morning is dark and windy. I struggle out of bed and grab my teddy bear off the floor. Pull apart his back seam and dig around for the little tinfoil rolls of whites. I only feel one and dig around, knowing I have to have more than one roll left. I bought six, with my last six dollars, just last week. But the bear's empty. I decide to only take two whites until I can figure out what happened to the rest of my stash. Wonder if Kathy knows where I keep them—whites in the teddy bear, reds in the toe of my old tennis shoes in the back of the closet, acid in the lining of my wool coat that I don't wear anymore. I don't even try to keep pot around; it's too bulky—my dad would find it for sure.

I don't think I've told anyone, not even Shirley where my stash is, so I had to have taken five rolls in the last week, minus the ones I shared with Kathy. I sit back down on the bed and try to remember taking so much. I remember digging in the bear all last week, when I got up, when I got home. Realize I must have taken it all. I go get my shoe and find all my reds are gone too, and remember I took them to come down from the whites every night.

I open the foil roll and put the two whites back inside the bear. I don't ever want to be like Muzzie; never want to take something and not remember taking it. I silently swear to stay off everything today and tomorrow. I wait to decide about the day after that.

I pull back the curtains and shiver. The wind's whipping the tree branches so hard I think one might snap off. I go to my closet and pull out a pair of dark blue, wool bell-bottoms I bought at the Navy surplus store. It takes a few tries to match up all the double buttons on the two halves of the pant's fly. I throw on a turtle neck, braid my hair back, and pull on a matching knit cap I lifted.

I call Kathy and tell her to wear pants, that we're going to show the Man that he can't make us wear skirts when the weather's this bad. She hesitates and I have to push her to agree. I grab a piece of beef jerky out of the kitchen cabinet, throw on my pea coat and head off to the battle ground. Hope I get sent home before lunch.

I meet Kathy in the F head, amazed I made it clear across campus without getting stopped by a teacher. She's wearing a matching pant and top set with little daisies and a short black coat that doesn't even cover her butt. I'm fucking freezing, she screams when I walk in.

What the fuck are you wearing sandals for?

My other shoes don't go with this! she says and puts a hand on her hip. You look like a sailor or something, she says and I turn and look in the long mirror behind me.

I'm all one color, from head to foot. I look like a dark blue pole. My eyes barely show under the knit cap, the collar of my coat is pulled up and my hands are tucked in the pockets. There's steam coming off me and I realize I'm boiling up inside all these clothes. I start peeling layers, but realize I don't have layers, just the coat and my clothes.

I'm fucked, I tell Kathy. I can't sit in class with all this on, I'll burn up.

Yeah. That's why I wore this. She looks down. At least my legs are warm. That's something.

The last bell rings and we run down the hall to first period. The teacher's late so there's just a woman from the principal's office trying to get everyone in their seat. We slip along the wall and get to our seats before she brings the class to order. When class is over we leave by the back door and feel pretty proud that we got away with wearing pants to school.

Second period is P.E. so there's no problem. We play volleyball in the gym. A few girls make fun of us when we put our pants back on, but we ignore them and hope they won't fink us out.

Mrs. Andrews seems to overlook our pants, looking only at our faces all through the class. I think we're home free when the bell rings.

Miss Conrad. I'd like to see you for a moment, please. You too, Miss Weston.

We walk up to her desk and stand on the far side, hoping she won't see our pants.

I realize that it is atrocious weather outside. However, you put me in an untenable position by wearing pants when they are strictly forbidden by the dress code. She looks up at us and we both look down at our hands. Did you think I wouldn't notice? We don't answer. And what do you expect me to do? If I don't report you then I am going against school rules when I am supposed to uphold them.

What if the rules are wrong? I ask quietly.

Then they must be changed, not broken.

How can you change them if everyone just keeps obeying them? I ask a bit bolder. I look up at her.

Ah. Well, yes that is a valid question. You start by bringing the subject up for discussion and pointing out your concerns before you disobey.

That never works, Kathy adds, still looking down at her hands.

I'm still looking right at Mrs. Andrews. Just report us and we'll head back home. It's no big loss missing school.

You think that? That there's no benefit to learning, to expanding your mind?

I expand my mind all the time, I tell her. Nothing you do expands anything but your pocket book.

She shakes her head and says quietly, I'm sorry you see no profit in receiving an education. I had hoped ... she pauses and looks down at her hands.

Stop hoping and get real, I say and turn away.

Stop, Miss Conrad! I have to report you. You leave me no choice.

I turn around and look at her. You have a choice.

She hesitates a moment, then shakes her head and writes out the yellow slip and holds it out to Kathy.

That's what I thought, I say and walk out without looking back.

I want to tell the Principal just what I think of his rules and his regulations. Tell him how unfair it is to make girls wear dresses when it's freezing outside, while boys stay all nice and warm in their slacks. Tell him his rules and regulations are all bullshit, that nobody who thinks could think his rules were fair. But I don't say anything.

He suspends me for two weeks and tells me when he sees me again I had better be wearing a skirt or dress that's regulation length.

I tell him in that case he won't see me again.

I go home and decide not to go back to school—ever.

I tell Muzzie about what happened when she gets home that night. She agrees with me and says she'll go talk to the Principal in the morning. I don't believe her. She'll get drunk and forget all about it by morning. But none of it matters; I'm not going back there anyway.

I don't sleep at all that night, spend it going over and over all the things I wish I'd told the Principal, and worry about what's going to happen when my dad finds out I got suspended.

Muzzie is gone when I finally get out of bed around eight the next morning. I turn up the heat to seventy degrees and spend the morning reading a book Ken loaned me, *Cat's Cradle*. It's very weird but I dig it, I think.

I hear Muzzie's car in the driveway around ten and think she must be drunk or sick or both; she's never home early unless she's drunk or sleeping off the night before. I put out my cigarette and climb onto one of the high stools at the breakfast bar and sit cross-legged, like I always do when Dad's not home. I can see her through the kitchen window fumbling with the lock. She doesn't look drunk, just cold. Her breath makes big wispy clouds between her and the door.

She finally manages to open the door and an ice cold wind follows her in. She doesn't take off her coat, just walks into the living room and starts calling me. I don't say anything; don't want to talk with her or anyone. My head hurts and all I want to do is drop some whites. But I told myself I wouldn't, so I won't, no matter how much I want to.

There you are! Muzzie says. What are you doing still in your jammies? Are you sick? She walks straight over and puts her frozen hand on my forehead.

I'm fine, I tell her and shove her hand away.

Then get yourself dressed and get to school.

I'm suspended! Or did you forget?! Anyway, I'm never going back.

Donna D. Conrad

All their rules and regulations and bullshit! I hate them all.

That might be, but you've won this round.

I look up at her not understanding what she means.

You won! Go put your slacks on and I'll drive you back to school.

What? I uncross my legs and drop them to the metal ring halfway down the stool.

The Principal agreed to let girls wear pants when the weather's bad. You won!

I jump down and throw my arms around Muzzie and kiss her. I won? I really won?

Yes, my little revolutionary! She smiles bigger than I've seen her smile in a long time. But only when the weather's bad. Otherwise it's business as usual. And now, if you get yourself to school, you can be the first girl to wear pants the first day it's legal.

I dash out of the kitchen and stop partway down the hall. I run back to the kitchen to kiss her and say, Thank you.

I'll always be there for you when you're in the right, sweetheart. That's what Muzzies are for. She laughs and kisses my cheek. Now go put on some pants and let's get you to school.

I turn and run down the hall.

And not those terrible sailor pants! She calls after me.

1969 in the news

- President: Richard M. Nixon

- Vice President: Spiro T. Agnew

- The population of the United States is 202.68 million

- The national debt is $353.7 billion

- Average income per year is $5,984

- Average cost of a new house is $27,900

- Average monthly rent is $135

- A gallon of gas costs $0.35

- *Oliver!* wins Best Picture

- *Mrs. Robinson* wins Best Song

- *By the Time I Get to Phoenix* wins Best Album.

- The following TV shows debut: *The Courtship of Eddie's Father*; *The Bill Cosby Show*; *The Flip Wilson Show*; *Hee Haw*; *Marcus Welby M.D.*; *The Brady Bunch*; and *Sesame Street*

- The manned spacecraft, Apollo 11, lands on the moon. Neil Armstrong is the first person to step onto the lunar surface. He exclaims, "That's one small step for man; one giant leap for mankind."

- An American teenager known as Robert R. becomes patient #1 in the U.S. HIV/AIDS epidemic

- The Woodstock Festival is held in upstate New York. It is a mecca for 500,000 anti-war activist and hippies

Donna D. Conrad

- ❖ **The first ARPANET link is established laying the foundation for the Internet**
- ❖ **The U.S. military goes to a lottery draft to select inductees**
- ❖ **The Cuyahoga River in Cleveland, Ohio, catches on fire due to massive amounts of pollutants and is credited as the start of the environmental movement**

A Time for Loving
Late-January 1969

Suggested listening:
Single—*Time Has Come Today*, The Chamber Brothers

I don't remember getting out of bed.

But I'm not in my bed.

Lights flash over my head.

I'm wrapped tightly in thick blankets.

They're soft and warm and I'm not hurting as bad as before.

His mom works all day. He asks if we want to see his room. Kathy says she'll wait downstairs. His room is narrow, with one window, one twin bed, an electric keyboard. He says he'll play for me. The cover never comes off the keyboard. Kathy throws a plate at me when we finally come down for lunch around one. I don't know why she's mad. But it doesn't matter—I like fucking.

Don't worry sweetheart. We're almost there.

I open my eyes and realize I'm in the backseat of the Galaxy 500. Muzzie's driving with one arm over the front seat trying to reach me. I smile at her, but am too sleepy to say anything.

I figure I'll know where we're going when we get there.

I don't notice at first. Kathy does because I don't borrow any tampons. I tell her I skip periods all the time. She raises an eyebrow. Does he use a rubber?

I don't think so.

You don't let him come inside you? she asks.

Donna D. Conrad

I don't know, I tell her.

Either he does or he doesn't! She tells me and puts a hand on her hip.

I look around her room, not wanting to admit I don't know what she's talking about. I don't know! I tell her again.

She looks at me and I start to tear up. What are you crying about? It's no big deal. You just can't let them come inside unless they're wearing a rubber. You could get knocked up.

How can you tell? I ask.

The lights are so bright, like spotlights. I squeeze my eyes shut tight. I'm rocking back and forth, real slow and I think I must be on a boat. Think that Muzzie must be taking us to Catalina Island for my birthday like she's always promising she will. It'll be great to be anywhere else than Covina on my birthday. I relax and float away on the tide.

We're on Chris's bed. He and his friends are already out for the night. Kathy's in her room with Frank. I show Ken the little square package, but can't find my voice to ask him to put it on.

I don't like those, he tells me.

Oh. I set the rubber on the bed stand and sit on the bed.

He kisses me. We don't need them. I always pull out before I come.

I smile and tell him that's great. I can hardly wait to tell Kathy I'm safe.

How long has she been like this? I almost recognize the man's voice, but not quite.

Since this morning. She was fine last night, Muzzie tells him.

I hold on tight to the blankets, but they slip through my hands. I'm so cold. So cold.

I want you to.

I look down at his dick wobbling around. You want me to kiss it?

He nods and smiles.

I scoot down and kiss the top.

No. Put it in your mouth.

Yew! No way!

*Hey. You don't want to make love without a rubber anymore, so this is the
next best thing. Come on. Everyone likes giving head.*

I shake my head and tell him we don't need to use a rubber.

Too many people are talking all at once. The man I think I know
is telling everyone what to do, like he's a big shot. I want him to shut
up. Let me sleep. But he won't.

He keeps asking me about school; wants to know what classes I'm
taking; if I like them.

There's a sharp pain in my arm and I drift off into a dream filled
with sunlight.

*You just put it in your mouth ... like a popsicle, Kathy tells me. The guys all
love it. I don't get it.*

So, that's it? You just put it in your mouth?

*She thinks about it for a minute. Yeah. Just act like you're sucking on a
popsicle. Or a fifty-fifty bar, the one with the cream center. She cracks up and
takes a hit of the joint and passes it to me.*

What are you laughing at? I ask.

You'll find out, she laughs and a big cloud of smoke fills the space between us.

She'll be okay won't she? Muzzie sounds really worried and I want
to tell her I'm just sleepy is all.

She'll be fine, Helen, the man tells her. I recognize his voice.
Wonder why Dr. Don is here.

Wonder where here is. But I'm too sleepy to really care. I'm warm
and I don't hurt anymore.

It's been two months! Kathy's pacing back and forth in my bedroom.

But he pulls out, so I can't be.

Every time? she asks. That's a drag. You should just use a rubber.

He doesn't like to. Besides we do all kinds of other stuff.

Like what?

*I tell her about the hand massager of his mom's. That I'm starting to like
giving him head.*

So, you don't fuck?

219

Of course we do! I still like the real thing way better. But it's nice other times, you know, when you can't do the other, 'cause y'know, he's tired or something ... I trail off.

Frank never gets tired, she sighs. Sometimes I wish he would.

Ken's always ready, too, I say a bit too quickly, feeling like there'd be something wrong if he wasn't. It's just that ... you know ... if we're together all day ...

Yeah, she says and grabs her coat off the floor. I remember you guys goin' at it all day. She looks at me and adds, You shouldn't let him know you like it that much! He'll think you're a slut. She turns and walks out the door.

Donna. Donna. A hand taps my face, but I don't want to wake up. Come on now. I know you can hear me.

I open one eye a little and see the outline of a man with a big bushy head of hair leaning over me. Where? I croak and realize how dry my throat is.

You're in my office. Do you know who I am, Donna?

I blink both eyes open and recognize our family doctor. Dr. Don? I ask.

He smiles and pats my hand that he's holding. You're going to be just fine now.

Why am I here? I look around. I don't ...

Just rest, he tells me.

I wait until Dad and Muzzie are both out and Shirley's staying over at David's. I light candles and put all my Joan Baez and Judy Collins albums on the spindle, one piled on top of another, even though Ken tells me it isn't good for the albums. I remember to remind myself not to think about him, that he has nothing to do with what I'm doing.

I take four of the six capsules I got from Kathy, and four reds to knock me out during the trip. Kathy swears she knows a girl, who knows a girl, who says this much mescaline always works. I save the extra two just in case. I turn on the record player and lie back on the bed and wait—hope it will be a good trip—a freedom ride. I laugh out loud at the joke I just made and realize everything will be alright. That I'll never have a bad trip, even when I'm doing it for this reason.

The bleeding starts during the night, while I'm sleeping. The cramps wake me in the early morning. I'm still tripping, despite the pain and the reds. I look around at the swirling colors on the walls of my room and think how wonderful life is when I'm tripping.

Dad coughs in his room and Muzzie says something in her sleep from hers. I drop my feet to the floor, the pain is so intense I follow them all the way down. I always have bad cramps, but nothing like this. I thought it would just be like a really bad period. But it's nothing like a bad period. I lay curled up on the floor and feel the blood draining out of me, but I can't move. I want to call for Muzzie, but am too afraid Dad will wake up.

You scared your mother half to death.

I nod and sip hot broth through a straw.

Want to tell me what you did?

I shake my head. Dr. Don takes a deep breath and shakes his head kinda sad. You could have died.

I nod—not believing him.

No. He takes my hand and looks me in the eyes. You could have died. You've had two blood transfusions. This isn't a game. If your mother hadn't brought you in when she did, you could have died.

What did you tell her? I ask, without much hope that he didn't tell her what I'd done.

He looks away and takes another deep breath. I told her these things happen sometimes with young women and that she needn't worry. That we caught it in time and that you'll be fine. He looks back at me, and his eyes aren't as kind as I remember them. I lied to her.

He drops my hand and stands up. She wanted to know why I didn't put you in the hospital. He looks at the ceiling. I couldn't have done that without everyone knowing what happened, now could I? So, I told her that you weren't that bad off and that it wasn't a problem to keep you here in my office.

He looks back at me. I've never lied so much in my life as I've lied for you. I delivered you sixteen years ago, right across the street, in that very hospital! You are dear to me, but I won't do what I've just done for you again. Not ever.

I'm sorry, I tell him, and quietly add, Thank you.

Get some rest, he tells me and turns off the lamp. Your mother'll be here in the morning to take you home. I'm headed home myself. Nurse Johnston will be here if you need anything. We'll talk more in the morning about how to keep this from happening again. He leaves and closes the door behind him.

I lie awake wondering how the hell I can avoid getting pregnant except by not having sex. Worry I'll never get to make love with Ken again. I cry myself to sleep, alone, on a cot, in a small exam room in Alhambra, California.

Death Knell Sounding
February 25 – March 21, 1969

Suggested listening:
Album—Joan Baez/5, Joan Baez

Everything is grey and wet and dreary. Neither Shirley nor I have recovered from my 3am nightmare scream that brought Dad and Muzzie barreling into our bedroom—ended with Dad yelling and Muzzie putting a cold washcloth on my forehead.

I'm so happy Shirley moved back home. I missed her so much. I cuddle close to her as she finally drifts off to sleep just before dawn. I count her breaths and pray for dawn. It comes, faint and dismal. A harsh February rain splatters the windows, making our room cold and uninviting. I lie in bed and listen to Dad coughing and banging in the kitchen. I stay tucked in bed hugging Shirley.

The day grows darker, and the rain is slammed against the house by a strong wind. I sit in the living room watching the almost horizontal rain through the sliding glass door, sip on my Double Cola and wish Kathy was in town, wish Muzzie was awake, wish the gray day would end.

The wind dies away and the rain falls in thick sheets. Laddie whimpers at the sliding door and I pull myself out of the deep armchair and let him in. I think it's safe; Dad won't be home for hours and Muzzie never cares if Laddie comes in, especially when it's cold and wet.

He takes two steps inside and shakes himself, spraying the dining room with dirty water and matted fur. I slap him on the nose and yell, Bad dog! He plops down on his butt and yelps at me. Bad Dog! I repeat. He leaps up and plants two muddy paws on my chest. I almost fall over backwards.

Laddie pushes off and dashes past me, romps through the living room and back around through the kitchen and back to me, plops on his butt and barks once. He pants and looks at me, his big golden eyes so hopeful. I forget that he's been a bad dog, forget the puddles and muddy paw prints—remember him when he was a little ball of fur. Remember how, when I'd let him in through the bedroom window in La Puente, he'd snuggle under the covers and keep my feet warm all night. Remember when Dad shaved him down to his skin so he didn't have to brush him. Remember all the times Laddie's run away, and how Dad always beats him when he finally comes home skinny and exhausted. Wonder why he ever comes back once he's free.

I sit on my butt with Laddie in the dining room and let him lick my face and stand on my crossed legs. He loves me even though I don't feed him, or brush him, or walk him; even though I yell at him and tell him he's a bad boy. I wouldn't love me if I were him. I'm glad Laddie is kinder than me.

A knock at the door has me grabbing Laddie's collar and shushing him, though he doesn't start barking. I stand up and see a soldier in a grey raincoat and hat through the kitchen window. He knocks again. I lead Laddie to the sliding door and shoo him out, wipe my muddy hands on my jeans and walk slowly through the kitchen. He knocks louder. I pull the door open a crack. Yes?

Is your Father home?

No.

Your Mother?

Whadda ya want?

I would like to speak with your Mother.

She's asleep.

Would you please wake her?

I shake my head no.

I need to speak with her. It's urgent.

Wait a minute. I close the door and go get Shirley. She's playing her guitar and singing *There but for Fortune*, really low.

There's a guy at the door. Some kinda army officer.

She stops singing and sets her guitar on the bed.

He wants to talk to Muzzie.

She gets up and pushes past me, walks down the hall with me on her tail. She pulls the door open a little wider than I did, but not much. Whadda ya want?

Please, Miss. I need to speak with your mother. It's urgent.

Water's dripping off his hat and pearling on his thick coat. I notice a black briefcase in his hand, and that his eyes are the greenest I've ever seen, like emeralds in sunlight. But there's no sun, only rain and the gray day matching his coat.

I'll get her, Shirley tells the man and closes the door on him. We both go to Muzzie's bedroom. Shirley taps lightly on the door and tells me to wait in our room. I ignore her and follow her in to the dark, stuffy room; try to make out Muzzie's shape under all the covers.

Mom? Mom? Wake up. There's someone here to see you. Shirley gently rocks Muzzie. She pulls back the covers. A shock of red hair rests against a faded white pillowcase, Muzzie's face is almost as white.

Mom. Shirley shakes her harder. Come on Mom, wake up.

And I wonder why she's calling Muzzie, Mom; she never does that.

Muzzie stirs and blinks her eyes open. They're glassy and not focused. She smacks her lips and yawns wide. What? What's going on?

A man wants to see you, Shirley repeats.

A man? What man?

I think he's from the Army. He's in a uni- ...

Muzzie jumps up and throws the covers off. Where? Here?

He's on the front porch.

You didn't let him in?

No ... I ... I don't know who he is ... and I didn't ...

For heaven's sake, Shirley. I raised you better than to leave someone standing outside in this weather.

She looks at me and points to her closet. Grab my good robe and slippers. How long has he been here? What does he want?

Just a minute or two. He wouldn't tell me what he wants.

Me neither, I add.

You both answered the door? she asks as she slips her arms through the sleeves of a red and blue flowered robe that nearly touches the floor.

No. I did first, and then I got Shirley.

Oh, girls. You didn't leave him out there freezing all this time?

I hand her the fur-trimmed slippers and sink back inside myself, hurt that I've disappointed Muzzie. She brushes past us and heads down the hallway, tying her robe and fluffing her hair. We follow close behind.

She opens the door wide and says, Please, come in out of the rain.

The man removes his hat and shakes the rain off. Thank you.

I must apologize for my daughters ...

Not at all. They were only being cautious. I appreciate that. Hope my own daughters are as circumspect.

He steps in through the front door. Shirley and I take a step back. Muzzie tells us to go to our room. We duck inside the living room and tiptoe along until we're just out of sight of the dining room.

Here let me help you out of that wet coat.

Thank you.

Would you like a cup of coffee?

No thank you, Mrs. Conrad. Please ... sit down.

I tap Shirley on the shoulder, wanting to ask her why Muzzie is being so nice to a soldier; she hates the war as much as we do. Shirley slaps my hand and shushes me.

Mrs. Conrad, I have terrible news about your son.

I know, Colonel. I know.

Has someone else already been here?

No. But a mother knows. No need to say more.

He died in the service of his country. An honorable death.

The room spins. I can't breathe. I feel Shirley shaking. The floor smacks me hard in the face.

A fire burns its way down my throat. I gag and cough and sit upright.

It's alright, sweetie. It's only brandy. I look around. I'm stretched out on the couch with Muzzie and Shirley sitting on the edge, hovering over me; but I don't know why. I try to sit up and Muzzie pushes me back down.

Don't. You've had a shock. Just lie there for a few minutes. She sets the small glass on the end table, and wipes her hands on her best robe. Their faces are tear-streaked and pale and it rushes back to me … the Colonel. *He died honorably.* I scream, No! No! NO! and burst into tears.

Muzzie engulfs me. I know baby. I know. There, there now, don't cry. Terry would want you to be brave.

Bullshit!

Shirley!

It's bullshit. My sister jumps up from the couch and points a finger at Muzzie. You thanked him! You fucking thanked that bastard for killing your son … killing my brother. You fucking thanked him!

Shirley! Do not use that tone of voice with me!

Fuck you! Fuck you and your manners, and your fucking "make-nice" bullshit. Her voice is shrill and tears are running down her cheeks. They killed him! They killed Terry! And you fucking thanked THEM!

Muzzie stands up and wraps her arms around Shirley. Shirley slaps at her and kicks and even tries to bite, but Muzzie pulls her into a tight hug; holds her and holds her and holds her and Shirley can't do anything inside Muzzie's arms.

They both sink slowly to the floor and I hear Shirley's sobbing and Muzzie coo, It's okay baby, it's okay. He's at peace now. Peace. Peace. And Muzzie starts to cry and they hug each other and I want to be with them.

Muzzie looks up at me and holds out her arm. I drop to the floor and squeeze between them and feel them surrounding me—but the hollow remains—the space that Terry filled.

Your dad's home, girls. Go on back to your room.

It's still raining and gray and cold. No one thought to start a fire in the fireplace or turn on the forced-air heat.

Shirley takes me down the hallway and closes the door behind us. I can't sit still, can't stand still, keep pacing up and down along the sliding closet doors, trying to breathe like Muzzie told me to. Shirley sits on the bed, not crying, not talking, not looking at me. Her eyes are red and swollen, her lips a tight straight line.

I look away. I want her to tell me it's all a lie. Tell me Terry will be home in less than a month, when his tour of duty is up. But I know she won't. Know it's all true. Know my big brother won't be coming home. Know he'll never pick me up and dump me in the pool, clothes and all, again. Know he'll never call me Punk again, never see me tall and thin and my hair long. Know he'll only ever know me as the fat little kid that cried all the time—the fat little sister he had to babysit instead of going out with his friends. The problem he couldn't get rid of.

I hear the front door open and close, hear Muzzie tell Dad to come into the living room, hear Dad tell her he's tired and needs a shower, hear Muzzie tell him it's about Terry, then silence.

I open the door and creep down the hall, dash across the foyer and into the kitchen, tip-toe into the dining room and peek around the corner. Dad's back's to me. He's bouncing up and down, like he's on a tiny trampoline. Why wasn't it me? Why wasn't it me? Why wasn't it ... He keeps saying the same thing over and over and over. Bouncing and crying and bouncing and crying, Why wasn't it me?

Muzzie's standing in front of him, her hands hanging limp at her side. I know, honey, I know. Her voice is so soft I don't think Dad can hear her. I don't want to watch him bouncing anymore; don't want to hear him crying anymore; don't want to see the pain on Muzzie's face anymore; so glad Dad's back is to me.

Girls, come on out. The package's here. My dad leaves the bedroom door open when he walks back down the hall.

We look at each other and can't seem to move. Do we have to? I ask Shirley.

Yeah. Hey, it's okay, maybe there's something in it from ... from ...

Okay.

I take her hand and we walk to the dining room table. A big manila envelope is there, creased and cracked and stamped with red and blue lettering: Classified Inspected Declassified.

They went through his stuff? Shirley's voice is a little too shrill.

Dad turns on her. Of course they did! He was C.I.C.

I tug on Shirley's arm, try to keep her from starting a fight. She backs down.

Dad slices through the tape with the silver letter opener we all gave him for his birthday just before Terry left. I look away.

Here girls. Dad hands us an envelope with our names written on it in Terry's scrawling handwriting.

Shirley takes it but doesn't open it. We both just stare at it. I see tiny marks on the outside—know they've looked at it already. Wonder if they've blacked out anything, like they always did with his letters. Wonder what Terry wanted us to know in case he died.

Dad takes another letter and sits down in the chair next to Muzzie. She takes the envelope and opens it, takes a single sheet of white paper out and unfolds it. I watch their eyes move across the page. Muzzie closes her eyes. Her hands are shaking. Dad reads and rereads the letter. Muzzie gently shakes her head, her lips are moving, but no sounds come out.

Shirley turns and runs from the room with our letter. I dash after her but she slams the door in my face. I look down at the knob, reach out and turn it, but it's locked. I wait, my nose pressed against the door, my eyes closed just like Muzzie's, my lips forming the same words, This can't be all. This can't be all that's left of him.

Shirley and her new boyfriend, David, are snuggled together in the big overstuffed armchair. I don't want to be alone so I'm sitting cross-legged on the matching ottoman. They're talking quietly. I'm trying not to think of anything, but thoughts keep coming. The report said he was assassinated—how, when, why? We don't know much. It's been three days since the Colonel told us, five days since Terry ... since he was killed.

We're the only ones home. Dad's on a case, Muzzie's working a split. It's like this never happened for them. They go on working and cooking and eating and sleeping. I can't do any of those things, haven't gone to school, haven't eaten hardly anything at all, only cream of mushroom soup when Muzzie insists.

You need to keep up your strength. Terry would want you to be strong, she tells me.

I want to shout at her that Terry can't want anything. HE'S DEAD. But I don't. I know she's trying to be strong and take care of everybody. I haven't talked to Dad since we opened the package. Couldn't face him after I read Terry's letter. Only four typewritten lines and one handwritten sentence added at the end: *I'm sorry I won't be around to see you married and happy.*

Dear Shirley and Donna,

Well kids, I just wanted to say goodbye and tell you that the only regret I have is not being able to see you both and Chong Cha again. Also, please for heavens sake quit playing around with drugs they're horrible and can only lead to trouble so lay off 'em uh. My love to you both.

Girls I'm sorry I won't be around to see you married and happy.

Love ya,

Terry

6^2

I shake my head, trying to stop all the questions, and look over at Shirley and David. I blink again and again, trying to bring them into focus, but they stay all fuzzy and look really far away. I hear someone clearing their throat, like they're trying to get my attention; but no one else is home. My eyes drift over to the long dark hallway. Terry is standing there, fuzzy and out of focus just like Shirley and David, but real—very real.

You're not dead! I knew it was a lie! I knew it! I shout, not able to control myself.

It's not a lie, Punk. There's no emotion in his voice, but it's his voice for sure. He's facing the wall, his left side to me. He turns his head slightly, looks over his shoulder, but doesn't turn to face me.

Whadda you mean? You're here. You're not dead!

Tell Dad it's not his fault. He'll blame himself, and it's not his fault.

What? I shake my head again, not believing what I'm hearing.

Promise me you'll tell him it's not his fault.

Stop it! I shout. You're scaring me.

Don't be scared, and don't be sad. You'll always be my little Punk. Tell Shirley I love her and that she has to be strong. She can't let them get her down.

He starts to glimmer and there's a light all around his body. Tell Dad, Punk. Tell him it's not his fault.

Terry bleeds away into the darkness. Don't go! I shout and reach for him. Hands are grabbing me, David and Shirley are holding me up, pulling me back onto the ottoman. Shirley slaps me across the face. I see her lips moving, but can't hear her.

Don't go! Don't go! Is all I hear—me trying to stop my brother from leaving me again—needing him to come back and say he loves me too.

The hall is empty. My cheek stings.

He loves you. My voice echoes, like in an empty room.

What? Shirley asks.

He said to tell you he loves you.

Who?

Terry. He loves you.

A box arrives. Shirley and I watch the box all morning, know we can't open it, know we have to wait for Dad and Muzzie to get home from work.

The sun comes out and we decide to sit on the patio even though it's still cold. We stay in our flannel pajamas, bundle on sweaters and robes and fuzzy slippers. The cold air feels good on my face. Laddie trots over and lies down between our chairs. Neither of us pet him. We don't say anything, just sit and look at the brick fireplace and the BBQ, the frost clinging to the clothesline, the way the smoke from our cigarettes hangs in the air a moment, drops low, then slinks away close to the ground.

Shirley doesn't say anything about Terry's visitation—not last night—not today. I don't know what to say. We spend the day together, but I feel more alone than ever.

We go back inside and wait for Dad to get home. He's taking off work early, something he never does. I heard him talking with Muzzie late last night, when they thought I was asleep.

I'll take some leave. I have quite a bit saved up, he tells Muzzie. She doesn't say anything. They're spending more time together, sitting next to each other on the couch, holding hands. Dad even fixed Muzzie a cup of coffee late last night. I saw tears in his eyes as he stirred and stirred the instant coffee in a small scalloped cup— Muzzie's best china. We never use the best china.

I stand in the foyer watching him, trying to get up the nerve to tell him what Terry said. A battle rages inside me—do what Terry asked me to do, do what I know is right—or get back at Dad for all the beatings I've watched, for all the screaming and fighting and rules and regulations, all the white glove inspections of our room, all the times I was grounded for no good reason, all the times he asked me to tell him why I did or didn't do something only to yell *Don't give me excuses,* when I try to explain—for killing Terry.

I turn away and walk back to my room, leave him stirring the coffee.

We open the box the next morning. Dad pulls out a small box covered in turquoise-colored linen. Inside is a tea set with cups that have no handles. Next is a tattered black address book with Terry's uneven handwriting. Muzzie looks through it. I didn't know he knew so many girls, she says, and sets it gently on the table with the tea set.

Dad pulls out a long thin pipe with a silver inverted cone at one end, and a matching silver mouthpiece at the other. The stem is carved with miniature wingless dragons dyed bright red, green lizards and white flowers on long wavy branches. Shirley reaches for the pipe. Dad hesitates, and then hands it to her.

Must be a souvenir, he says and looks over at Muzzie. You can pick up the craziest things in the markets over there. Once I found a coat made out of cat fur. All mismatched and stinking to high hell.

Condie! Muzzie puts a hand on his arm and shakes her head. He stops talking.

Can I have it? Shirley asks.

We all look at her.

I don't know. Can you? Dad answers.

Shirley huffs and corrects herself. *May* I have it?

Let's wait and look at everything before I decide.

She lays the pipe gently on the table and leans back in her chair, but her eyes remain locked on the pipe.

When everything is laid out, Dad puts the box on the floor and we all just sit there looking at what's left of Terry. A hat, a tie, some cufflinks, the tea set, some books and papers, his black-rimmed glasses, the pipe—not much.

Okay … well, Dad starts. I think your mother should have the tea set, and I'll keep his papers and books. So Skinny, he smiles at Shirley, you'd like the souvenir pipe? She nods. Punk?

I look at the remains of my brother and don't want anything that's there, but I know I should take something. His glasses, please, I tell him.

He hands them to me. Good choice. He always wore them. He pulls out a white handkerchief and blows his nose like it's a bugle.

I hate him all over again. Hate him handing out Terry's stuff like he had some right to do it. Hate his tears. Hate his keeping Terry's books and papers and address book, keeping Terry's friends from the rest of us—feel justified in not telling him what Terry told me to tell him.

I take Terry's glasses back to my room and close the door before Shirley gets there. She's as bad as they are. She doesn't even cry anymore, sleeps all night, doesn't hug me or tell me it's alright when I wake up screaming. Probably doesn't really believe Terry came to me and not her.

She pushes open the door. What are you doing closing the door on me?

I shrug and scoot over to my side of our bed. Nothing.

Nothing? Well don't shut the door on me again. This is as much my room as yours. Even more 'cause I'm older.

You moved out! I shout. You only came back 'cause you couldn't make it out there on your own. Couldn't make it 'cause you're stupid, and can't keep a job!

She's on me in a second, pushes me back against the wall. Take it back! Take it back!

No! I try to slap her but she grabs my wrist and twists it. Take it back or I'll break your arm, you little jerk!

No!

What the Hell's going on in here! Dad's at the door, his hands bunched in fists on his hips, Muzzie right behind him.

Shirley lets go of my arm and sits next to me. Nothing. We're just goofing around.

Yeah, just goofing around, I add, rubbing my wrist.

Don't you dare lie to me! You're both grounded for a week.

Donna D. Conrad

Condie, Muzzie interrupts, they're just upset about all this.

I don't give a good god damn what they're upset about. They're not fighting under my roof! Acting like a couple of wild animals. Not in my house.

It's our house too, Shirley yells back.

Your house? Your house? Dad advances on us and I cower tight against the wall.

He's never hit us, or even spanked us, but his words bruise us and beat us down. I feel tears welling up in my eyes and wish I were dead like Terry. Wish I didn't have to live with Dad's temper, didn't have to live with Muzzie's drinking, didn't have to live in this house at all.

Condie, Muzzie's hand's on his arm. Please. They're just upset, like we all are.

Don't you dare defend them! He turns on her, his hand raised to strike. They act like this because you didn't raise them right. What kind of a mother are you? A lousy stinking drunk. Your own son would rather kill himself than come home to you!

We all freeze in place. Muzzie's mouth is open, her eyes big and round. Dad drops his hand.

What? Muzzie takes a step back. What do you mean?

The report I received today! Dad yells. They say your son killed himself. Shot himself in the head rather than come home to a drunken wreck like you!

Muzzie looks at Shirley and me. It's the first time, since the day the Colonel told us, that I've seen tears in her eyes. She doesn't say anything. The silence gathers in the room until it's unbearable. Everyone's like statues. I don't think we're even breathing.

I look from one to another and wonder why I'm here, in this family, if I ever really belonged to them? Dad—skinny, bald, with a big fleshy nose, a scowl twisting his lips, making him look like some mask in a horror movie. Muzzie—her skin dull and listless, her face showing her age, her big boobs and tiny waist, her red dye-job, eyes swollen from too little sleep and too much whiskey, a bruise on her upper arm starting to turn purple right next to one fading away to yellow. There have been too many days and nights in this family. Too many lies and secrets. Too many years pretending that we'll all live happily ever after.

Shirley is behind me. I can't see her, but I can feel her, know that she doesn't belong here anymore than I do. But I can't help her, wouldn't know where to begin let alone end.

Terry killed himself. It makes sense to me. Maybe he's the only one to get it right.

Muzzie doesn't come out of her room all the next day, except to pee or throw up. Shirley tells me Muzzie deserves a good drunk, after what Dad said. She doesn't believe him, thinks he only said that to hurt Muzzie—as if he needed to do anything extra to make her hurt.

I'm going to ask him for the reports, Shirley tells me. We're back on the patio even though it's raining again.

You can't. He won't give them to you.

Then I'll break in his room and take them.

He'll throw you out if you do.

It'd be better than living here anymore. God I hate him! She flicks her lit cigarette across the patio. It lands in a puddle, hisses and goes out. I'm goin' back in.

I'll stay here awhile.

As you like. Don't catch a cold. You don't want to be sick at the funeral.

I nod and look out at the yard, a deep expanse of grass we rarely use anymore. The stagnant swimming pool, filled with algae and who knows what else under the slick green-black surface. The tall, cinderblock, back wall that separates our backyard from the school's yard.

I can almost see us all on any given sunny day in mid-summer before Terry went away. Laddie bouncing across the grass chasing his worn tennis ball; Terry and his friends drinking sodas and laughing, wrestling like puppies, pushing each other into the heated pool; them all chasing Shirley and me around the yard until they catch us and dump us in the pool. Muzzie in a summery print blouse and peddle-pushers, setting the picnic tables on the fresh mown lawn. Dad in short-sleeves and slacks next to the BBQ and ice chest filled with beers and sodas.

My stomach churns and I think I might throw up again, try to breath deep and turn my thoughts away from the latest report we received.

Autopsy report: Terry Jay Conrad, age 23, height 6'4 and 3/4", weight 245 pounds. Hair brown, eyes brown. Active service U.S. Army Intelligence Corps. Station: Seoul, Korea. Dad reads it all to Shirley and me just as it's written. Just the facts. Jack Webb and Dragnet—my dad and the autopsy report on his only son. I wonder if everything isn't just a TV show.

A single gunshot to the right temple. 35 caliber pistol found next to the deceased.

I close my eyes and realize that's why Terry stood sideways. Why he didn't show me the right side of his face when he was in the hallway that night. I feel tears burning my eyes, air escaping my lungs and not coming back.

Cause of death: Dad pauses and I take a breath. Murder by person or persons unknown.

What? Both Shirley and I ask at the same time. He didn't kill himself? Shirley adds.

Evidently not, Dad sighs.

Then why did you tell Mom he did? Shirley is out of her chair, facing him down, her hands planted on the table.

The first reports indicated the possibility of suicide. There must be new evidence.

You bastard! Shirley shouts runs from the room.

Dad looks at me, and I feel like a mouse trapped in a corner. He quietly folds the report and looks up at the ceiling. I didn't know. I thought he might have … He looks down at his hands and adds, Why would he want to come home to all this?

It's like I'm not there, like Dad doesn't even see me. I want to leave, but don't want to draw attention to myself. He pulls an ever-freshly starched handkerchief out of his pants pocket, bugles his nose and wipes his eyes.

Well then, Punk. Your big brother didn't kill himself after all. He died protecting his country. He died a hero.

He's still dead, I whisper.

What?

I shake my head. Nothing.

No. You said something. Now what did you say? He's staring at me hard, like he does just before he explodes.

He's still dead, I tell him.

The wave crashes over me. I don't pay attention to him, stop myself from covering my ears to block out the yelling, because that'll only make things worse. I sit and stare at the table.

The storm dies away. Dad stomps out of the kitchen and I'm alone again. I hope the storm is over, and I'm not just in its eye.

I don't like the man. His hair is all slicked back and he never looks at me or Shirley; doesn't really look anyone in the eyes, looks just in front of them.

The gravesite is well placed, near the top of the hills, overlooking the valley. He leans across his desk and taps on the brochure Dad's holding. There is one space open next to it. Should you wish to reserve it for another family member.

Dad looks at Muzzie, but neither one says anything.

Will there be a viewing?

It will be a closed casket, Dad tells the man.

I look over at Shirley. We're thinking the same thing, we won't even get to see Terry one last time.

Very well. A closed casket viewing for family and friends.

Dad and Muzzie both nod.

We're not crying anymore.

The limousine backs into our driveway. We sit in the back, all in black, Muzzie, Shirley, and me with tiny black hats with black veils and short black gloves. The road swishes past. I have a window seat. There's nothing to say. They're putting Terry in the ground today. There's nothing worth saying.

Sunlight pierces the stained glass windows and throws splotches of colors on the flag-draped coffin. The minister talks on and on about Terry, even though he never met him. Terry's best friend, Drew, says less, stopping every few words to keep himself from crying. Lee, his other best friend, tells about Terry breaking up a fight once at a garage party. Says Terry was peace loving and gentle and kind and the best man he would ever know. Our next-door neighbor, Bob Tabler, tells everyone that Terry was a gentle giant. That he was peace loving, wouldn't hurt a fly. That knowing him was an honor. That he will be missed.

Everyone knows Terry was peaceful, loving, kind, generous. Everyone knows he was forced to go into the Army, forced to be what he wasn't. But nobody's saying that today. They all say he died nobly, heroically. He's dead is all I know, and their words can't bring him back. I wish they would all stop talking, put him in the ground so I can forget him. I don't want to see his face in my dreams anymore, hear his voice in my head. I want him to have never existed.

Soldiers in dark dress uniforms are at the gravesite. I stop and won't go down the hill from the chapel. Muzzie looks back at me and begs me with her eyes not to make a scene. I told her back at the house I wouldn't go if Terry's murderers were there.

I stop on the curb.

Shirley takes my hand. I know, she whispers. I don't like it either, but we can't let Muzzie down. She tugs on my hand. Come on.

I follow her to the grave. Stand next to Muzzie's chair, chew on my lip to keep from crying, dig my nails into my palm when that fails, look up at the sky and try to pretend it's all a dream—the casket, the soldiers, Dad looking so proud—his son died in the line of duty.

FUCK HIM! I scream silently. Fuck them all …

A bugler plays taps and two soldiers take the flag from his coffin, fold it with crisp clean movements. They've done this too many times, I think. They're too good at it for it to have any meaning.

I hear rifle bolts thrown and look around. Several rows of gravesites away, three soldiers aim at the sky and fire a volley, throw back the bolts, aim and fire again. The noise is deafening. I plug my ears.

Shirley pulls my hands away just as the third volley is fired. A solider walks forward and kneels in front of Muzzie, offers her the coffin flag. I know she'll slap his face, throw the flag on the ground. I wait for her to tell him that she'll never forgive them. I know she could never forgive them. But she takes the flag, thanks the solider.

I look away. I don't know her anymore. The guns blast through the silence surrounding the crowd at the graveside.

Dad shakes hands with the Colonel in charge of the honor guard then salutes, sharp and clean. Turns to the honor guard. They salute. He returns the salute and they stand back at attention.

I close my eyes and remember to breathe, tell myself none of it matters, all their pomp and ceremony and pride and honor, it's all a lie. My brother's dead. Where's the honor in having your brains blown out in Korea? Where's the honor in all the kids dying every day in Viet Nam? Where is the honor in Terry leaving me?

A shadow falls across my face. I open my eyes. The Colonel has his hand out, his hat tucked under his other arm. I look into his green, green eyes and realize it's the same man who came to our house that gray day more than a month ago. I look down at his white-gloved hand, back at his face, and take a step back, shaking my head. I know it's a futile gesture, not shaking his hand; know the war will continue, that young men will keep dying. Know nothing can bring Terry back—but I couldn't live if I took the Colonel's hand in mine.

I understand, he tells me in a soft voice.

No you don't, I tell him. And you never will.

He turns sharply, takes two steps, stops in front of Shirley, turns to face her and holds out his hand. She tucks her hands under her arms and shakes her head no.

He nods once and says, I understand.

Desert Dreaming
April 1, 1969

Suggested listening:
Album—Living the Blues, Canned Heat

The acid's mellow, the weed from Mexico heavy, the guys very cute. I raise my hands up high, clapping in time with the music, and do a little shimmy—grab for my halter top as it rises above my tits—too late. Three girls around me scream, All right, and whip off their tops and start dancing, boobs bouncing, hips swinging. I tuck my tits back inside the halter and move away, drag Kathy with me.

Hey! Where we going? That spot was hot!

Let's find Shirley, I yell over the music. Kathy blinks and looks back longingly to the spot right in front of the stage. Some older guy had broken through the barricade and we all rushed the stage. Kathy and I were first, but now everyone's there. It's not where I want to be—where everyone else is.

I wander through the bodies. Most guys have their shirts off—after all, we are in the desert and the night is clear. I pause and look up at where the stars should be, wonder if they're there even when I can't see them. I suddenly feel a deep need to see them. I dive through the crowd, further and further from the stage lights, the psychedelic light show flashing across the drive-in screen—desperate to make sure the stars are still in the sky above.

Kathy's voice, telling me to slow down, wait for her, dies away. I don't care about her, I only care that the stars are waiting for me to see them, waiting for me to know they're there—know if I don't see them, they'll vanish.

I reach the fence, but the lights are still too bright. I see a flood of kids pouring in through a hole. I push against the current, out into the desert calm. I keep walking out into the flat expanse of dirt and tumbleweeds, into the crisp, lean night.

I stop when the first star winks back into existence, breathe a sigh of relief that I made it here before the last star died. Soon others join the survivor, the sky pulsates back to life, a few flamboyant stars streak across the sky trailing green and blue streamers. I breathe a sigh of relief, knowing I saved the stars from extinction.

Some bluesy rift floats across the desert and I find my feet tapping. I still them, want to just be here with the stars. Share this moment with the entire universe.

Where the fuck are you going?

I spin around. Kathy is tiptoeing through the field of rocks and tumbleweeds. She looks pissed. I take a step backwards and find there's no ground under my feet.

A hand grabs me and I sit down hard on top of a pointed rock. It bites through my hip huggers. I squeal.

Jesus! Are you that stoned? You almost stepped off a fucking cliff!

I look over my shoulder and see a wide, black chasm, sharp rocks lining its edge.

Didn't know it was there, I say, but my voice sounds far away.

Yeah, well … Kathy plops down beside me. Look at me! I turn and look into her eyes, notice how incredibly blue they are, like big sapphires. Wow, your eyes are blue, I tell her, astonished I hadn't noticed before.

Hey! Stop it! You're starting to freak me out!

No. No. I try to calm her, it's all cool. I'm cool. I just didn't know your eyes were blue. Really. It's cool.

Fuck! Why'd you take that acid from that guy? You already dropped some back at the motel.

The day flashes up in front of me, like it's on the drive-in movie screen back at the concert.

Our Grandparents live in Desert Hot Springs, a small retirement town across the desert valley from Palm Springs. At night, if there's no wind kicking up the sand, and you're on the second floor of almost anything, you can see the lights of Palm Springs; like a mirage offering food and drink to wanderers stuck in the dry Desert Hot Springs wilderness.

We find a motel with a pool and settle in. Shirley calls Grandma and explains that we came to see them, but that I came down with strep throat. Yes, we went to March Air Force base and the doctor said it was strep and that I shouldn't make the drive home until my temperature breaks. Yes, we're disappointed we can't see them, but know it wouldn't be good for Grandma to be exposed to strep. No. No need for Grandpa to bring us anything, besides he might take the germs back to Grandma. Well, no. Not really. Ah well, Okay. Thanks. See you soon.

I'm off the edge of the bed before the phone hits the cradle. What do you mean, see you soon? What the fuck?

Shut up! What could I do? Grandpa's bringing by some of his chili.

What? We're busted! Fuck!

Oh stop it. Take off your makeup, put on your robe and look sick!

What? What about Kathy? He'll never believe I'm sick! I don't even look sick!

He's only gonna see you from the parking lot, dumb-shit. Stop whining and get your makeup off! He's on his way. Kathy, if he looks like he's coming up get the fuck under the bed, and don't mess around. It'll blow the whole thing if he sees you.

Kathy nods and finishes off a glazed donut. I head for the head and scrub my face clean and put baby powder all over my face, trying to look pale, but it just cakes and makes me look like I have leprosy. I scrub again and climb into my nightgown and throw my robe over everything, realize I didn't bring my slippers.

I don't have my slippers, I yell through the partially opened door.

What the fuck do you need slippers for? It's a hundred and ten degrees!

But I always wear slippers!

Fuck the slippers and get out here. Gramp's just pulled into the parking lot. Shit! He's getting out. Kathy! Under the bed. Now!

Donna D. Conrad

Kathy drops her second donut on the floor and dives under the bed. Shirley grabs the half-eaten jelly roll, stuffs it back in the two-dozen sized box, and slides it under the bed with Kathy.

Cool, leaks out from under the bed.

Shut the fuck up, Kathy. And don't you dare eat even one of those under there. Hear me!

Yeah, I hear you, Kathy moans.

And shut up!

There's a knock on the door. I dive into bed, pull the covers up to my chin, and try to look sick, which isn't too hard. I wish I could be as cool under pressure as Shirley. She never panics, always pulls off whatever scheme we're working. But as she tucks a pipe full of weed under a chair cushion, and throws a lavender shirt over her bikini top, I wonder how we're going to get out of this one.

Gramps! She says as she throws open the door. You shouldn't be here. I would have come down to the car.

Ah hell. I'm strong as an ox. Brought you some chili. Guaranteed to kill any germs. Where's Punk?

Shirley swings around and points to me. In bed, right where she should be. She squints at me and I can almost hear her thoughts, she's thinking so loud. Don't blow it for Christ's sake.

I pull my hand from under the covers and wave at Gramps and croak, Hi, and force a weak cough, which sounds fake even to me.

Hey, hey there, Punk. Don't say a thing! You just lay there and get well, now. He turns to Shirley. She looks fevered, awfully red and chapped.

Oh, yeah, well ... ah.

You should get some cold rags going. Here let me ... He turns around looking for the bathroom door and Shirley jumps in front of him.

It's ok, Gramps. We just finished a round and ... and ... and have to wait another ten minutes. She's already feeling better. Shirley points to me and I smile and nod.

Well. If you think so. Pity you can't come on out and see your grandmother. She always looks forward to seeing you kids.

I put on a pout and nod again. Shirley gives Gramps a quick kiss on the cheek. Kathy sneezes and I pull up the blankets trying to cover for her.

You got a cold, too? Gramps asks.

No. Probably just the dust. The wind was really blowing when we got here.
Shirley tells him and tries to steer him towards the door.

Always blows in the spring, Gramps tells us and looks over at the chairs. I
could stay a while and make sure Punk's feeling better. He heads for the chair
with the pipe under the cushion and I let out a moan.

Shirley's fast on the uptake. I think she needs to sleep, Gramps. Maybe she'll
feel better tomorrow and you can come back over then.

Well, if you think you're okay out here. You better keep your door locked,
though. There's a bad element in town 'cause of that freak show over in Palm
Springs. Wish you girl's picked a better time to come all the way out here.

But it's Easter vacation, Gramps. It's the only time we could come out to see
you and Grandma.

I know. I know. You girls watch out now. And don't talk to any strange
boys. Promise?

Shirley crosses her heart and hopes to die. I bite the covers to keep from
giggling, can't imagine how Kathy's not cracking up out loud; figure she stuffed
another donut in her mouth to keep quiet—weed always gives her the munchies.

I think it's over, Kathy says, and I flip back to the desert night and
the black emptiness in front of me. There are voices floating across
the desert from the concert, but no music, just shouting and what
sounds like bullhorns. *Clear the field. Move aside. Stop right there.*

What the fuck?

I don't know.

Let's go see.

A strong wind's kicking up dust and papers. Kathy tugs on my arm,
yells, *Run* and takes off across the parking lot. A beam of light strikes
me and I freeze where I am. It streaks past me and shines on three
boys tipping a car from side to side.

Halt! a voice like the Wizard of Oz booms from above and I look
up. A black dragonfly is hovering above the parking lot, a beam of
light coming from its head. I blink the insect away, knowing it has to

be a helicopter.

Whoop, Whoop, Whoop fills the parking lot as the copter lowers, the light holding steady on the boys. They flip the car on its side and vanish. The copter moves towards me and I dive under the nearest car. The beam of light searches the parking lot, almost touches me under the car. I pull my hand in tight just as the beam sneaks under the car a few inches. The sound is deafening, the wind pushes a filthy newspaper into my face and I'm too scared to brush it aside.

Stop messing around! Get your ass out here, we gotta get outta here. I brush the paper aside. The whopping has drifted away, so has the light. Shirley's on her hands and knees looking under my car. Come on! Hurry up before the pigs get here. She offers me her hand and I slide out, scraping my belly on the asphalt.

Jesus, you're a wreck! What the fuck were you doing under there?

There was this cop copter that was following me …

How much acid did you take? she asks.

I shake my head and try to explain it's not the acid, that they were looking for me, that some guys picked up a car and tipped it over.

Come on. Let's get back to the motel. Shit! You look like you were in a car wreck.

She takes me by the arm and shouts to Kathy to cut it out.

Kathy breaks away from a longhair she's kissing and bounces over to us. He's so cute. Can he come back to the motel with us?

No!

Please, please, please, please, please. Kathy's tugging on Shirley's arm and bouncing and begging and I can't believe no one else is worried about the copter.

Please! Kathy begs one last time.

Shirley caves and says, No trouble though!

No, he's cool.

We make it to where the Galaxy 500 is parked. I climb in the passenger seat, Kathy, her longhair, his two friends, and three other kids needing a lift, climb in the back. Another guy, with a guitar slides in from the driver side, followed by Shirley.

Everyone keep cool, the pigs are everywhere. Is anyone holding?

Two guys in the back say, *Yeah*. The guitar guy nods.

Shit! Well, stash it good and keep cool. They probably won't stop us. She turns and looks over into the back seat. Shit! Where'd you all come from?

They're cool, Kathy says.

Three of you have to get out. Can't have seven in the back seat, against the law. They'll bust us for sure.

How about the floor? One of the guys offers.

Two drop to the floor and curl up into little balls, another stretches out flat across the four laps.

Yeah, that works, Shirley tells them. Be sure you stay down till we're out of the city.

No problem, someone moans and I think it has to be the guy on the floor behind me.

Here. Shirley hands me a rubber band. Tie you hair back and wipe the blood off your cheek. You, she points to the guy in the middle, keep that guitar outta sight.

We'll take it, someone from the back offers.

The hell you will, he says and lays the belly on my lap and puts his hands over the neck.

Cool. Let's go! Shirley turns the ignition and the blue bomb roars to life. Everyone keep cool, she warns and backs out of the parking space and into the beam of a helicopter.

See! I told you! I yell. They're looking for us.

No they aren't. They're looking for freaks on the ground. Stop being paranoid.

She eases out onto the street and is waved through an intersection by a cop with a helmet and rifle. I look back and see a mob of kids in a gas station surrounding a cop car. One guy has the nozzle of the gas pump inside the window and is pumping gas straight into the cab.

Shit! We better get moving, I shout. They're gonna blow up that cop car.

Don't panic, Shirley says. You know what the old man always

says, the pigs don't pay attention to people acting normal. They go for the ones that are running.

I look over the back seat, the guy on the laps is craning his head to see what's happening, so are the two guys on the floor. Kathy is making out with the longhair.

They're looking out the windows!

What? What the fuck are you doing? Shirley reaches over the seat and smacks at the guy behind me. Get the fuck down, you jerks! she yells and goes over the center line in the road.

You're gonna get busted if you don't drive right, the guitar guy tells her calmly.

You wanna drive? she spits back.

Sure! he says.

Too bad! Just shut the fuck up or get out!

I'm hoping they'll get out, but the car quiets, except for Kathy giggling and the longhair mumbling something I can't make out.

Once clear of the city we roll down all the windows, and the guys climb off the floor. Kathy hops onto the longhair's lap and everyone settles down. The guitar guy turns away from me and starts strumming, the neck of his guitar poking over the back of the seat.

There's something happening here, what it is ain't exactly clear ...

Everyone joins in, Stop, children, what's that sound ...

The desert night is calm and clear. The stars twinkle in time to the song.

The longhair pulls the screen off the bathroom window and crawls through. The others follow. The room gets smaller and smaller. Kathy's on the bed with the longhair, Shirley's shushing everyone— no one's listening. I wait for the bathroom to clear out, and let Shirley wash all the cuts and scrapes from my stomach and arms.

Don't think you'll be wearing the hip hugger tomorrow she says.

Why not?

Look at you. She points at my belly. You're a wreck. Better keep it covered till they heal.

I pick a piece of asphalt out of a cut just below my bellybutton and toss it out the screen-less window. You gonna let them stay the night? I ask.

Yeah. Why not? They'll settle down in a few minutes. I saw one of them handing out some downers. They'll crash soon.

Then what?

We take 'em back to the city in the morning and go to the concert. Why you so concerned? Acid going bad?

Nah. I just don't like them so much.

You don't like anyone anymore.

That's not true ... I pause a second and realize she's right, I don't like most guys, think all they want is to get into my pants.

Of course, they do. What's new? Shirley says and I realize I was talking out loud. You turning all holy or somethin'? Staying true blue to that Ken dude?

I blush and shake my head no. I just don't like them, I say, jutting my chin at the bathroom door.

Sure. Just them, she says and dabs my shoulder. She leans over and kisses my cheek. You just be you, Punk. It's okay.

Games of Chance
April 1969

Suggested listening:
Single—*Mobius Trip*, H.P. Lovecraft

A fast click, click, click—rhythmic and metallic. A sharp snap, and a chill runs up and down my spine that stands the hair on my arms straight up, and drops me to the floor. I look around and see two guys playing with my dad's revolver.

Another spin of the cylinder and I hear a long low wail, like a banshee from some Irish fairy tale. What's wrong with her? It's fucking empty! one of the guys says and they both walk down the hall and into my dad's room shaking their heads.

What a fucking nut case!

No kidding!

I wonder who they're talking about.

Shirley pushes me into the hall closet of our house in La Puente and tells me we're playing "hide-n-seek" and that I have to be very, very quiet and not come out even if Dad tells me to. I nod and snuggle in behind all the big furry coats and hope I can get "home-free" before I'm found. After a few minutes I wonder where "home free" is and push my way out to ask Shirley before she starts to count to one hundred. I never get to be It because I can't count that high very well. But I don't mind because I really like hiding and don't like seeking at all.

I step outside the closet and Dad grabs me by the arm and marches me to the living room. Terry and Shirley are already sitting in the straight-backed dining room chairs that are set all in a row facing the front door. I know better than to try to get away, but my stomach does a flip-flop as he sits me in the chair at the end of the row. I hate it when dad makes us play this game. It scares me. I wish mom wasn't sleeping. Dad never makes us play with him when she's awake.

He always does the same thing. If we look away or close our eyes he yells at us, he even slapped Terry once. So I have to watch him or get in big trouble. He leaves us sitting, all straight, like grownups—goes into the den. When he comes back he stands in front of us and shows us his revolver. He cracks it open and spins the empty drum, then holds out a bullet for us to see before he puts it in a chamber and flips it closed, then spins the cylinder again.

He walks around behind us and I get even more scared 'cause I know what he's going to do next.

Who's going to be the lucky one, he asks in a sing-song voice.

I know better than to turn my head, but look as far to the left as my eyes will go. Dad's holding his gun's at Shirley's temple. There's a loud click and Shirley lets out a breath she's been holding.

Guess it's not you, Skinny. How about your little sister? Dad asks and I feel him move over behind my chair.

Shirley takes my hand and squeezes it. I feel the cold metal against my head. Dad presses the gun tighter against my temple. The click seems louder than anything else. Louder than Shirley's sobs, and Terry breathing like he's just got done running. I can feel the gun shake a little when it goes off, like it does every time Dad pulls the trigger, and I wonder what would happen if the bullet was in my chamber. I've seen people shot on TV, but know they're not really hurt, because I see them in other TV shows later on. Still, it scares me more than anything else every time Dad makes us play this game with him.

I push past the guys coming back out of my dad's room and take the revolver out of his underwear drawer. I open his safe in the closet and take out one bullet and walk back out to the living room.

Kids are spread out on the floor, on couches and chairs. The two guys that had the gun are standing by the fireplace sharing a joint. I walk up to them, flip open the cylinder, put the bullet in a chamber, snap it close, spin it and put it to the blonde's temple.

Donna D. Conrad

Want to play, fuck-head? I ask, and squeeze the trigger.

The guy sinks to the floor crying like a baby. Didn't think so! I spit at them. I turn and walk away. I open the cylinder and take the bullet out of the active chamber; am glad I didn't bother with the second guy.

I tuck the gun back in the drawer, put the bullet back in the pack, and wonder why the hell I just did what I did. Figure it must have been because of something I'd seen on TV.

The Invasion of Inchon Harbor
May 1969

Suggested listening:
Album—Yellow Submarine, The Beatles

A pair of flies is dancing across the classroom leaving fluorescent trails of orange and green in their wake. They remind me of Fred Astaire and Ginger Rogers, a wingspan apart, twirling and soaring, spinning and dropping. *They fly through the air with the greatest of ease ...* The words to the song buzz in my head and I laugh out loud. Realize too late I'm in Mr. Decker's classroom.

You find this subject amusing Miss Conrad?

Uh ... no, I tell him and look around. Everyone is staring at me, everyone except Kathy, who's watching the flies. I follow her gaze and get distracted by the bright purple streamers the flies are trailing.

Miss Conrad!

I tear my eyes away from the light show and look at Mr. Decker. He's never looked more like a hawk—piercing blue eyes, long, narrow nose and tight, thin lips—I ... um ... no not amusing ... I was just ...

You were just off in your own little world. A world where nothing matters, where you are a queen and everyone has to do what you want, when you want it!

I almost agree with him, but some part of me knows better. He's been waiting for any excuse to flunk me. Hasn't found one yet because I score all A's on his tests. But, since I never pay attention in

Donna D. Conrad

his class, he wants me to fail.

I know he's never forgiven me for not saluting the American flag at the start of each class—never forgiven me for winning the battle with the school board over saluting the flag—never forgiven me for not caring what he thinks or what he believes in—never forgiven me for not acknowledging his authority.

Each day is a new insult to him and his patriotism. Each day he has to watch as I remain seated during the pledge of allegiance. Each day he has to face the fact that a student has won. I knew he was going to be trouble the first day of class.

Everyone please stand. Everyone stands, even me. Face the flag. Everyone turns, puts their right hands over their hearts. It takes me a moment to figure out what's happening, a moment longer to marshal the courage to put my hand down, a moment more to sit back in my seat.

You. Stand up.

I shake my head, but don't say anything.

Stand up now!

No.

What is your name?

Donna Conrad.

Miss Conrad, you will stand and salute the flag with the class, or you will be sent to the principal's office.

I stand. He looks back to the flag. I walk forward. He looks confused. I wait for him to understand. He turns to his desk and pulls out a yellow slip, scribbles something on it and snaps the paper taut between his hands before handing it to me. And don't come back until you're ready to salute the flag!

I'm back in his class the next week, sitting through the pledge of allegiance. Muzzie told the Principal that they couldn't make me take the pledge if I didn't want to. That this was a free country, that freedom of choice was our greatest liberty. The Principal gave me the chance to go back to class and just stand during the pledge, told me that I didn't have to even say the words. I refused. Muzzie took my suspension to the school board that same week. The school board said that it wasn't legal to require students to recite the pledge of allegiance in the classroom. I didn't know that—Mr. Decker did. The board upheld my right and he was told not to press the issue for any student. I agreed to continue in his class; he agreed to allow students to choose whether to join in the pledge of allegiance.

It's an uneasy truce.

We are all waiting, Miss Conrad. Please come forward, Mr Decker tells me.

What? I ask. The acid is peaking and I can't remember why he's even talking to me.

Come forward this instant, he shouts.

I stand and walk to the front of the class, expecting another yellow slip, looking forward to grabbing a quick smoke in the *F* head on the way to the office.

I stop at the far side of his desk.

No. Over here. He motions for me to come to the chalk board.

I'm confused and look back over my shoulder at Kathy.

Miss Weston cannot help you, Miss Conrad. Please come over here.

I walk around the desk, and come to the blackboard, staying as far away from Mr. Decker as I can.

Class, Miss Conrad is a perfect example of the fringe element that is trying to destroy this great country of ours. She cares nothing for rules, abhors order, and scoffs at anyone who seeks to better themselves through morality and education.

I look out at the sea of faces—flips and crew cuts nodding up and down, eyes avoiding me, looking with admiration at Mr. Decker. I look for Kathy's, but jets of brightly colored mist shoot from the ceiling and I can't see past the first two rows.

I look over at Mr. Decker. His nose curves and folds down over his lips, his dark hairline retreats and turns pure white, his eyes stay true blue and piercing. A bald eagle. How perfect, I hear myself say.

I've had enough of this insolence! Mr. Decker shrieks. You pay no attention in my class, you are a disruptive influence, and I will not tolerate your disrespect another moment!

I haven't done anything!

You haven't done anything is right! I don't know how you pass my tests, but I know you're cheating. You know absolutely nothing about modern history. You care nothing for knowledge, for learning, for anything but anarchy.

I smile at him, thinking how small he really is, how tight his mind is squeezed, how free I feel at this moment.

The Eagle has me by the arm, is squawking in my ear, I have you this time, Miss Conrad.

How's that? I haven't done anything wrong.

He blinks twice, opens his beak, ruffles his neck feathers, and then turns away. Class, Miss Conrad will continue today's lesson. He turns and looks at me over his shoulder. Since she *obviously* knows so much about the subject that she doesn't feel it's necessary to pay attention. So please, Miss Conrad, the class is yours.

He sits on the corner of his desk, looking more like a vulture now. Please, he points to the board. Tell us about today's subject. Oh, and by the way, since you've missed the last three pop quizzes, consider today your make-up. It will be 30% of your grade.

I start to protest, but don't want to give him the satisfaction; hope I know something about today's subject—don't have too much hope that I do. I turn and look at the board: *The Invasion of Inchon Harbor* drifts across the board, the perfectly straight capital letters evenly spaced, a rough drawing of a harbor with hills at the right side floating beneath the letters.

The image of my Dad at the dining room table flashes through my mind, his voice droning on and on about his top secret mission to plan the invasion of Inchon Harbor, plays in the background like an old 78 record on a gramophone. I stop breathing, wonder if this is some weird trip—wonder if I'm really at home listening to my dad tell the same old story again.

Just as I thought. You are a stupid girl with nothing going on in your head, Mr. Decker says.

My mind snaps back to the classroom. I realize this is real, that I'm being asked to talk about something my dad has told me about more times than I can remember. I clear my throat and begin, The invasion of Inchon Harbor marked the turning point in the Korean War.

Mr. Decker sits down on the corner of his desk, his beak dissolving into a mouth once again, his nose straight and pointed, his eyes not quite so piercing.

In my mind I hear my dad talking about the Korean War like it was the only thing in the whole world worth talking about. He'd trap us at the dining room table and drone on about how the war was as good as lost; how General MacArthur cooked up a plan to land troops behind the North Korean lines and launch a huge surprise attack on the enemy's rear, at Inchon Harbor.

I can hear my dad's voice loud and clear. It's like I'm simply repeating what he's saying as he's talking, like interpreters on TV at the United Nations. I find I'm rather good at it, and wonder if I might like being an interpreter.

My confidence grows as I continue: By July 1950 the allied forces were in trouble. The Chinese were backing the North Koreans and together they were closing in on Seoul, the capitol of South Korea. Our chances of winning the war were almost non-existent. As it stood we'd be lucky not to get pushed off the peninsula all together.

General MacArthur sent Trudy Jackson, and a small team of intelligence operatives, a hundred miles behind enemy lines to map the tidal surges at a narrow, undefended harbor called Inchon. They were supposed to figure out if a surprise amphibious landing was even possible.

I turn to the rough map Mr. Decker had drawn on the board and erase his lines and redraw the harbor. There were high seawalls running the length of the narrow harbor, which has tidal surges of up to thirty feet …

That will be all, Miss Conrad!

I turn away from the blackboard and tell him, But there's more. I haven't gotten to North Korean troop placements and how the C.I.C., that's what they call Army Intelligence, was able to determine

...

That will be enough!

I set the chalk back in the tray and wipe my hands against each other to brush away the white chalk.

Quite enough! Mr. Decker adds and I notice his face is flaming red, his lips white. I look in his eyes, and feel like I'm looking into a cloudless sky.

There is a clap of thunder and I duck behind the desk. Realize it's the class applauding me. I peek out over the desk. Some kids are standing up, a few boys whistling with their fingers in their mouths. I feel as red as Mr. Decker, and don't quite know what to do.

Take your seats this instant! You, all of you, be quiet! Sit down this instant! I will not tolerate this behavior. Sit down!

No one's listening to him. They slap me on the arm as I pass down the aisle, flash me the peace sign, a few thumbs up. I make my way back to Kathy. She's watching the flies, doesn't look away when I sit down behind her. The class quiets down just as the bell rings. We all wait ...

Class dismissed!

Kathy looks over at me, her eyes big black disks. How do they stay up in the air like that? she asks.

They have wings, I tell her.

Way cool. They have wings. She looks around the empty class. Wow! Class is over. Cool, let's snag a smoke.

We stand up and I glance back at Mr. Decker. He's standing at the blackboard looking at my drawing of Inchon Harbor, shaking his head and muttering to himself.

Come on! I need a smoke, Kathy whines and pulls my arm.

I take a last look at the back of Mr. Decker's head, notice a bald spot starting to form near the crown. I feel somehow sorry for him. Sorry for all the squares that can't accept the fact that they're getting older and the freaks are getting stronger.

A Place to be Me
June 1969

Suggested listening:
Album—Woodstock, Various Artists

Woodstock. Everyone who's anyone's talking about the rock concert being held back on the east coast. It might as well be on the moon. Ken can't get his mother's car for the time it would take to get there and back, and Bear's car wouldn't make it as far as Arizona. I don't even try to think up a story to tell Dad about where I'd be for that long.

No one at Charter Oak has even heard about the concert. Shirley thinks it'll be a total drag, like the Monterey festival last year, with bad sound and you couldn't even see the stage, let alone who was on it.

I don't care about seeing the stage, I just want to be there with everyone who's cool and turned on. I want to be with people who believe in love and peace and being free—want to be something other than a kid who can't get permission to go.

School ends. The long summer ahead feels like a prison sentence. Kathy's so wrapped up with Frank that she doesn't even want to go anywhere, especially if it means she can't see him for more than a day. I don't get it. I'm going with Ken, but I'd take off to New York without him at the drop of a hat, if anyone I knew was heading that way.

Dad's home all the time, trying to get his business going; *A Conrad*

Investigations. The A's so his business gets listed first in the Yellow Pages. He doesn't get many calls, and most of them want him to do things at night, so I'm stuck with him all day. Muzzie works splits so she has the afternoons off and works again at night. It doesn't matter, we don't go out like we used to. She's always faking it, acting all happy, but she's not happy. She drinks all the time, but not enough so she passes out, just enough to get through the day—which is too much for me to want to be around her.

How about Big Sur? Ken and I are in the living room, lying on the floor looking at the ceiling. We could go for just a couple of days. You could get away that long.

It's not Woodstock, I sigh and turn over on my stomach. I prop my chin on my folded hands and sigh again. Nothing's like Woodstock.

It might be a real drag, Ken offers and turns over, draping an arm over me.

No. It'll be totally cool, and I won't be there. I shrug out from under his arm and get up, wander into the kitchen and open the fridge. Want a beer?

Sure! Where's your old man?

Who cares? You want a can or a bottle? I ask.

Doesn't matter.

I grab two cans from the back of the row, pull off the teardrop tabs. I stuff them way down in the trash so Dad won't see them when he takes out the garbage. Ken'll take the cans with him, and toss them once he's out of the neighborhood. We have the routine down. I never take more than two beers at a time, figure Dad will think Muzzie drank them, if he notices them missing at all. He doesn't seem to care as much about things since Terry died. I don't mind, means he's not always spying on me. He doesn't care what I do, as long as I don't talk back, keep the house clean, his shirts ironed, and stay out of any trouble he can find out about.

But he's still here all the time. I don't ever feel like I can just be me when I'm home. I walk back in the living room and hand Ken his beer, sit on the edge of the couch.

There's no way we can get there, so just forget it, he tells me and downs his beer.

I study the tear shaped cutout in the lid and know he's right. I just don't want to accept it; accept that I'll be the only freak on the planet that isn't at Woodstock. I take a sip and really want a joint, but I'm grounded for two more days because of my grades, so I can't drive with Ken anywhere.

I'll be back, I tell Ken and head for my room. I dig in my closet, way in the back, and drag out my good dress shoes. I peel back the insole and take out the flattened tinfoil pack.

What you got?

I jump at the sound of Ken's voice and tip over backwards. End up in the back of my closet with my feet in the air, clutching the foil tight in my hand.

Jesus Christ! What are you so wound-up about? Ken offers me his hand and drags me out of the closet.

Nothing. I was just getting my stash and you freaked me out. I show him the tinfoil pack. I've got some groovy orange sunshine. Wanna drop? I stand on my tiptoes and give him a quick kiss on the lips.

I can't stay that late. I have to have the car back by ten.

I fall back on my heels still disappointed that Ken's Cougar is really his mother's and he only got to use it when she didn't need it.

I have some grass, Ken offers. We can go out in the car and smoke a reefer. I'm parked in the driveway, so you're not technically breaking the rules.

Cool! I give him another kiss and head for the bedroom door.

What about your neighbors? It's still light out and they can see the car from their kitchen window.

They don't care. As long as we don't let their little boy see, they're cool. Shirley told me she's smoked with Bob. But, I'm not supposed to know.

Smoking in his car, Ken gets me to agree to go to Big Sur with him as soon as I'm not grounded.

At least it's not all the guys that went on the Rotta Run, but almost. Bear and Larry, and Andy and Ken's little brother, David, are all crammed in the backseat. I have the whole bucket seat up front to myself—Ken told the guys that he wasn't going to have his girlfriend sit on the floor between the seats. They didn't like it, but they wanted to go to Big Sur, so they piled in the back. I smile most of the way up the coast.

The sun is still high when we make camp and head up the path that runs along the river. There's music up ahead. We pick up the pace. I climb over a big boulder right behind Ken, shimmy down the far side and stop dead in my tracks. People are laying out in the sun, swimming in the deep river where it pools between boulders, smoking and playing guitars and singing, some dancing, some just grooving to the sounds—all of them stark naked.

Bear slides down next to me and heads off towards the swimming hole stripping as he goes. The other guys follow, leaving me alone by the boulder. I don't have any problem wearing hardly anything, but wearing nothing's a different story.

Ken's already on top of another boulder right at the water's edge. He kicks off his cut-offs and dives out into the middle of the stream. I take a deep breath, undo the strap of my halter top and join the boys in the river.

I'm still shivering, even though I'm right next to the fire. We didn't leave the river until well after dark, and I had nothing but my soaking wet cut-off jeans and a dry halter for the walk back. Ken offered me his t-shirt. I wish he'd offered his jeans.

The next day I'm determined to strip to the bone. I make it as far as my underwear. The sun feels good after the icy water and I drift off into a dream where I'm floating high above the ocean, sailing over the cliffs, and on inland to a farm where everyone's a freak. I finally feel at home. I take a big hit off a joint and hold it in, feeling at peace with the world—realize it isn't a dream. Open my eyes to find a woman with thick, curly, blonde hair blowing smoke in my face.

She smiles at me and I'm not at all afraid, even though I don't know her. She takes another hit and leans in closer and puts her lips against mine, gently releasing the smoke into my mouth. I take a deep breath and realize this weed is different than any I've had before. I hold it in a long time, with my eyes closed. When I open them, she's gone. I prop myself up on my elbows, but don't see her anywhere.

Ken sloshes out of the river and comes over to me. He nods and asks, You let just anybody kiss you?

I smile at him, suddenly wanting him to make love to me. Not just anyone, I tell him and hold out my arms to him.

He looks around kinda nervous like and shakes his head. You that stoned?

I smile and nod, then lie back on the warm pebbles and drift back into my dream of the farm and life being good.

She's at the swimming hole the next morning. She motions me over to her stretch of shoreline, I sit down next to her. She doesn't have anything on but a silver peace sign dangling from a long chain around her neck.

She brushes my hair behind my shoulders with her hand. You're so beautiful. You shouldn't be ashamed of your body. She looks down at my shorts and then at my halter. You don't need to hide behind clothes.

She hands me a lit joint that's so slim I can't imagine anyone could have rolled it. I take a hit and sink back against the pebbled shore, not believing how strong it is. She smiles and takes the joint back, passes it along to a guy with frizzy red hair down to his waist, who's sitting next to her.

What is that shit? I ask.

Maui Wowie. Like it?

I nod—about all I can do.

You staying in the campground?

I nod again.

Want to buy some?

How much?

Twenty a lid.

Four-fingers?

She nods and passes the joint back to me.

I haven't seen twenty dollars all at once for so long I can't even imagine finding that much. My allowance of two dollars a week is always gone before the week hardly begins. I take a hit and wonder if Ken has that much on him.

She leans in close and whispers in my ear, Five if you take your clothes off and leave' um off …

It's as good a reason as any for getting naked.

A Small Step for Man
July 19 - 20, 1969

Suggested listening:
Album—Led Zeppelin, Led Zeppelin

Ken has a job at a tire store. I'm on my own for all of July. Woodstock is all I think about. Shirley tells me to stop being a baby. Even she can't get away for that long, and she's almost twenty. She's working at a ballpoint pen factory with Sandy, and they have a new place together—a big old house way out in Azusa. They hate their jobs, but have really good stash now that they have money.

I tell her it's too bad she's not still with Eric, what with how much pot is selling for now.

It's fine, she says. He dealt crap anyway. She hands over some black beauties I asked her to get. I always keep a stash of really strong downers on hand just in case a trip goes bad. I had to use my entire stash last week when Bear took a whole handful of acid on a dare.

He's so big it took five black beauties to knock him out. Ken joked that it was like trying to sedate an elephant. I didn't think it was funny and told Ken he had to pay for the next round of downers. He gave me twenty dollars. I scored a lid of decent pot, five black beauties, and five hits of orange sunshine. I made out like a bandit. Kinda hope Bear freaks again so I can get another twenty from Ken.

Dad's working on a case way out in Northridge and won't be home for a week, so Shirley hangs out with me at night. I sort through my new stash. You staying the night? I ask Shirley.

Maybe. Got anything planned?

Naw. I just wanted to know what I should take. If you were headed home, I'd do a rainbow. But, if you want to stay I'll split a tab with you. I hold out the orange sunshine she just gave me.

She takes a gulp of beer and shakes her head. I already did some before I came over.

I can't help but look disappointed.

Hey. She socks me in the arm playfully. I can't wait to see if you're gonna be with Ken. I never get to see you hardly at all since you hooked up with him.

I don't think I'm with him that much, but don't say anything. He's got a full-time job for the summer, I tell her.

She nods at my stash. I'll split a tab with you. This shit isn't coming on at all. I think I got burned.

Bummer.

Yeah. Hand over some of the real stuff, chickie. She snaps her fingers and I break a tab in half. Put half in her mouth and half in mine. We clink our beers and down them.

Muzzie gets home around midnight. Shirley and I are listening to Led Zeppelin, a new group outta England that has a wicked lead singer. He's singing about being dazed and confused and we're both swaying to the music and digging what he's saying. The acid is nice and mellow and we're feeling groovy.

Sounds like he's having a good time. Muzzie sets her purse on the end table.

Shirley turns down the volume and I'm a little embarrassed because it does sound like he's making love to someone. Not that Muzzie thinks I'm a virgin or anything, but still … you don't listen to that kind of stuff with your mother!

I have the weekend off. You two want to go with me to see your grandparents? We can stay in a motel, just the three of us.

I can't believe my luck, not only getting out of this place, but staying in a motel. Staying in motels is so groovy—nothing like being at home. Sure! I answer and wait for Shirley to say she'll go, too. She doesn't say anything. You have to go! I tell her and slap at her. It'll be so cool. You have to come!

Okay! Okay! Don't flip out. I was just trying to figure out how to get outta work. I told 'um I'd work overtime Saturday.

Call in sick, Muzzie suggests.

And it's settled. We're going to Hemet to see our grandparents for the weekend. But really, we're going just to have fun and be with each other like we used to do before Shirley moved out.

I wake up Friday morning with a bad sore throat, but don't say anything—I don't want to be the one to spoil the fun. I fall asleep in the backseat. Shirley taps me on the knee and passes me some whites before we're out of L.A. By the time we get to Hemet I'm feeling really bad. I can't stop shivering and my throat is so sore it's hard to swallow.

Muzzie checks us into a motel on the backside of the trailer park where our grandparents live. I fall into bed with all my clothes on. They leave me to sleep and go see the grandparents. Even the whites can't keep me awake. I drift off into a dream about astronauts and the ice cold of space, no air and no gravity—no up or down.

It's pitch dark in the room when I wake up. There's a Double Cola on the nightstand and a note: *Gone to find you some chicken soup. Be back soon. Muzzie Pooh.* I take a sip of my cola. It hurts so bad to swallow I don't take another. I stumble into the bathroom, pee, wash my hands and face and hurry back to bed. I'm so cold I grab an extra blanket from the closet and all our sweaters to pile on top of me.

Someone is trying to pour something into my mouth. I shake my head and croak that it hurts too much and turn over. Someone rubs my back softly and sings my favorite bedtime song, *The Great Silkie of Sule Skerry.* I drift off into dreams of seal men walking up on shore and dancing with me and me going back into the sea with them. We swim to their Skerry and it feels like home to me, even though it's just bare rock in the middle of the sea.

Muzzie wakes me up with a cup of hot tea. She feels my forehead with the inside of her wrist. You're burning up! she tells me.

I'm okay, I croak and get dizzy trying to sit up.

You stay down. She turns to Shirley. I think we should take her to the base. I don't like the way she looks.

Shirley agrees and they start getting me up. I don't remember putting on my jammies and sit on the edge of the bed looking at the swirls of colors and random patterns. The room tilts sideways and the bed bumps up against me. I close my eyes and feel like I'm floating on air.

Random noises try to bust apart my warm, lazy dreams, but I ignore them. There are voices I know and some I don't. A lot of men it seems for Muzzie and Shirley and me in Hemet. I'm jostled and prodded and start getting really pissed that Shirley's hogging so much of the bed. I push back and hurt my arm. I open one eye and close it right away the lights are so bright and right overhead. I wonder what the hell kinda trip this is, wonder if Shirley gave me some acid to make me feel better.

I crack open one eye and see all the lights flashing past overhead. Decide she had to have slipped me some acid.

It's okay, sweetie, Muzzie's voice floats along with the lights. We brought you out to the Air Force base, sweetie. The doctor is going to see you in a minute.

I open both eyes. Muzzie's on one side of the gurney, Shirley on the other. I can tell by their tight smiles that I must be pretty sick. I raise my head a little and see a medic pushing the gurney, figure another one's at my head. But I don't care. I don't want to do anything but sleep. I sure don't want to swallow anything; my throat's so sore it hurts just lying here.

She's worse than I thought, Shirley whispers across me.

I don't care. I just want to sleep.

Some man is reading off a bunch of numbers. I want to change this dream, don't want to be stuck in fucking math class in a dream.

They'll be here soon, sweetie. It sounds like Muzzie's voice real close. Where the hell are they? Excuse me! Excuse me, we've been waiting quite a while … Her voice drifts away, but the man keeps rambling off numbers.

All kinds of men start yelling one after another, we're go, we're go, we're go. Then they start counting again. Someone says the eagle has wings. I laugh and regret it instantly.

There's a sharp pain in my arm and I try to pull away, but can't seem to move my arm. A man's voice says, That should help for now. We'll keep an eye on her for a couple of hours. Please wait in the lounge. There's a TV in there.

We'll wait here, Muzzie says, and I drift back off wondering what kinda acid Shirley gave me to make this trip so strange.

A man's counting again, but this time it sounds like he's giving measurements, 400 feet, 200 feet. Then the eagle is back and they say it's landed. I laugh, wondering what the hell an eagle is doing here.

I wake up and realize I'm feeling a little better. Think I might have a sip of my Double Cola. Open my eyes, but I'm not in the motel room. I try to sit up but my arms are strapped down and there's a tube running along my left arm and up into a glass bottle that's hanging in mid-air. I close my eyes and tell myself this is the strangest trip yet. Think that maybe I've been watching too many Ben Casey and Dr. Kildare re-runs on TV.

I open my eyes again and look around. There's a crowd of people in white uniforms in a tight group around a high counter. A man's talking all scratchy like on a short-wave radio. I can't make out his words, but everyone in the group suddenly explodes in cheers and starts clapping and hugging each other.

I look around and don't see Muzzie or Shirley anywhere. I'm cold again and thirsty and don't understand why my arms are strapped down, why I have a needle in my arm, why everyone is so excited—why I'm all alone?

I lie there watching the drip, drip, drip of the bottle into the long, clear tube for what seems like forever. The man on the short-wave keeps talking and everyone in the group is quiet, not looking anywhere but at the counter.

Hey! You're awake. Shirley leans over my head and kisses my forehead, then walks around beside my gurney.

Several doctors and nurses quickly turn and shush her.

She leans over me and whispers, Fuck them! How ya feeling?

What's going on? I croak.

She looks over her shoulder and whispers. Some patriotic bullshit. I think they landed on the moon or something. Muzzie's been furious that they've just been standing around. Took 'um close to an hour before they even saw you the first time. Then they hooked you up to this thing and went back to their fucking TV. Fucking bastards.

She leans over and gives me another kiss on the forehead.

Water? I croak.

Sure. Hang on a second. She turns to the group and asks, Can we get some water over here? Excuse me! Her voice raises and I see one nurse turn and look at us.

They're on the moon! the nurse says.

And we're on earth, Shirley shouts back. She needs some water.

That gets a doctor's attention. I'm going to have to ask you to wait in the lounge, Miss. He looks around and adds, Where's your mother? You shouldn't be in here alone.

Shirley shrugs and stays put.

Do I have to have someone escort you out? He takes a step away from the counter and I see a TV with a fuzzy black and white image that makes me think I'm still in a dream.

Shirley backs away and lets go of my hand. See ya in a couple of minutes, she tells me and disappears over my head.

The doctor and nurse go back to watching the TV and I don't get any water. After a while the group breaks apart. The same doctor says, One small step for man; one giant leap for mankind, and everyone sighs and smiles and a few nurses hug each other.

I watch the last drop leave the bottle and work its way down into my arm and wish Muzzie was here to tell me what the hell is going on.

Lunacy
July 20 - 21, 1969

Suggested listening:
Single—*A Day in the Life*, The Beatles

Muzzie turns on the car radio. It's a long drive back to Hemet from March Air Force base and no one is happy. Muzzie found some whiskey somewhere and is pretty smashed. Shirley's coming down off whatever she was on and doesn't have anything else on her. She never dreamed we'd be at the hospital for six hours. I'm still feeling sick, but my temperature dropped from 104 to 102, so they let me go home.

It's getting dark by the time we make it back to the motel. Muzzie tucks me in bed then leaves, telling us she's going to check in with the grandparents because they'll be worried about us being gone all day. She adds that she'll stop off somewhere and bring back food so we can enjoy what's left of the night.

The only thing on TV is the moon landing. We try all three channels with no luck, so we don't watch anything.

I can't believe we didn't know about that, I croak at Shirley.

Why should we? Just a bunch of establishment freaks trying to distract people from the war. They do this shit all the time just to cover their ass. God I hate Nixon.

I nod, but still think it's pretty cool that we made it all the way to the moon. I remember my dream about floating in space and wonder how I knew they were in space, even when I didn't know about the moon landing.

Car lights flash in the window and Shirley pulls back the curtain. Fucking great! She drops the curtain and leans her head against the wall.

What?

She's got a bunch of freaks in the fucking car with her.

Fuck no!

Fuck yes!

Shit! I dive under the covers.

Shirley starts tossing clothes and stuff off the floor and into the tiny closet. She looks in the mirror. I see tears welling before she can blink them back. Damn it! she says, still looking at herself in the mirror, then pulls the rubber band out of her hair and goes to unlock the door.

Muzzie waltzes in followed by a pack of freaks with long hair and beards and sandals and jeans. Not one of them is carrying anything, except Muzzie, who's arms are filled with shopping bags. Shirley takes two and sets them on the low dressing table next to the TV.

There's more in the car, Muzzie tells her. Be a doll and grab them.

Shirley slaps two guys on her way out and tells them, Help me out.

They just look at her and flop on the bed closest to the door.

She kicks one in the shin and tells them, Get the fuck up and help or get the fuck out!

They both get up and make their way out, bumping into other freaks still pouring into the room.

A guy with straight, black hair almost down to his waist sits on the side of my bed and looks at me. I scoot over so I'm not so close to him. You the sick one? he asks. I nod. Cool.

How'd ... I mean, why ... no ... I mean ...

Your mom came on to us at the park and said she had two daughters that wanted to party. Invited all the guys back here. He scoots a little further onto the bed, as more guys arrive. Some have to hang around on the sidewalk outside because the room's already full.

I'm sick!

Donna D. Conrad

Yeah. I know. Anything contagious?

Strep throat.

He stands up and plops back down on the other bed. I pull the covers up under my chin and cross my legs under the blankets to keep freaks from sitting on them. More guys sit on the bed, talking together, snagging beers out of the six packs on the dresser. No one seems to be paying attention to me and I wonder if I'm invisible again—hope it just happens naturally now that I've been practicing for so many years.

Hey! You got any sounds? someone yells.

I see Shirley go over to the radio and turn it on. She dials through the stations and finally finds a faint KRLA. *Sky Pilot* weaves in and out of conversations until someone cranks up the sound. It's a flood of Doors, and Stones, and Hendrix, and Joplin until the phone starts ringing and Shirley shouts for everyone to shut up.

Muzzie's passed out in the arm chair by the bathroom. Shirley and I just stare at the phone, hoping it'll stop ringing. It does and everyone starts talking again and someone turns up the radio.

The freaks outside start drifting away until everyone left can fit in the room. Shirley closes the door and pushes her way through the crowd to me. You okay? she asks.

I motion for her to lean in closer. She kicks the foot of a guy sitting between us. He leans way back and Shirley leans in. I have to pee, I tell her.

So go.

I can't. I have my pajama's on.

For fuck sake! She looks around the room quickly. You think they care? They won't even notice. Here. She gives me her hand and pulls me out from under the covers.

My legs are still crossed, my ankles sitting on top of my thighs. I fall flat on the other bed and some square guy with a crew cut. Wonder how the hell he got here. Shirley helps me untangle my legs and I hobble to the bathroom on feet completely asleep.

Nice jam-jams, the black-haired dude says as I pass him.

I stay in the bathroom until someone starts banging on the door. Go away! I try to shout, but only manage a weak croak. It feels like I just peeled the skin off the inside of my throat.

You're too old to pull this shit! Unlock the damned door, Shirley yells from the other side. I lean way far out and manage to turn the lock and still stay on the toilet.

Come on. I'll help you back to bed, Shirley sighs and offers her hand.

The phone starts ringing again and Muzzie stirs in her chair. Why doesn't someone answer the phone? she asks all groggy.

I look around and don't see Shirley anywhere. Muzzie struggles out of the chair, someone turns down the radio. She looks over at me all bleary-eyed and asks, Where's your sister? I shrug and don't even try to say anything. I haven't spoken since my stint in the bathroom—think I might have fallen asleep for a while despite all the noise.

Hello, Muzzie says into the phone. She sounds wide awake and very telephone operator like. I wonder if she's talked on the phone for a living so long it's like me being able to become invisible without really trying—it just comes natural.

No, she says into the phone. No one but me and my children. No. I'm certain. Now it's late. Good night. She hangs up and waves her hands in the air. Everyone listen. They're on to us, so we have to keep it down. She turns toward the door. And you! she snaps her fingers at a guy who's looking out the window. Hey, Looky-Lou. You behind the curtain.

The guy looks back into the room.

Drop the curtain and don't open it again. And someone get me a beer. She drops back into her chair and looks all wiped out then asks me again, Where the hell is your sister?

I shrug and think about writing her a note.

Well. Go check the bathroom. She nods towards the closed door.

I get out of bed, grab a sweater off the closet floor and try to ignore the guys and my pajamas. I turn the handle and push hard on the door, expecting it to be locked. It flies open and I stop dead in my tracks. Shirley's in there with an older freak who has a thick rubber strap tied around his upper arm and a needle in his other hand. I can't breathe. The room starts to swirl around me, but I can see Shirley's eyes clearly—they're glassy and not focused. She has a stupid smile on her face and her arms are all limp in her lap.

I back up and pull the door behind me. The junkie looks over his shoulder as the door closes. He has the same stupid grin on his face as Shirley. I want to cry, but I don't. I've learned not to freak-out at other people's trips. Learned that sometimes I have to be the one to hold it together when stuff comes down hard—that this is one of those times.

I pull the door shut, shuffle through the dozing guys on the floor and over to Muzzie's chair. I lean over and tap her on the shoulder.

She jolts awake. What? What? She looks around, like she's forgotten where we are. What's wrong? she asks.

I whisper, Shirley's in the bathroom.

Why are you whispering?

I have strep throat, I say a little louder and my throat feels like it's on fire.

She looks at me a second, then pats my face. You should be in bed, she tells me. You still have a fever.

There's a loud knock on the door and everyone looks at it.

Hide, Muzzie hisses really loud. Kids start diving under the beds, into the tiny closet, down on the floor on the far side of my bed, a whole group crowds into the bathroom.

Shirley stumbles out of the bathroom holding hands with the junkie. I can tell she's too stoned to care, but she asks Muzzie anyway, What's happening?

They're at the door, Muzzie whispers. The knocking gets louder.

Shirley drops the junkie's hand and looks around, kicks a guy's foot that's sticking out from under my bed. Spins around and flips on the TV and turns the radio down. She looks around once more, pushes the junkie back in the bathroom, pulls the door closed, turns back and nods at Muzzie. I slide under the covers and try to look sick, which isn't hard.

Muzzie pats her hair down, brushes off her blouse, and opens the door a crack. Yes?

What in tarnation are you up to in there? The man is practically shouting.

What do you mean? Muzzie pulls the door open a little wider. My daughters and I are just settling in for the night.

The man looks past Muzzie. Shirley's sitting at the end of one bed watching the TV, I'm in the other. Why are both the TV and the radio on?

I have two daughters. They like different things. Now if you don't mind … She starts to push the door closed.

The man puts one foot inside the room. I pull the covers up to my chin, Shirley just keeps watching the TV. But I can tell she's not seeing anything.

My wife saw several young men leaving this room not long ago.

The bathroom door opens and the junkie walks out, his pants unzipped. Hey, there's a shit-load of people in there, he slurs and points back at the bathroom. No room to piss. I'm gonna go outside.

The Galaxy 500 drifts along the empty streets of downtown Hemet, Muzzie driving real slow. The junkie and the guy with the long black hair are still with us.

I tap Muzzie on the shoulder and croak, That one says *Vacancy*, and point at a long narrow motel.

She pulls over to the curb and tells us to stay put.

I turn and look at Shirley and the junkie, crashed out on the back seat, their legs and arms all tangled together and don't think Muzzie has to worry about that. But I'm worried how we're gonna get them in the room—wonder why the guys are even here at all.

Donna D. Conrad

She slams the door closed, then opens it again. On second thought you better duck down, she tells the black-haired guy.

Sure thing, Mrs. Conrad. He curls up with his head in my lap.

I push him off me and he slips to the floor.

Stop that right now, young lady. We're in a heap of trouble. I don't need any more trouble from you, Muzzie scolds.

I don't say anything, feeling bad that I've caused Muzzie trouble; wonder if all this isn't my fault. If I hadn't gotten sick then we'd have seen the grandparents and swam in the pool at their trailer park, had dinner, and gone straight to bed. Realize that because I got sick, we're in a heap of trouble.

The motel owner gives us ten minutes to clear out, before he calls the cops. Kids start pouring out of the room as he watches. I have to pack everything because Muzzie's pouring instant coffee down Shirley's throat.

She's not drunk, I tell her, stuffing clothes in our duffle bag.

She stops in mid pour. She looks drunk, she answers.

I shrug my shoulders not sure enough to know—not wanting to tell Muzzie Shirley's mainlining smack, even if I am sure.

I take my hip-huggers and a t-shirt into the bathroom to change. The room stinks of piss and sweat and something else. I breathe through my mouth and get dressed, all the time feeling like I might pass out. When I come out the longhair and the junkie are helping Shirley out to the car.

The motel room is still cluttered with beer cans and potato chip bags and all the ashtrays are full to the brim. I start picking up beer cans.

Don't bother, Muzzie tells me. They kick us out in the middle of the night … they can clean the damned room themselves!

Muzzie opens the car door and slips inside. We're in luck! They only had one room with two beds left. And it's around back! She pats the long-hair's butt. Scoot over, honey, but keep your head down. They think it's just me and the girls.

The long-hair slides further across my lap and grins up at me. I look out the window, not wanting any of this to be true—know it's all too true.

The guys get Shirley up the flight of stairs and into the room. Muzzie and I carry our bags and follow them. They dump Shirley on the bed. She smiles up at the junkie and holds out her arms to him. He rolls her over to the other side of the bed, pulls back the covers, rolls her back over and climbs in.

Guess it's you and me, Punk, Muzzie says and pulls back the covers on the second bed. You look terrible, baby. Get into bed. I'll make some hot tea for you.

Where am I supposed to sleep? the long hair asks.

You're an Indian, Muzzie tells him. You should be used to sleeping on the ground.

Christ! the guy cusses and grabs a blanket and pillow out of the closet and throws himself down on the floor at the foot of the bed.

I have to pee but don't want to walk over him. I climb into bed with my clothes on and watch the dawn break through thin white curtains as everyone sleeps off the night.

Past Present
August 1969

Suggested listening:
Single—*We Will Fall*, The Stooges

The road looks familiar, a scene from a dream I don't quite remember. I scoot down lower in the bucket seat, study the joint squeezed tight between my fingers. Can't will myself to raise it to my lips. Can't will myself to do anything but hope the dream passes. Hope I'll wake up soon.

I don't ever look for the place it happened. Don't want to know where they took me; where they took everything from me. But each time I drive along Valley Boulevard and see the low hills off to the side, I shiver.

It seems like Ken is always driving Valley Boulevard. I wish he'd take another street, but he says Valley is the best street, and doesn't even ask me why I don't like it. Not that I would know what to say—wouldn't dream of telling him about that night, a year ago this weekend.

The car banks hard and starts climbing. The joint burns my fingers, but I can't move.

Is this it? Ken's voice brings back feeling, brings back the pain of scorched flesh. What the fuck are you doing? He snatches the roach from between my fingers and pinches it out, drops it in his shirt pocket. Hey! He slaps my arm, but I still can't move. Hey! Snap outta it! Another slap on the arm and I raise my eyes, but try not to see outside the car. This look like the place?

I force myself to look out the window as the Cougar crawls along a deserted road that has no curbs, no street lights, a road with hills on one side, gullies on the other. I nod.

Did you turn left or right?

We went up, I say in a whisper.

The Cougar turns sharply and I lean into the door, trying not to lean towards Ken—telling myself I should wake up now, wake up!

We drive the flat land between Covina and La Puente to pick up Bear before heading to the beach. I didn't know we had to pick up Ken's little brother out in Whittier. Didn't know we were taking the back way along Turnbull Canyon.

I dig my nails into the leather seat as we climbed the steep canyon road; blinking back tears; stuffing down memories; willing myself to listen to the music—a new tape by Credence Clearwater. The road turns black as night, the Cougar's headlights flashing on scrub brush hills that spring up in front of us and then drop away, leaving us in a black void.

Turn it up! Bear yells from the backseat and suddenly the car is filled with a man warning us that there's a bad moon rising, that trouble's on the way. The headlights catch a road leading up into the hills. A road I never wanted to see again. The car slows and I start screaming and tearing at the door, trying to get out while there's still time.

Do we have to? I ask Ken. It happened a long time ago.

Just last summer, he says.

All these roads look the same. I can't be sure.

There aren't that many roads that run off the canyon. The last two didn't go far enough back to be the one.

It really doesn't matter does it?

He doesn't say anything. I study the burned skin on my finger, surprised it doesn't hurt.

We leave Bear at his cousin's house in Whittier and head straight back to Covina. What the fuck is wrong with you? Ken keeps asking me; but I can't tell him—can't tell anyone.

Nothing. I just got scared driving around those curves in the dark.

Yeah, well you almost got yourself killed for Christ's sake. If Bear hadn't stopped you, you'd a fallen out the door and been road kill. That's the most fucked up thing you've ever done—and you've done plenty of fucked up things!

I can't look at him, but want to ask what he means. I don't remember doing anything fucked up, don't believe I have, at least not around him.

I can't breathe. I want to roll down the window, but can't seem to move. This is the place, I tell him. I know the long curve after the rise. Have seen it in nightmare after nightmare over the last year.

Don't make me get out, I beg Ken.

My dad's not home. I invite Ken in and tell him I'll tell him what scared me. We sit in the living room on the curved sectional. I can't look at him. I can't say everything, but say enough so he knows what happened, knows I couldn't get away, knows there was no place to run, knows they hurt me.

He doesn't say anything for a long time. I scoot back on the couch and wait, know he'll understand and not be mad at me for freaking out.

He takes a deep breath and looks down at his clasped hands. What were their names?

I shake my head, confused about why he wants to know that.

What were their names? He asks again.

I don't know.

You got in a car with a bunch of guys, when you didn't even know their names?

I thought they were Shirley's friends. I didn't ... didn't think.

No you didn't think, did you? He stands up and tells me he'll pick me up in the morning. He wants to see where it happened.

I dig three reds out of my teddy bear and crash for the night.

He opens the car door for me. Come on, get out.

I shake my head no. I can't, I whisper.

He grabs me by the arm and pulls me out of the car and starts off down the road. I trudge along behind him. We round a small bend in the road, right where I fell and was dragged back to the car.

He stops walking. No place to run? he says with his back to me.

No place to get help?

No. There's nothing up here, I tell him.

So what's that? he says and steps aside. Just around the bend the road fans out into a long cul-de-sac with three houses at the far end.

They weren't here last year! I say, not really believing what I'm seeing. Nothing was here.

He walks past me back toward the car. Those aren't new houses. They've been here for years, he says as he passes.

I didn't see them! They must have had their porch lights off! I run to catch up with him. You have to believe me! I plead and grab at his sleeve.

Oh I believe you, he says and turns around to face me. I believe you jumped in a car with five guys you say you didn't know. That you went on a drug deal with them. That you ended up here, within fifty yards of three houses. That you say they raped you.

He turns and walks back to the Cougar.

And I know why I've never told another living soul about what happened that night—why I'll never tell anyone else for as long as I live.

Decline and Fall
September 1969

Suggested listening:
Single—*Rainy Day Women*, Bob Dylan

It's not fair. I can't take another year of Mrs. Andrews. I do everything I can to get out of her class. I even go see the counselor, who hates me, and tell him I have a personal conflict and need to change classes. He's no help at all, tells me I'm stuck with Mrs. Andrews—it's like a bad acid trip that just keeps going on and on and on.

Kathy has the same class as me. I'm glad for at least that. We drop mescaline at her house the first day of school. It's the only way I can face Mrs. Andrews.

Class! Mrs. Andrews taps the edge of her desk with a ruler. Class!

We quiet down.

Welcome back to most of you, and for those who are new to my class, welcome. You will find that what you learn in this class will be of value to you the rest of your lives.

I spit out a short laugh. Mrs. Andrews ignores my outburst and continues yapping for the whole hour. After ten minutes I tune her out and wish I could go home and read some real books, books by Vonnegut and Bradbury, books about the real world. But I know she'll make us read more Shakespeare and stuff that doesn't mean anything to anyone anymore.

The week drags by and I stare out the window of third period English and wish I were anywhere else.

Friday finally shows up and I think I might just make it through the first week of school. Kathy and I split a tab of acid even though Ken doesn't like me dropping acid when he's not around. He thinks people freak out all the time on acid. He doesn't believe me when I tell him that I've never had a bad trip—that I'd stop cold if I ever have a bad one. He makes me promise I'll only drop mescaline. But facing Mrs. Andrews calls for stronger stuff. Kathy swears she won't tell him.

I'm tripping along, enjoying the scene from the window, when Mrs. Andrews's words float by and grab my attention. You are all approaching adulthood now and I feel, as Juniors, you should take an active role in your education.

The class starts buzzing and I look at Mrs. Andrews, thinking she can't be serious.

Class! She taps the ruler again and picks up a folder from her desk with papers in it and starts to hand them out to the front row students. Please fill out these forms, listing your favorite subjects and personal interests and I will endeavor to structure our class work so it will have relevance to your lives.

I take the paper from the guy in front of me and roll my eyes at him. He smiles and says, I can't write what I'm interested in, and winks. I look away and wish I hadn't looked at him.

The paper's filled with questions. I look the page over and settle on: What is your favorite movie? I scribble Romeo and Juliette, and crack up. Kathy looks over at me and I show her. She giggles and writes the same on her paper. I'm going to have fun with this one, I whisper. She nods and we both dive into the paper, giggling and looking around between scribbles.

The last question is: What is your favorite book? I think and think and think but can't come up with anything good. I think about putting down some of the books Ken loans me, but I don't want her to know that much about me. I try to remember some of Terry's books I've read. But I don't want to put down anything that isn't ridiculous. Then it comes to me: *The Decline and Fall of the Roman Empire.* It's one of Terry's first edition books that he loved. I read some of it with him. It's still on the book shelf, but I can't bring myself to read it now that Terry's dead.

I jot the title down and laugh to myself, Let's see her assign that book!

Miss Conrad, would you please see me after school today?

Why? The last thing I want to do is end my day with Mrs. Andrews.

I'll discuss that with you in private at three o'clock sharp … today.

I nod and grab my books off my desk, can't believe my bad luck. Kathy's not even at school today. She ditched with Frank, left me alone at school for some guy. I'd never do that to her.

I tell my sixth period teacher I have a headache. He writes out a note to the nurse. I toss it in the trash and hang out in the F head, smoking and waiting for my three o'clock with *Julie.*

I push my way in through the group of freshmen pouring out of her classroom and feel so sorry for them if they get stuck with Andrews for four fucking years. I have a sinking feeling that I might get her next year too and almost turn around. Being expelled might be better than two more years of her!

Miss Conrad! she calls, and I have to go in.

She's sitting on the corner of her desk smiling. I look over my shoulder to see who she's smiling at, realize it's me. Please, sit down, Miss Conrad. She motions to a chair she's pulled up next to her desk. She takes a paper from a folder on her desk as I sit down and pull my dress a little lower, trying to cover my knees without any luck.

Don't worry, I won't report you for your skirt length. You're pretty talented at bending the rules and getting away with it, aren't you?

And I know why she's doing this—it's to get back at me for

winning about girl's wearing pants to school. They changed the rules last year, but only when the weather's bad. Then we got a letter during the summer saying girls can wear matching slack's outfits any time of year. But the skirt length stayed the same, so I've worn skirts an inch too short every day so far.

No matter, she adds and tips the paper so I can see it. It's my questionnaire from last week. She taps the paper and tells me, I'm interested in some of your responses and would like to know more about your selections.

I just made everything up, I tell her and fold my hands in my lap.

Interesting. Yes, I can tell you're very creative. But this last question about your favorite book? *The Decline and Fall of the Roman Empire?*

I made it up.

You made it up? She smiles again and I'm getting really nervous all of a sudden. I can take her sending me to the office, but not her smiling.

You know what I think? she asks all smug like. I think you've read this book, or at least parts of it. And I also think you are smart enough to fool everyone into thinking you're stupid.

I look up at her and then away again, don't understand what she's getting at or why. You can just flunk me right now if you want, I don't care. I made up the name, that's all, I tell her.

She stands up and holds out a lined piece of bluish-white paper that's typed on. I've never seen this form before; wonder if it's expulsion papers.

You're too smart to be in my class Miss Conrad. Too smart to be in dumbbell English, or any other dumbbell classes. I pulled your junior high records. You were an A+ student. So, there's no need to tell me again that you just made up the name of a book you obviously know, and perhaps have read.

The room starts spinning and I think I might throw up, but I won't give her the satisfaction of thinking she knows anything about me. What I did in junior high doesn't mean anything, I tell her.

It means quite a lot Miss Conrad. I won't let you keep ruining your chances to get a good education. Look at me!

I look up and see real concern on her face. See that she might really mean what she's saying.

I've spoken with your counselor.

You what? I ask, infuriated that she would talk with the man that wouldn't let me out of her class. You have no right!

I have every right to see that you get the education you need. I won't stand for you wasting the best years of your life, acting like you're some mindless fool who wouldn't know a good book if it bit them.

You have no right to talk to my counselor, no matter what you think!

She's quiet for a moment, looking at me intently. Thank you for letting me know what I can and can't do. But no matter what you think, you're out of my class, Miss Conrad, as of today.

It's like a splash of cool water, her words. I relax a bit and think, I'm out of her class … that's just what I wanted and now I've got it.

You will start on Monday with Mr. Sundstrand in College Prep English. The water turns to ice and I can't think of anything to say, can't think past *college prep*.

You have to be kidding, I tell her.

I've never been more serious in my life.

Farther Shore
September 1969

Suggested listening:
Single—*Flowers Never Bend with the Rainfall*, Simon & Garfunkel

I don't shower, I don't eat, I don't brush my hair all weekend. I don't want to go to school, to the new English class, but my dad's home and I can't stay here. I can't ditch at Kathy's either because her dad's on vacation.

My mind flashes back to Mrs. Andrews and her smug little smile. How dare she kick me out of class and put me with some stuck-up snobby cheerleaders and jocks? I rant on in my head, damning her and my counselor and the new teacher, whatever his name is! I won't go! They can't make me!

I stick my leg through a bright orange and purple pair of hip-huggers—a new gauntlet to throw at the establishment. Maybe, just maybe, I'll get sent home before third period? The idea gets me moving.

My dad catches me just as I'm walking out the door. He's never up this early after working a week-long case. Where the hell do you think you're going in that god damned hippie outfit! I drop my hand from the doorknob.

Get back in your room and put on your school clothes right now, young lady!

I duck my head and turn around, walk past him and down the hall;

don't want to look at him, all skinny and wrinkled, in his white BVD standard issue underwear and matching t-shirt. God, I hate him.

He rants on and on and follows me to my room pointing and yelling and I just stand there waiting for him to shut up and let me change. And make it a decent dress! And the hem better be touching your god-damned knees or you're grounded for a week! And brush your hair for Christ's sake. Get it out of your eyes. I'm surprised you're not blind already! He pulls my door closed and I hear the bathroom door slam.

The day can't get any worse, I think then remember I'm in a new English class, a fucking college prep class.

I might just hate Mrs. Andrews more than my dad; but it's a close call.

The bell rings and the F head clears out. Kathy didn't show up today so I'm there all alone trying to figure out what I should do. If Kathy were here I'd walk into Andrews' class with her and sit down as usual. What could she do? Nothing!

I toss my cigarette in the toilet and don't bother to flush it. Fuck 'um all! I tell myself and pull the ends of my ponytail apart to scoot it higher on my head. Fuck it! I'm going back to Andrew's class anyway! I shove the door open and start down the hallway. I want to storm in there, tell her off and get expelled. I could go live with Shirley and Sandy; or run away completely—head to San Francisco—live in a crash pad with other freaks who stand up for their rights; freaks who don't cave the first time they get cornered.

Instead I chicken out and turn around, head back up the hallway. I round the corner, hardly breathing. I keep walking, not knowing what I should do now; the second bell's already rung and the halls are empty.

I stop, look around, wondering where the hell I am. A door's open and a bunch of students are talking all at once. A man is laughing at something and I wish I had *him* for a teacher instead of

Mrs. Andrews, who wouldn't know how to laugh if her life depended on it. I look down at the slip of paper in my hand and back at the open door and start to walk away real fast.

Miss Conrad? It's the man that was laughing, standing in the doorway.

I turn around. Miss Conrad? I nod. Welcome. We've been waiting for you.

My heart starts beating way too fast and I can't seem to breathe. He takes a step towards me and asks, Are you alright? I nod. He smiles and asks, Care to join us?

I know I'm busted. I walk past him and into the classroom, stop next to his desk not knowing what to do next. I tell myself I'll sit through this one class and then never come back.

Class, this is Donna Conrad.

I can't believe he told everyone my name! I hate the way my name sounds! How could he do that? I don't look up, study my boots and hope he doesn't say anything else. He does.

Miss Conrad just transferred over from Mrs. Andrews' class. I expect you all to make her feel at home and help her catch up on her classwork.

He touches my shoulder, but I can't look at him. I know you'll be a great asset to our class, Miss Conrad. I steal a glance at him to see if he's making fun of me, but he's not. I can tell he means it, that he wants me in his class. I'm too confused to say anything and so nod and duck my eyes again.

Please take a seat. Here's one right in front. My eyes flash around looking for any other seat. I see an empty desk in the back corner.

Or that one in the back is fine, too. He touches my shoulder again and gives me a little nudge towards the desk. He follows me down the aisle and waits until I'm seated, then hands me a thick book, holds on to it until I look up at him. He smiles and lets go.

Alright class! He announces and walks back to his desk. Who can tell me why Richard of York thinks he has a legitimate claim to the English throne?

Donna D. Conrad

I look down at the book and silently groan. *The Complete Plays of Shakespeare*—

I'm doomed for all eternity.

A Long Way Home
October 6, 1969

Suggested listening:
Single—*Come Together*, The Beatles

The sun turns deep orange, like the acid we took when it was still piercing yellow. The ocean swells and shrinks, but creeps ever closer. It's a long way back to Covina, even further to home—a place I've never known. But it's time to start for there or face being restricted for two weeks.

Our thumbs are stuck out like necks waiting for the axe, or a reprieve. The cars swish past without slowing. Ken pushes me out further on the road and hides behind a low billboard.

But it doesn't trap the big fish—me as bait wearing cut-offs and halter.

The sun fades until there's no color left in the world except the streaks of car lights and the harsh street lamps. Flashes of light continue to illuminate before they abandon us on the shoulder.

Hey! You want a ride or not? A call from a faded green sedan sets us running.

The back seat is cavernous, soft and spongy, like moss in some underground cave. I sink in, hearing the men rapping in the front like they're old friends, and I know Ken is working on the driver to get us all the way home.

The seat begins to thud. Bass reverb and a shushing sound from a voice I know well.

John Lennon is singing to me, from the walls of the cave, telling me to come together … come together … everyone—freak and straight—cool and uptight—beautiful and ugly—everything and everyone—Come Together, over him.

He sings it over and over, all through the night, all along the wide, bright highways flowing inland from the beach; through the blacked out canyons of La Habra; the flat lands of Covina, right up to the dead-end street that leads to my parents' house.

The front seat flips forward, Ken tells me I'm home, while Lennon keeps telling me it can work, we can all come together, and I wonder, truly wonder if it could be real—this world the Beatles sing about.

The faded green sedan glides away. I watch its lights streak blue and red under the golden rays of streetlights before walking the straight narrow sidewalk to the hedge where I hide my clothes.

I pull my hair back in a ponytail, shrug into my long pants and plain blue blouse; hope my dad is out on a case; that Muzzie is out too, in her room. I walk up the driveway, open the front door to darkness—know for certain I'll always be a long way from home.

Wings of Love
Late November 1969

Suggested listening:
Album—Moby Grape, Moby Grape

The Magic Kingdom is afire tonight. Dad is on a case out in Northridge, so Muzzie tells us we can bring our boyfriends. She brings her best friend, Arlene. We split once we're past the general store on Main Street. Shirley and David, Ken and me, rush to Fantasyland. On our own for the whole night in Wonderland.

We duck into the empty sentry post in Sleeping Beauty's castle. Shirley digs the mescaline out of her cigarette flip top box and divvies it up. We each get one cap, which we down with the lemonade Muzzie bought me before we spilt up.

It's gonna be a magical night in Wonderland, David announces with a big smile and heads us straight at the Matterhorn.

I'm alone at school all day, every day since Mrs. Andrews told the councilor about how I knew that stupid book, and got all my classes changed. Wish I'd never tried to be a smart-ass. I sit in the back of the college prep classes, try to follow the teacher's lectures, try to keep up with kids smarter than me, try to figure out how the hell I'm going to survive a whole semester of teachers who want real answers to real questions. I can't even hang out with Kathy during the week 'cause we don't have the same classes or homework, so I only see her once in a while, on weekends when she's not with Frank and I'm not with Ken 'cause they don't like each other.

We wait and wait and wait just outside the graveyard, then surge forward all at once, then wait again. Shirley and David are kissing all the time and one family lets a whole group of college students cut in front of them so their little kids can't watch. I look at Ken and wonder if I'd ever want to kiss him that much; decide I wouldn't—especially on mescaline.

The graveyard is starting to freak me. I think I'll skip this one, I tell Ken, who turns around, his eyes all wild and unfocused, his mouth hung open with his tongue dangling out the side. I scream and Shirley smacks me. David tells us to cool it before we get kicked out of line.

The next surge shoves us all inside a big wood paneled room with high ceilings. When the floor starts dropping and a lightning flash shows a person hanging from the ceiling, I scream again. I'm not the only one.

They're all laughing. I'm crying. Ken keeps trying to kiss me in the black "doom buggy" until I'm crying so hard he can't. I curl up on the seat with my eyes closed and cover my ears until it's over.

I get my first tests back from English and Social Studies. I get A's on both and think the teachers must be cutting me some slack since I'm new. I re-read the teachers' comments and realize they're not bullshitting me. That I passed their tests with A's.

I still sit in the back of all my classes, still hate the cheerleaders and jocks, still get stoned every morning before class, but for some reason, what these teachers are saying, especially Mr. Sundstrand, is beginning to make sense; makes me want to read the books they assign; makes me want to show them I can do even better.

Crocodiles, Headhunters, Indians, Fairies, Princesses, Frogs, Pirates, even the Abominable Snowman, scamper through the clear, cool night erasing the terror of the Haunted Mansion. But the little singing dolls in *It's a Small World* are still running through my head, and everyone I see looks like a doll on a twirling metal stand. I keep laughing and spinning around and around and around, until Shirley takes me into the restroom and splashes cold water on my face.

Now cut it out! She tells me. I just laugh and try to kiss her.

Stop it!

Why? What's wrong with laughing and singing and dancing? I spin around again and she pushes me into a stall just as a mother and daughter walk in. We both start laughing so hard we have to pee. I hold it while she goes.

We burst back out into the night, but can't find the guys. Fuck 'um, Shirley says, and we take off skipping arm in arm singing, *it's a small world after all,* at the top of our lungs.

I spend all of P.E. in the library reading because I slipped when I was wasted on reds and fell hard on my knee; the same knee I broke three times when I was in fourth grade. The doctor at the Air Force base said I'm not supposed to suit up for a month. Instead, I have to turn in essays about sports every week. They're so easy, I finish them on Monday and have the whole week to look up stuff my other teachers mention in class. The librarian even recommends books, brings them over to me and sometimes sits next to me for a few minutes explaining why she thinks a particular book is good. She lets me check out more books than I'm allowed.

Ken's working nights and weekends now, so I'm free to read all the books I get from school. My dad doesn't yell at me as much anymore—doesn't do much of anything except sleep all day unless he has a case.

Kathy calls once in a while and we still hang out when Frank's not around. But all she talks about is getting married and having kids, and how great Frank is. I think he doesn't treat her very well, that he only likes her 'cause she's blonde and has big tits. Her dad says she can't get married until she's a senior, so she and Frank stay at his apartment a lot.

I thought I would miss Kathy more than I do—sometimes I miss her more than I thought I would—when the weather's cold, or when Muzzie's drunk and my dad's yelling, or when Shirley doesn't pick me up and take me places for weeks at a time—when I get my first C on an assignment.

The Great Depression. I've heard Muzzie and my dad talk about it forever; think I can ace the test just from their stories. So I read The Jungle by Upton Sinclair, instead of the dull text book.

Now I know better than to believe everything Muzzie and my dad tell me— something I should have known before.

You got to keep it secret, Shirley warns me.

I shrug, Okay, no problem. What?

We're going to Vegas tonight to get married.

What? I shout and Shirley grabs my arm and steers me away from the tram stop where we're waiting to catch a ride to the car. Muzzie shoots us a look to keep it down. I can tell by her limp lower lip and glassy eyes, she and Arlene have been drinking. Not easy to do at Disneyland. I figure Muzzie must have snuck a bottle of Old Grand-Dad in her purse. I'd bet my life it's empty now.

Married? In Vegas? How groovy. Can I come? Can I be there? I mean I don't care if I miss school.

She clamps a hand over my mouth and talks in a whisper. Of course you're coming! I wouldn't get married without you. Don't tell Muzzie. I don't want anything to go wrong.

I sneak out of the house at two in the morning and meet Ken at the corner. It's a five-hour drive to Vegas from Covina. We figure David will drive, he always drives, so we take another hit of mescaline, this time from Ken's stash and drive over to Baldwin Park to meet Shirley and David at his apartment.

Sandy and David's roommate, Ron, are drinking sloe gin fizzes with *Abbey Road* playing full blast. Sandy hands us fizzes and yells, Shirley get your butt out here.

Shirley comes out with a small suitcase and takes the glass Sandy offers and holds it up for a toast. Fuck it all! We're getting married today come hell or high water. There's twenty dollars riding on this and I plan to win the bet! She downs the whole glass, as do we all. It's so sweet I don't believe it's booze, but my head starts to spin and I know it is. David wanders out of the hall with a knap-sack, downs his drink and heads for the door.

The sun's rising. Pale pink and tangerine clouds line the horizon and heat waves are already shimmering close to the ground across the empty expanse of desert. The car in front of me keeps disappearing, reappearing in different shapes—sometimes a huge army truck with soldiers, sometimes a family sedan with wide tail lights—but it always changes back into David's El Camino—at least I hope it's David's.

We left David's family house in Barstow an hour ago, Ken said he had to crash. I told myself I could drive on mescaline … no problem. All I had to do was keep David's car in front of me and we'd get to Vegas just fine. That was before sunrise. I study the flat, even space between me and the horizon and wonder if I could just drive the Cougar out over the desert floor and meet the sun before it clears the horizon. The car drifts towards the desert, tempting me.

The room is huge, with mirrors on all the closets. I'm not looking in them, know that I won't like what I see—it's bad enough seeing everyone as they pretend to be, I couldn't stand seeing the real them in the mirrors.

She called Muzzie from David's parent's house in Barstow. Asked her to come to Vegas for the wedding, asked her to bring Dad. I thought this was all just a game—that David bet Shirley twenty bucks she wouldn't marry him—that all Shirley wanted to do was win the bet—but it's not. Even David's parents are here, fussing around and acting important.

Shirley's wearing a lacey, pale blue, almost white dress that comes even with her knees. David has a suit and tie on. I'm still in my hip huggers, haven't changed into the paisley dress Muzzie brought from home—the one I wore my first day of high school. I'm still trying to figure out how she has it—thought I'd tossed it. I told her I wasn't wearing it—not my style anymore.

I'm still tripping, Ken's still sleeping, Muzzie's still telling me to change or we'll be late for the ceremony. Shirley walks over and hands me the dress. For me, she says in a kinda sad voice and I see tears clouding her eyes.

Dad lets me have a glass of champagne, makes a big deal outta how I need to sip it; how he doesn't want me getting drunk on his watch. I'm tripping nicely on a new hit of mescaline and everything is cool; even my dad making a big deal outta a glass of champagne.

They're gone, all of them. It's just Shirley and David, Ken and me, at a totally trippy casino called Circus, Circus. I'm still in my high school dress, Shirley in her wedding dress, David in his suit, and Ken in jeans. He slept through the wedding back at the hotel, so finding him dress-up clothes wasn't a problem. We almost don't get in because of Ken's jeans, but they relent and let us in when Shirley tears up and tells them she just got married and that thirty people are inside waiting for the reception. It's worked at four other casinos; it works again here.

We laugh until I start hiccoughing once we're inside. Shirley spins me around and around until I'm so dizzy I can't stand up. Ken guides me to a chair and hands me a glass of water, right out of thin air. I drink it down and start laughing hysterically at Ken prancing around like he's on a horse.

We get kicked out when I put a nickel in a slot machine.

Shirley's married now. Kathy doesn't talk about anything but getting married. I stay in my room over Thanksgiving break and read *Cat on a Hot Tin Roof* and *A Streetcar Named Desire*—swear to myself that I'll never get married.

For Good and All
December 22, 1969

Suggested listening:
Single—*Birthday*, The Beatles

She's gone—moved to Barstow with David. She's going to have a baby in July. She sounds happy about it all.

I'm alone. For good and all.

I take a tab of orange sunshine out of my teddy bear and spin it on its side, watch it twirl on the floor and fall flat. I drop the needle on the album. Wait for the words to start.

So you say it's your birthday. Well it's my birthday too, yeah.

Pop the tab in my mouth, down it with a beer, settle in for a trip on my own. For good and all.

1970 in the news

❖ The population of the United States is 205.05 million

❖ The national debt is $370.9 billion

❖ Average cost of new house is $26,600

❖ Average monthly rent is $140

❖ Average income per year is $6,186

❖ Minimum wage is $1.60 per hour

❖ A gallon of gas costs $0.36

❖ First class postage is $0.06

❖ *Midnight Cowboy* wins Best Picture

❖ *Aquarius/Let the Sunshine In* wins Best Song;

❖ *Blood, Sweat & Tears* wins Best Album

❖ New Movie Releases: *M*A*S*H*; *Patton*; *Woodstock*; *Hello, Dolly!*; *Catch-22*; *On Her Majesty's Secret Service*

❖ Paul McCartney announces that the Beatles have disbanded

❖ Simon & Garfunkel release their final album together, *Bridge Over Troubled Water*

❖ 600,000 people attend the Isle of Wight Festival. Artists include Jimi Hendrix, The Who, The Doors, Chicago, Richie Havens, John Sebastian, Joan Baez, Ten Years After, Emerson, Lake and Palmer and Jethro Tull

❖ Jimi Hendrix dies of barbiturate overdose in London at the age of 27

❖ Janis Joplin dies from a heroin overdose in Los Angeles at the age of 27

- ❖ U.S. Invades Cambodia
- ❖ 100,000 people demonstrate in Washington DC against the Vietnam War
- ❖ Four students at Kent State University, two of them women, are shot and killed by a volley of National Guard gunfire. At least eight other students are wounded
- ❖ The Nuclear Non-Proliferation Treaty goes into effect after ratification by 43 nations
- ❖ At least 27 states have reduced the status of first-time possession of marijuana from a felony to a misdemeanor
- ❖ The U.S. Environmental Protection Agency (EPA) begins operation
- ❖ First Earth Day is celebrated
- ❖ The first New York marathon is run in New York
- ❖ Actress Sharon Tate, 8 1/2 months pregnant, and four others are brutally murdered by members of the Manson Cult. The following night Leno LaBianca and his wife, Rosemary, are also murdered by Manson cult members
- ❖ Chicago Seven defendants are found guilty of intent to incite a riot at the 1968 Democratic Convention
- ❖ Concorde makes its first supersonic flight (700 mph/1127 km/h)
- ❖ The Soviet Moon Rover becomes the first remote-controlled robot to travel on the moon's surface
- ❖ The Liquid Crystal Display (LCD) is invented by George Gray of England

People's Parties
March 1970

Suggested listening:
Album—Ladies of the Canyon, Joni Mitchell

I've never seen Laurel Canyon in the daylight. I like it. It's warm and dry and soft and quiet; not at all like when I was here after Hendrix's concert. I told Ken I didn't want to come with them today if it was in Laurel Canyon. He promised me it wouldn't be a wild party, just a bunch of groovy musicians hanging out and playing tunes.

It'll be like Big Sur, only closer. We can be there and back before your dad gets home, he tells me on the phone. I agree because even Laurel Canyon has to be better than sitting at home alone all day.

I'm grounded again. All because I won't wear a bra to school. Not that my dad would notice, but my P.E. teacher did and suspended me for a week. He didn't even ask why, just being suspended was enough for him. I'm actually glad he didn't find out, it would be too weird to talk with my dad about bras, let alone why I won't wear one.

I went to demonstrations last summer, women burning their bras and talking how high heel shoes are modern day foot binding and girdles no better than strait-jackets. I never wore heels 'cause I'm already too tall, and I never liked how girdles felt around my stomach, so I never wore them either—but bras! I've hated them since the first time I had to put one on. So I stopped wearing a bra right then and there.

Everything was fine at school, no one seemed to even notice, not

306

until we came back from Christmas vacation and Debbie Morris saw me changing in the locker room. She went straight to the gym teacher and complained about me being braless. Muzzie got a note asking her to make me wear a bra. Muzzie wrote the teacher back, told her to tell the offended girl to stop watching me undress in the locker room or she'd file a complaint against the girl for indecent behavior.

They settled on my not suiting up for class and I'm back in the library writing about sports, like when I hurt my knee. It's fine with me. The librarian seems glad I'm back and keeps me stocked with books I'd never think to read all on my own. I even take to coming into the library during lunch and after school. I kinda wish I'd been coming in here the last two years.

The sun is warm on my bare arms and legs. I stretch out on the wooden deck, my head in Ken's lap. His brother David is playing a pretty cool lick on his guitar, while Bear and his younger brother, Jamie, sip beers and nod along.

Shit! I'm supposed to follow that? Ken says and slaps my shoulder to move aside as David passes back the guitar.

I sit up and cross my legs, resting my ankles on my thighs, the most comfortable way I know how to sit, and flip my hair behind my shoulders. We're the only ones on the deck, everyone else is either in the house or down by the pool.

I wonder again how Ken knows these folks. He didn't really say much, only that they were cool. They're all way older than me, but I can dig it. The dudes are dressed in jeans and t-shirts, the chicks in long, flowered dresses. I'm the only girl in cut-off jeans that I've seen, one of the reasons I'm still on the porch and not inside.

Fuck! Ken slaps the face of the guitar and tries the lick again. He hates to look bad in front of his friends. But the guitar isn't his main thing. He plays the piano, teaches kids how to play, even gives concerts. He's good, but no matter what he's good at musically, his younger brother is better. Ken says David's a prodigy and doesn't have to hardly practice, that it all comes easy to him. But David always has a guitar in hand, seems to always be practicing some new lick, let alone if there's a piano around—you can't keep him away from it.

Bear gets up and stretches and looks out over the railing. Hey, some chickies are skinny dipping, he announces and slaps Jamie on the arm. Let's go, he calls and kicks David's knee.

David looks away from Ken's fingering and shakes his head. Naw, I'll stay. And looks back at the guitar all serious.

Spider Chickie, Bear calls to me, You in?

I shake my head, no. He shrugs and doesn't bother asking Ken; knows nothing can drag him away from an instrument he's having trouble with. They jump the rail and disappear.

I lean back against the warm, wood wall, and close my eyes.

Shit! She's here! She's here! Bear's back, whispering really loud. I've never seen him so excited.

Where? David asks. Even Ken stops playing and looks around.

She just walked in. Look, look, look. Bear ducks down and points to the wide bank of windows that look out over the deck.

I scoot over and look. A reed-like woman with long golden hair is standing with her back to the windows, facing a crowd of folks. The windows are open and I hear them congratulating her, and I know it's Joni Mitchell.

She's just won a Grammy for her album, *Clouds*. I play it over and over and over. It's the most beautiful thing I've heard in years. I can't believe she's standing right there. I could almost touch her.

Let's go in, David says.

In there? I gasp

Yeah. Why not? That's why we're here, to see her. She always plays at people's parties. I want to watch her fingering. She has the most wicked chords of anyone! David's on his feet, taking his guitar away from Ken, brushing his long hair back with his free hand.

Let's go, Ken tells me and slaps my leg.

I can't, I tell him. I mean look at them all. I nod over my shoulder at the window.

What?

They're all dressed up 'n all, 'n I don't know them. I can't just walk in and … and …

Stay here then, he tells me and walks away.

I want him to come back and tell me it's okay, that I look fine to go in, that it doesn't matter they don't know me, that he'll take care of me in there.

He doesn't.

I scoot back against the wall and hear chords strummed on a guitar, rich and wonderful. And then she plays and sings. It's like nothing I've heard before; not even when I saw her perform in Big Sur last summer after Woodstock.

I chance a look through the window and see David sitting cross-legged right in front of Joni, watching her fingers like a hawk, silently mimicking them on his guitar. I don't see Ken, hope he's coming back out for me.

He doesn't.

She sings about Morgantown and ladies of the canyon and I know that it has to be Laurel Canyon, a place that is sweet and peaceful and safe.

Mr. Sundstrand
March 1970

Suggested listening:
Single—*There are Times*, Janis Ian

You trip, don't you? Why? You have a brilliant mind. Don't waste it.

I look away not knowing what to say. He's a teacher, part of the establishment, thinks he knows me.

He doesn't.

We have no common ground.

How can someone who sees the best in everyone, no matter how they dress or wear their hair, understand my need to escape the hell of every moment of every day, waking or sleeping? How can he understand the reprieve I'm granted each time I pop little orange pills, or chew long and hard on bitter mushrooms?

He teaches me the classics. Brings out the writer in me. Makes me believe I'm someone other than the weird freak dressed in black, who sits at the back of his class. He's the first teacher I've ever really talked with. The first adult I've ever truly trusted. Now he asks, *why*, and I can't tell him. He could never understand, and I can't bear the thought of him not understanding.

He lectures on Dante and Kafka and Poe; talks long and lucidly about hell. But never realizes he's speaking to one of its inhabitants. He could never understand that when acid washes over me, all the bullshit and hate and hypocrisy are stripped away. When I'm tripping there is only me, the universe, and peace. I know *this* is how life should be. Know the other world—the world of beatings and rapes and cops and wars and drunken mothers and psychotic fathers—is the dream.

When I'm tripping with other freaks is the only time I'm with people who are honest and open. We touch each other with our minds, and words are no longer necessary. But some words are still important—some words reverberate throughout our world: *All we are saying is give peace a chance ... Love one another right now ... The love you take is equal to the love you make*—words that have meaning.

When acid is peaking, I have hope. But it always abandons me, leaves me adrift in a world I don't understand. So I smoke a joint, drop a tab, sit in the back of the classroom. Hope no one calls my name.

I still hate the sound of my name—even when *he* calls it.

Do I trip? I smile and ask, Do you really want to know?

He shakes his head and says, No. He touches my arm and adds, Just be careful.

I laugh and tell him, Tripping is safe. It's being straight that's dangerous.

I leave his classroom, but cherish his concern. He's the only one of *them* who cares about *me*-whoever me might be.

Take a Chance
April 1970

Suggested listening:
Single—*Déjà Vu*, Crosby, Stills, Nash & Young

Spring is here, meaning summer is still a long way off. Ken doesn't like me dropping acid so I switch to mescaline most school days—can't take class straight up–when the world is being torn apart.

The peace rally at UCLA turns into a riot, with pigs throwing tear gas and pulling out their batons, swinging on kids that just want to stop the war. I turn to face them, flip them off screaming "pigs" at the top of my lungs.

I get busted when I trip and fall trying to get away. The pigs take me to the L.A. County Sheriff's Office. I'm still a minor so they call my dad. I wish they'd just throw me in jail and leave me there.

He walks in all serious and has a talk with the pigs behind the high counter; keeps looking over his shoulder at me. He gets me out of there but stops in the long, grey hallway, turns to face me.

Do you know how embarrassing it is for me to come down here to bail you out?

I'm still flying on speed and angry about the pigs attacking a peaceful rally so I tell him, No, even though I do understand how he must feel walking into a place where everyone remembers when he was the big Man, who didn't have to wear a uniform. Fuck them all.

He shakes his head kinda sad and asks, Couldn't you just run a little faster?

I can't face sitting in a classroom listening to teachers who think it matters—what they teach, what I learn. It's all bullshit and won't stop a pig from hitting me with his baton if I dare to stand up for my rights.

I spend the day in the F head, smoking and sipping Double Cola. I haven't slept in three days so the mescaline comes on strong, and the bathroom is getting pretty creepy. I figure my dad should be gone to his new rent-a-cop job by now, and decide to head for home. I wait for the second bell to ring, then walk quickly down the F wing hall, trying to look like I'm just late for class and not ditching.

I round the building and start to cut across the oak tree forest that skirts the campus, think I just might make it through this fucked-up day when I hear my name. Hear Mr. Sundstrand calling me.

He keeps after me to fill out all kinds of forms, write essays and book reports. Wants me to try for a scholarship I know I can't get. Only really top students get scholarships. But he keeps pushing me and pushing me, until I read the stupid books he suggests, write a few papers, and two essays on why I think I deserve to get a scholarship to go to college and learn to be a teacher. I don't even know if it's my dream, or if it's really Mr. Sundstrand's dream.

I don't turn them in for a long time. Don't think they're any good. Don't want to see the disappointment on his face when he reads them.

But he keeps asking, so I give them to him just to make him shut up.

You headed off somewhere? he asks. I nod and look at my boots, slipping my hair behind my ear. You haven't been in class all week, he says. I was worried about you. You okay?

I nod to the ground.

I read your papers. They're very good. I look up at him and see he's holding a bunch of papers in his hands. I was just headed to the office to turn in your scholarship applications.

Applications? I ask him.

Yes. I copied your essays and book reviews and took the liberty of filling out two additional ones that I think you stand a good chance of winning. He looks down at the papers. I hope you don't mind.

He looks back at me and I'm sorry I ditched his class all week. I clear my throat and say, No, it's cool. I pause and add, Thank you. I think ... I mean ... Do you think I stand a chance?

He smiles and says, You have to take a chance to stand a chance. Don't you now?

Thirteen Seconds
May 4, 1970

Suggested listening:
Single—*Ohio*, Crosby, Stills, Nash, & Young

Now we're killing each other.

Doesn't matter that they're working for the Man, the National Guard troops. The soldiers who shot those students are just kids too. I can't wrap my mind around it all. Nothing makes any sense.

How can they be dead? They were only standing up for what is right, now they'll never stand up for anything ever again. My body aches, pain stabs through me when I think of bullets from M-1 rifles tearing through my body—tearing those kids apart—killing their dreams of living in peace.

Someone should take Nixon out on the White House lawn and shoot him and all his cronies who order kids to die—makes no difference if it's in the jungles of Nam or on the campus of Kent State. The old men are the ones who should be dying.

I lie back against my pillow and know in my heart that killing people, even Nixon, isn't right. But I don't know how to change hate into love, don't really want to—not now, not with four dead in Ohio.

I think of Martin Luther King, wonder if he had time to hate the man who killed him? And Bobby Kennedy, shot dead in a hotel kitchen in Los Angeles. Did he hate his killer?

I know I hate them all—the killers of dreams.

Family Ties
June to July 1970

Suggested listening:
Single—*Can't Find My Way Home*, Blind Faith

School ends for the year and it can't be soon enough for me. Shirley's coming home to live with us. She says they'll find a place soon, but I hope they don't, even if it means I have to give up my room and sleep with Muzzie. I don't think she should be alone with the baby almost here. Dr. Don's going to deliver it, just like he delivered me, almost eighteen years ago.

My job through the work-ed program means I'll be earning two whole dollars an hour. I tell Muzzie I can help with groceries and stuff, but she tells me to save every penny for college—I don't know how she knows I want to go to college, we never talk about it and she never talks to my teachers.

I clean out my room, move all my clothes into Muzzie's closet after she packs most of her good clothes away in big round barrels and stores them in the garage. I even paint my old bedroom a really pretty lavender.

I check out half a dozen books from the public library, so I can have lots to read during my breaks and lunch, and set off to work the first day knowing this summer is going to be the best ever.

David and I order breakfast at the all-night Denny's about a mile from the hospital. He looks at his watch, and says, Two-thirty, and sighs. I can't believe she's not going to have the baby till morning. David, Muzzie, and me had piled Shirley into the big back seat of the Galaxy 500 and rushed her to the Alhambra hospital around eleven. Dr. Don came over and said it would be awhile, but he'd sleep at his clinic right across the street, just in case. The hospital nurse told us the baby wouldn't come before seven or eight in the morning, and that we should go get something to eat. Muzzie stayed behind, not wanting to leave Shirley alone.

David shakes his head and opens another sugar pack and dumps it in his coffee, ignoring his scrambled eggs and sausage. She looks horrible, he says and opens another pack.

I carefully drag my fried eggs up and onto the uncut pieces of toast, relieved they don't break on the way. Then systematically slice the egg-toast combo into neat little squares. I sprinkle salt and just a little pepper and dig in. Nothing's tasted this good in I can't remember how long. I don't stop until it's all gone, down my glass of orange juice and sit back against the padded booth.

We should get back, David says and stamps out his cigarette.

We hear Shirley screaming as soon as we push through the doors. David takes off down the hall with me on his heels. We skid to a stop outside Shirley's room but she's not there. The screams are coming from the operating room at the end of the hall, behind the two big doors marked "Medical Personnel Only Beyond This Point."

Fuck that! David says and heads for the doors, but he's overtaken by Dr. Don, who's moving so fast I don't think he even sees me standing by the empty room. He's in checkered pajamas and doesn't even have his slippers on. He pushes past David and bangs through the double doors. I can see nurses scurrying around inside. One grabs a smock and holds it out to Dr. Don. He strips off his pajama top and jabs his arms through the arm holes as the doors close on him

317

and Shirley's screams.

She's the most perfect thing I've ever seen. We decide to name her Michelle, which Shirley says means love, and David comes up with Paxx, Latin for peace. Michelle Paxx—Love and Peace—there couldn't be a better name in the world, or a more perfect baby girl. David sings the Beatles *Michelle* to her day and night. I dress her in all the tiny outfits she got at the baby shower and think there just might be hope for the world.

Kathy comes over one Saturday to see Michelle and it's like I don't even know her. She's wearing a bow in her short blonde hair. But it's more than that. Something I can't quite name. She's different and I can't imagine us doing all the things we did. I know for certain there's no going back—she's going to marry Frank come September, before she even graduates, and once I graduate I'm going to college. It's a far cry from when we thought we'd run away to San Francisco and wear flowers in our hair and get stoned forever.

The room's always dark, Muzzie snores and talks in her sleep and I lay awake hearing all the night noises. I never knew there were so many. I don't want to take reds anymore because they make me stupid the next morning when I'm at work. I wonder what changed—they never made me feel stupid at school.

David and my dad don't get along. They try to avoid each other, but the house isn't that big. When they get started the yelling goes on and on and on. Little Michelle always cries. Shirley and I hide in our childhood room together, tell the baby it's all okay, that nobody will ever hurt her.

I try not to cry along with her. I've learned that tears don't help anything; never did.

Just when I think everything will turn out fine, that I'll have enough money saved to start college, I mess up at work. My boss calls me into his office and tells me that he's disappointed. He thought I was a decent young lady. Thought he could trust me. I don't know what he's talking about. I can't think of anything I've done to make him say that. He holds out a round flat disk and I realize my birth controls pills must have fallen out of my purse.

He drops the disk on his desk and tells me to gather my personal belonging and leave. He doesn't employ my kind of girl. I reach for my pills and he takes them back, asks me if my father knows I have them.

I tell him our family doctor prescribes them. He shakes his head slowly, telling me again what a disappointment I am to him. I hold out my hand for the pills. He drops them in his trashcan and tells me to leave.

It's Friday and I don't know how I'm going to get more pills by morning.

I don't tell anyone I've lost my job. I leave every morning at the same time and drive to the public library—spend all day there. School's still a month away and I feel more alone than ever.

I think about the scholarships I applied for and am so afraid they'll think I'm no good, just like my boss did—that the whole dream of going to college and becoming a teacher is like all my other dreams ... nothing at all. I blow all my money on mescaline and reds. Start each morning with mescaline. End each night with reds.

I'm lost and I know it.

Choices Made or Stolen
August 1970

Suggested listening:
Single—*Spinning Wheel*, Blood, Sweat and Tears

Griffith Park is the coolest place in the world. I love the large mellow meadow with gentle swelling knolls surrounding an old fashion Carousel. *Catch a Painted pony let the spinning wheel turn* ... The song, sweet, like the day, runs through my mind.

I come here every Saturday. My dad doesn't watch me as closely as he did before. Doesn't even ask where I'm going every Saturday morning. I drop Muzzie off at work in the morning and head for Griffith Park. It's not very far from Covina. But it's a whole different galaxy once I'm out of the car and grooving with real freaks in L.A.

I lean back into the arms of Alex, a long, bronzed freak from back east somewhere, who ran away from home and didn't stop until he reached the Pacific Ocean. He said he hitch-hiked all the way and found that people everywhere are groovy. I think he's groovy. I met him the first time I came here.

Ken works every weekend, so I'm free to hang out wherever I like. And I like Griffith Park. Alex is always in the meadow without a shirt, his long blonde hair loose and glowing in the sunlight that bathes the meadow, making it look like an impressionist painting.

Alex hangs with a group of older freaks that are really cool and talk with me like I'm one of them. We talk all day about art and books and music—share our food and stash and acid, like a real family.

Alex and I have been hanging together since that first Saturday. Nobody back home seems to miss me. Shirley and David found a place to rent way out in Baldwin Park. Kathy's into Frank so bad I hardly ever see her, and Ken is starting to be a real downer; always lecturing me about dropping too much acid, my skirts being too short, my jeans too low cut. One thing I don't need is another father.

Alex puts a joint in my mouth, his hand cupped around it so anyone passing won't know it's a joint. I suck hard, sip the air and hold my breath.

I think it's out, Alex sighs. He shifts and I hear the click of his zippo lighter, just like the one my dad uses. He tells me it was his dad's. That he liberated it on his way out the door, along with $5,000 his dad kept in a lock box in the bottom drawer of his desk.

Alex has good stash, and even takes me out for food before we go to his pad and make love. I don't eat much, but he does. He eats everything I leave and everything else on the table, bread, crackers, everything. I don't eat meat anymore, not after reading a book about industrial animal farms earlier in the summer. I threw up and swore never to eat another dead animal the rest of my life.

Try again. Alex sticks the joint between my lips and rubs his thumb along my chin.

I smile and suck hard. That's a good girl, he says and leans over me, puts his lips to mine. I let the smoke rise from my lungs and push it into his mouth. He breathes it in and then pushes it back to me and me to him again. It's a ritual of sorts, sharing the high, sharing the dream of being one.

He lets the smoke ease its way out between his lips as he looks out over me at the park. This whole scene is starting to be a real bummer, he says and takes the joint.

My nice, peaceful high takes a dive. I sit up and cross my legs, try to act like I don't really care; look around the crowded meadow and think I've never seen anything so groovy in my whole life.

A bunch of us are heading up to Canada next week. Why don't

you come along?

Canada? Wow, that's cool ... Why Canada? I try to sound like my heart isn't breaking; like I'm cool with anything, especially change which is supposed to be cool. But I've never been a big fan of change, it fucks everything up, even when everything's already fucked up.

Marcus and me both turned eighteen last week and we have no intention of ending our days in Nam. So we're heading to Canada.

Will they just let you in? Let you stay?

Fuck yeah! Everyone knows that. Where have you been? Oh yeah ... Covina. I forgot for a minute you live in the squarest town in the universe.

Marcus and the two girls lying next to him laugh. I blush and let my hair fall in front of my face.

You can come along if you want, he offers.

How long will you stay?

How long is this fucking war gonna last?

Long time passing, Marcus sings out and Alex laughs kinda sad.

A long fucking time as I see it from here, he adds and takes another hit.

I'm still in school.

The Man won't teach you anything you need to know, he tells me and I remember he had dropped out. He kisses me and blows smoke into my lungs and I wish he wasn't leaving.

Come with me, he sighs. We could make it together up there. I really dig you and you don't have anything keeping you here. Do you? He looks into my eyes and I know he doesn't know me at all if he has to ask.

I'm not eighteen until December. You'd get busted for all kinds of shit if they catch us.

He sits up and looks out over the meadow. You want to stay here with your old man the Narc and your mother the drunk?

It's not them. I told you, I'm still in school. And when I say it I realize that I want to be in school—want to go to college and become a teacher—think I stand a chance—think that this time the dream might come true.

He leans forward and kisses me. Is staying in school better than that? he asks.

But we both know the answer. I grab my bag and stand up. He doesn't try to stop me. I walk away through the freaks and hippies and teeny-boppers and on past the Carousel with the little kids all excited about riding the big shiny horses.

I realize I'll really miss the park.

Legal Tender
December 22, 1970

Suggested listening:
Single—*White Rabbit*, Jefferson Airplane

It's supposed to be special, my eighteenth birthday. Shirley and David want us to come over to their place. I don't like it much, it's old and dirty and damp and smells like my sleeping bag when I get back from Big Sur.

Muzzie stopped drinking about a month ago, so she's all excited about doing something special too. I wish she was drinking so there wouldn't be a fuss. Hope to hell my dad won't be home until after we head off to Shirley's. He's working with a man who trains attack dogs, beautiful German Shepherds. I wish we had one to keep Laddie company. Dad says they aren't good family dogs because they're always on duty, don't know how to "stand-down" as he puts it. He told a story to his poker buddies last month about one female that his boss keeps at home for protection. Lady, the dog, was sleeping one afternoon when the boss's kids came home from school. They surprised Lady and both kids needed stiches, the girl almost lost her eye. I still wish we could get one to keep Laddie company.

I climb out of bed, stretch and wonder if anything has actually changed overnight. I'm still in high school and living at home, so I still have a curfew, homework, chores around the house including ironing all my dad's white shirts and starching his white handkerchiefs. God how I hate those handkerchiefs! Spray, press flat, fold in half, press flat, fold in half again and press flat. I feel like the Greek King, Sisyphus, pushing a fucking rock up a hill only to have it roll back down … forever and ever and ever.

I go to the bathroom, comb my hair, wash my face, look at myself in the mirror and wonder if anything is different. Can't think of a thing. Wonder why anyone has to celebrate my fucking birthday, wish they'd all go away and leave me to sleep the day and night away. Sleep away the day that's supposed to make a difference, but won't.

I hear my dad's car chug into the driveway. It's a Ford Cortina he bought thinking it would be less obvious on stakeouts than the Galaxy 500. Not that he has that many stakeouts anymore, doesn't have much work at all. The car backfires and keeps sputtering even after it's turned off. It needs work, but since he left the State and lost his private-eye business, he doesn't even have enough money to buy new handkerchiefs. There're holes in the ones I iron but he won't let me throw them away.

The front door slams and I wish I wasn't stuck in the bathroom, know he'll catch me when I cross the hall. Wish I'd gone over to Kathy's, even if Frank's living there now that they're married. It couldn't be any worse over there than it is here.

Punk. You home? My dad calls from the dining room.

Yes, I lean out of the bathroom and shout down the long hall.

Come on out here.

Shit! Shit! Shit! I silently scream. I pull my hair back in a low ponytail and walk down the hall trying to figure out what the fuck I did wrong this time. Run through all my chores and am sure I did them all.

He's standing on the other side of the tall breakfast bar that divides the kitchen and dining room. It's the Birthday Girl, he says and waves for me to come closer.

I tuck a loose strand of hair behind my ear and study the patterns in the linoleum.

Come on over here, he says a little louder.

I look up and see he's sitting on one of the high swivel stools, pointing to the one next to his. I really want to be at Kathy's now. Hell, I'd take Shirley's house, smell and all, rather than sit next to him. But there's no way out.

I wander over, slow enough to put off the inevitable, but not so slow it'll piss him off.

Here ya go, he says and pats the seat of the stool next to him.

I tuck another stray hair behind my ear and slide onto the stool, balance the balls of my feet on the metal rail that runs around in a circle half way down. Wonder what the hell he could want. He doesn't seem mad, even maybe a little happy.

He whips out his pack of Viceroys and taps the bottom. Two cigarettes slide out of the jagged opening at one end. He takes one and hands it to me. I shake my head, not knowing what he wants.

Go on. Take it. You're eighteen today and I want to be the one to give you your first cigarette. It's legal now for you to smoke and I want to make sure you know how.

I try to keep my mouth from dropping open, but it's not easy. I can't look at him, know he'll see the utter disbelief in my eyes. I sneak a look up through my eyelashes, trying to figure out if he really believes I've never smoked a cigarette in my life. I can tell he does, and stopping myself from laughing in his face is harder than anything I've ever done.

I smile sweetly and wait for him to talk me through lighting up and inhaling. I don't cough and he's proud of me.

We finish the cigarette together, me and my Narc father, there at the breakfast bar—and I realize that being straight around my dad is sometimes trippier than tripping.

1971 in the news

- The population of the United States is 207.66 million
- The national debt is $398.1 billion
- Average Cost of new house is $28,300
- Average income per year is $6,497
- Average monthly rent is $150
- Minimum wage is $1.60 per hour
- A gallon of gas costs $0.40
- First class postage is $0.08
- Movie ticket costs $1.50
- *Patton* wins Best Picture
- *Bridge Over Troubled Waters* wins Best Song and Best Album
- Jim Morrison dies of an apparent drug overdose in Paris at age 27
- The 26th Amendment to the US constitution is ratified lowering the voting age to 18
- Prisoners riot and take hostages at Attica Prison in New York, resulting in the death of 10 hostages and 29 inmates
- Charles Manson and three of his followers receive the death penalty for the Tate/LaBianca murders
- Australia and New Zealand pull all troops out of Vietnam
- China is admitted to the United Nations
- Harris public opinion poll claims that 60% of Americans are against the war in Vietnam

- ❖ The New York Times begins to publish sections of the Pentagon Papers showing the US Government had been lying to Americans about the Vietnam War. It states that "... the Johnson Administration had systematically lied, not only to the public but also to Congress, about a subject of transcendent national interest and significance."

- ❖ Greenpeace is formally established

- ❖ Cigarette advertising is banned on TV

- ❖ National Public Radio (NPR) broadcasts for the first time in April 1971

The house on Nearglen in 2010. Our bedroom is on the right.

Charter Oak High School, 2010

Shirley and me, 1970

Laddie at Nearglen, 1970

Me in my peacoat, Shirley, and a friend, 1969.

1971 Shield Dedication

The yearbook staff dedicates this volume of the Shield to Mr. David Sundstrand. He has earned this recognition by conveying to those around him the idea that he really cares about his work and his students. As depicted on these pages, he is a person of many moods. Although he is completely serious about his job, he uses humor to its best advantage. To reciprocate for all of his efforts, we dedicate this book to one who has dedicated himself.

Mr. Sundstrand, a teacher who made a difference.
Reprinted from the 1971 Charter Oak High School *Shield*.

My high school graduation photo, 1970

Muzzie, me, and Condie, 1971

1971

Me, Shirley, and Conde, 1971

Me in one of my longer dresses, 1971

Me, Muzzie, and Shirley. Survivors.
San Jose, Calif., 1984

The Game of Life
May 1971

Suggested listening:
Single—*Venus in Furs*, Velvet Underground

When does the game become real?

When you play so long and so hard you forget it's only a game. When you don't have to remember your lines anymore, you just make them up as you go. When you tell yourself that you know the difference between the truth and the lies, but you don't. When you know the game has to end, but you can't give it up because it's become everything you are—in the game, in the lie, in your life.

When does the game become real? When you play so long and so hard you forget it's only a game.

So you want to be a teacher now?

You want to play a new game?

Or is this time the one time that's real?

How could you ever tell? You've played too long and too hard to know.

Shifting Sands
June 1971

Suggested listening:
Single—*Remember*, John Lennon

Kathy and I get dressed at her house for old times' sake. My gown is too big and Kathy's too small. Her belly is so huge I think she's going to fall over every time she takes a step. She's bigger than Shirley ever was with Michelle. We put our caps on for each other. I have to sit on the bed for Kathy to reach my head.

You grow more? She asks.

I shrug. Don't know … maybe.

She drops to the bed next to me. Want a hit of hash … for old time sake?

Is it okay? I ask and point to her stomach. I mean with the baby and all.

She puts both hands on her belly and sighs, Shit! I don't care. I'm so fucking sick of being pregnant. It's not like everyone says. They say I'm supposed to be beautiful and glowing and content. I hate it! I hate it every single day!

I put an arm around her and she lays her head on my shoulder. I wish none of this had happened, she sniffs. I don't want a baby. Shit, shit, shit! She bursts into tears and I hold her and rock her and don't have any words of comfort.

335

I know they're out there in the bleachers, Muzzie, Ken, Shirley, David, baby Michelle, and my dad. Watching me sit in the hot sun in my blue cap and gown. And I wonder what Shirley's thinking. I wonder if she wishes she'd graduated, wishes she'd never had that joint in her purse, never been sent to San Francisco, never dropped all that acid and smoked all that pot—wonder if she wishes she never had Michelle, just like Kathy wishes she'd never gotten pregnant.

I don't think anything would be different, no matter what I did when I was young. I'd still be here, graduating high school and heading to college, having a steady boyfriend, living at home, trying to get a job that will allow me move out—don't know how it could be any different.

My row stands and we walk up the wood stairs, wait for our names to be called, take our diplomas and shake hands with the Principal, and walk away … walk away from our youth. Become adults in an instant.

Pictures are snapped, backs slapped, the cheerleaders and jocks head off to the gym for some rally Kathy and I weren't invited to. We take our robes back to the locker room and make sure our names are checked off the list. We hug each other and swear we'll go see a movie before she has the baby—know we probably won't.

Everyone is milling around waiting for me, wanting to do something special on my special day. I just want to go home. Shirley and David finally take Michelle and head back to their place. Dad opens the car doors for Muzzie and me, waits to close them and then walks around to his door, honking his nose in his starched white handkerchief and I can't believe he's actually crying out here in public. I scoot down in the back seat and hope to hell nobody sees.

We get back to the house and I head for my room, but Muzzie calls my name. What? I turn around and hope she doesn't want to take more pictures.

I have to talk with your father and I'd like you to be there.

Why?

Please, is all she says. She turns her back on me and walks into the kitchen where I can hear my dad blowing his nose and running water for coffee.

Our baby girl's all grown up, he says when I walk in the kitchen. Muzzie just stands there staring at her hands and I wish she'd just get it said, whatever it is, so I can go lay down before Ken picks me up. We're headed to Big Sur for my graduation night. The rest of the graduating class is going to Disneyland, as if it's some big deal.

I walk over to the breakfast bar and sit on one of the high stools, waiting for Muzzie to say something. My dad turns the water off and everything is silent, like the calm before a storm. My stomach does a flip-flop and I want to leave, know something terrible is about to happen.

Muzzie slowly opens her purse, the one that she's carried all day and matches her dress and shoes. She reaches inside and pulls out a thick envelope and hands it to my dad.

What's this, he asks, and turns it over, breaks the seal and pulls out a bunch of paper.

It's divorce papers, Condie. Donna, you are my witness that your father has been served.

Her words echo and I'm not sure I'm hearing them right. My dad must be having the same problem because he's shaking his head slowly, shuffling through the papers. He looks up at her and says, You can't mean it.

I most certainly do, Muzzie answers and motions for me to come to her.

I can't move, can't believe she's doing this. After all these years, it can't be true.

My dad what I'm thinking, This can't be true. Then asks, Why?

Muzzie laughs, a cold ugly laugh, and motions for me again.

I get up and walk to her side. She tells me, Go wait for me in the car. You don't need anything; our suitcases are already in the trunk. Go on now, she tells me and gives me a little push towards the door. Wait for me in the car.

I don't move, don't trust my dad not to hurt her, hear myself say so out loud.

Don't worry. Your father won't ever hurt me again. I promise you that.

And I know she's right, know she's finally safe.

The Midway
August 1971

Suggested listening:
Single—*Baba O'Riley*, The Who

The County Fair is a yearly ritual. The whole family used to go when I was little. When I started high school Shirley, Sandy, Kathy, and I would drop acid and trip at the fair. But now Sandy's moved away to Ventura, Shirley has David and Michelle, and Kathy has Frank. I suppose I have Ken, but he's always working or playing some piano gig, so I'm alone come the weekend.

The summer wears on and I decide that I don't need anyone but me to trip at the County Fair. I score some killer acid from Eric. I've never told Shirley I still see him, get most of my dope from him. He's living with Barbara now and they have a new baby together. They seem happy with each other, though I'm never there very long. Barbara doesn't say much to me, never asks me to sit down or anything; not since I blew it by leaving little Christopher crying upstairs while I was making out with Ken downstairs. I can't really blame her now that we have Michelle. I'd do the same thing if some stupid kid left her crying.

I drive over the Pomona pass and down into the neighboring valley, through a maze of dirt parking lots, following glowing sticks of fire and cute guys waiving me on to my very own parking space. Feel like the world is spinning just as it should this sultry summer night.

I leave my leather jacket in the car and take off into the surrounding brush to smoke a joint before venturing onto the Midway—the only place at the fair I ever go.

The barkers keep yelling for me to come on over. I keep walking, digging on the lights and sights and noises—big kids and grown-ups screaming on the fast rides, little kids all excited about being in a toy airplane whirling a few feet off the ground.

I realize the whole world is just a carnival, complete with fun houses that distort everything we see, roller coasters and tilt-a-whirls that throw us off balance, and barkers that tempt us to try our luck at winning a prize we didn't know we even wanted.

There's a bird what could put her ring round me bott'l anytime.

I look around for the British accent. 'Ere littal chirpy. I look over at a ring toss booth, one of many on the Midway. There's a blonde with wavy hair that could pass for Robert Plant of Led Zeppelin, except he's too stocky. But that doesn't stop me from wandering closer.

He leans back against the side of the booth and smiles at me, raises a bushy eyebrow. Care for a toss, Lass? Bet you'd luv to put a ring 'round me bott'l.

I like him. Like that fact he's so out there. Doesn't hurt that he looks like Plant. I tuck my thumbs in the belt loops on my hip-hugger and say, Oh, I don't know ... I lean over the low divide and look intently at the rows of bottles, then glance sideways at him. Looks like an awfully small bottle from where I'm standing.

He whoops and claps his hands together, passes me three rings and starts yelling at the top of his lungs, Come 'n watch the lass ring me bott'l! Three tries and she wins the prize of her choice. Come watch the lass ring me bott'ls!

He draws a crowd and I know I'm red all over, but I can't back down now. I take one ring and turn to face the crowd of Looky-loos and kiss the ring. For luck, I say and turn back. I've always been good at this game. I land the ring dead center around the back bottle. The crowd erupts in applause, I blush again.

Sure'n th'lass 'tis lucky, but she'd need t'lead a charmed life t'make anothu', he calls out to the crowd.

Not when the bottles are this small, I shout and flip my hair back over my shoulder. The crowd laughs. I fire off the next two rings one right after the other and both land solid around the bottles. The crowd erupts and the carnie bows deep from the waist with a theatrical flourish of his hands.

People crowd the stand waving dollar bills at the carnie and I realize I didn't pay for the toss. I hold out a dollar bill. He slides his index finger down the side of his nose and walks over to me, slips a hand around my bare waist and whispers in my ear, th' throws on me. Come back at closin' and I'll give ya your prize.

I step to the side and watch the carnie, who has a big-ass grin on his face, take all their money and hand out rings. I drift to the back of the crowd and feel strangely excited by the whole exchange. Wonder if I will drop back by at closing—doubt that I will.

The bar looks like someplace my parents would go, dark red, tucked upholstered booths, worn out waitresses that look like their feet hurt, Elvis on the jukebox. But they served me hard liquor without a second glance—since I'm only eighteen, it's a great place to be.

The carnie says he comes here every night after the midway closes; thought I might need a drink as much as he does. He orders two Drambuie on the rocks without asking me. Tastes like cough syrup, but I down it and lean over to kiss him. I'm losing my nerve but don't want to chicken out now that I've come this far.

The motel rents by the week. He makes sure no one's in the hall and slips me into his room. It's tidy, bed made, no clothes on the floor, no take-out boxes on the night stands. He tells me to make myself comfortable and goes to take a leak. I kneel on the bed facing the bathroom, wondering what the fuck I'm doing here. I don't even know the guy, other than he looks and sounds like Plant, and is different than anyone I've ever known.

He comes out with his shirt off and I catch my breath. He makes Plant look like a little girl. His chest is covered with curly blonde hair and bulges with muscles—definitely different from all the druggies I hang with. His waist looks narrow in comparison and I wonder why I thought he was stocky. I really want him to make love to me—no, to be honest, I want to fuck him.

He comes close and lifts my hair away from my face with both hands and studies me for a brief moment. You could do nice, he says. A lit'al makeup an'some curls, I could put ya out, easy.

Put me out? I ask, wondering if I should maybe leave.

He drops my hair, tells me not to listen to anything he says. Then he kisses me—I don't care what he says after that kiss.

We share my last joint. The acid is long worn off and I have a headache from the booze. He swigs at a bottle of Jack Daniels between puffs. The smell makes me sick to my stomach. I wish he wasn't drinking because I'm hoping we can fuck again before morning and I can't kiss him if he smells like Muzzie.

Stay put, suga', he tells me and rolls out of bed, shrugs into his jeans. I have a quick call t'make and I'll be right back t'finish what we started. He leans over and I turn my head so his kiss lands on my cheek. Oh so it's like that? Ye'll change ye toon when I get back, he says and smiles that killer smile of his. He pulls his hair back and I see the tight muscles of his chest and stomach and figure he's probably right.

He closes the door and I'm alone in the room. I hear the clink of coins in the payphone down the hallway and wonder who he's calling at this time of night. I wrap the sheet around me and walk to the door, pull it open a crack.

Yeah, baby, I miss you too. No, just some rides broke down and I had to work late.

I shake my head a little and wonder if I'm hearing wrong—but no, the carnie's lost his British accent. I close the door and wonder who he's trying to fool, me or "baby?" Know it's me. Know I'm just another ring toss—one of many games played along the Midway.

And that's alright with me—nothing wrong with playing the game as long as you know who the players are.

Stairway to Heaven
September 13, 1971

Suggested listening:
Single—*Stairway to Heaven*, Led Zeppelin

The morning light doesn't penetrate the leaves of the big walnut tree outside my window. My room in the attic is dark and cold. It fits my mood. The first week of college was tougher than I dreamed possible.

I'm working part-time at a book depot, every afternoon from three to six, taking a full load of classes, and helping around the house here 'cause Muzzie started drinking again and doesn't do anything all day long but stay in her half of the attic, passed out.

And now I have to put in more hours with tutors 'cause I'm so far behind everyone else, especially in math—I remember being so good at math in junior high—wonder why I'm not anymore.

I slip on my jeans and a guy's sleeveless white t-shirt—standard issue for college. The first day I got all dressed up only to find most girls wearing either long hippie dresses or jeans and t-shirts. I hate long hippie dresses.

No one else is up yet. I stuff my arms into my pea coat, duck out the back door, and head for my car on the far side of the parking lot that sits between the big front house Shirley and David rent and the single units that form a horseshoe behind us. I hear a car door open and look around. Ken's Cougar is parked on the street. I can't believe he's waiting for me at six in the morning.

You're up early, he says and slips an arm around my waist.

I shrug away. What are you doing here?

Wanted to see you.

At six in the fucking morning? I turn and walk over to my Karmann Ghia, a car Ken found and fixed up for me when I graduated in June.

I never seem to catch you at home any other time, he says to my back.

That's because I'm either going to school or working. I don't have time to do anything else.

Not even return my phone calls?

I stop and turn to face him. Look. I'm sorry, but this whole college scene is heavy.

I work and go to school, too, he tells me. Doesn't mean I don't still want to see you. He slips an arm around my waist and draws me close. Doesn't mean I don't miss you. He leans down and kisses me.

I don't want to hurt his feelings, especially when I'm not sure about my own feelings, so I don't pull away. He stops kissing me and looks pleased with himself.

Listen, you can't be hanging out all night and ambushing me on my way to school.

Why not? He smiles at me.

I twist out of his arms. It's weird. You're starting to act like my old man. It's freaking me out. I slip the key in the door and wrench it open. It creaks and groans. I stop and look back at Ken with a hand on my hip. If you have so much free time, why don't you fix this fucking door like you promised? It could wake the dead.

I just might do that for you, if you do something for me.

What? I don't really want to know, but figure it can't hurt to ask—might be something easy, like a blowjob.

Go to a concert with me tonight.

Where? Who's playing?

Led Zeppelin, he says and digs two tickets out of his coat pocket.

Show's sold out, but Bear scored these for me.

Zeppelin isn't playing anywhere tonight.

Nowhere around here, they aren't.

He's looking even smugger and I'm starting to get pissed off. Stop playing around. You don't have tickets to Zeppelin!

He hands me the tickets. I look at them and can't believe what I'm seeing. Berkeley? Are you outta your mind? Tonight in Berkeley?

He jumps in the air, spins half way around, lands on both feet and then leans against my car. It'll be their last show in the States on this tour. I hear they're gonna play some new stuff that isn't released yet.

He has me and he knows it. Led Zeppelin is my favorite band. He knows I wouldn't miss this for the world. But Berkeley? I whine and slam the noisy door closed. I can't miss school.

He looks over his shoulder, a slight smile playing along his lips. Come on! He turns and takes my hands. It'll be like it used to be. Remember last year when we drove down to San Diego for Zeppelin then spent the night at the beach?

I lean against the car and look at the tickets and nod. Okay. But I can't stay overnight. I can't miss any classes. I'm already so far behind I can't believe it.

Ken whoops and I shush him. You'll wake up the whole fucking neighborhood.

Go grab your stuff. If we leave now we can take the coast route and stop in Big Sur for lunch.

I start for the house and stop, turn around and stuff my hands back in my coat pockets. Fuck!

What? Ken walks towards me.

I can't go.

Why?

No. I mean, not this morning. That's why I'm headed in so early. I have my first session with my German tutor. If I cancel on him he'll probably dump me, and I really need him!

Whaddaya mean? You were raised in Germany. You spoke German till you came to the States. That's why you took German—

you already speak it!

Yeah. I came here when I was six years old.

So?

So I speak German like a fucking six-year-old. This is a college class. And my teacher's a fucking Nazi!

'Scuse me for asking. Ken throws his hands up and takes a step back. You need to chill! He grins and adds, A Zeppelin concert would make you forget all this bullshit.

I turn back around and stomp my boot on the asphalt. I can't fucking believe I have to have another tutor. And this one sounds like a real square.

Why? Wha'd he do?

When I called on Friday to make sure where we're supposed to meet, he answered the phone, Preacher here.

Preacher?

Yeah, and he sounds old. He's probably some bald-headed church freak who's tutoring students so he can convert them to Calvinism. God. I hope he doesn't start trying to convert me or anything.

Just drop him and let's take off now!

I can't. He's the only German tutor available and I'm not failing any classes my first semester … Not ever for that matter. I plan on getting straight A's and more scholarships so I can get the fuck outta Mount Sac and into a real college. Christ, I hate all this fucking bullshit!

Come on. Blow it off. What's one day, one fucking German tutor? You'll find another guy who'll teach you to say Ich bein ein Berliner. He slides an arm around my waist. I'm tempted.

Stop it! I slap his hand and throw open the car door, not caring about the noise. I'll meet you at your place at eleven. We can still make the concert.

Barely, Ken leans back against the bumper and puffs out his cheeks, lets out a long breath. Okay, have it your way. He pushes off and walks to his car. See you at eleven, he calls to me without looking back. If you're late, I'm leaving without you. I'm sure I can find someone in Berkeley who wants to see Led Zeppelin.

I flip the bird to his back and climb in my Ghia. Think to myself, Fucking Nazis everywhere I look!

I make it to Ken's around 11:30. Knew he'd wait. I settle back in the leather bucket-seat and start to drift off before we're out of Covina.

Ken taps my leg and holds out a small tin-foiled roll of whites. Want some?

I take one to hold off passing out before we're over the Grapevine.

Only one? Ken asks. You look wiped-out.

I want to sleep once we're over the Grapevine.

What is it with you and the Grapevine? I'll drive safe. If you want to sleep, sleep.

I know. It's just that I've never seen it in the daytime when I wasn't tripping.

What's to see? he sniffs and tunes the radio to KRLA.

I take another sip of my Double Cola and lean back, start drifting to Jefferson Airplane's *Today*.

Ken wakes me as we start climbing. I sit forward, watching everything swish past, wishing he'd slow down around the curves. But I know better than to say anything, only makes him drive faster.

The Grapevine is bleaker than I thought it would be. Dry scrub grass and grey rock outcrops tumble down the hillsides, butting up against the asphalt. I shake my head and sit back wishing I'd left the Grapevine to how I remembered it when Kathy and I went to San Francisco in her dad's car last summer. I remember tiny rivulets of sparkling water flowing through emerald green tufts of grass and shiny rocks of purple and gold as we sped past them—I was stoned on acid, but hoped it wouldn't make a difference—hoped when I was straight everything would be exactly like I remembered it from that trip.

We break out through the final pass and begin our descent. I'm disappointed to see a thin layer of grey smog spread out over the valley as far as the eye can see. I chalk it up to another encounter with reality.

Ken clears his throat and asks hesitantly, Could you ... uh. Would you?

I turned eighteen at the end of December. My consensual sexual experiences are limited to Ken, Alex, and the carnie, but I already know what that husky lowering of the voice and the vague pleading tone that goes with it, means. Know that a blowjob, which is easy enough for me, goes a long way. And judging by the response from Ken, I must be getting pretty good at it.

Sure, I tell him. As I lean over the empty space between our seats and unzip his jeans, I wonder if all men are the same, and it occurs to me just how limited my experience really is. For the briefest instant my mind flashes on my German tutor, Preacher, who I met just a few hours ago. He wasn't at all what I had thought. Pretty good looking actually, with thick, wavy, black hair down past his shoulders and green eyes that look younger than the rest of him. I figure him to be around thirty and wonder why he's just now in Junior College. He walked me to my car and, after a few false starts, asked me if I'd like to go for a ride on his BMW motorcycle.

Another time, perhaps, I told him, and thought to myself, It might be fun, once I get to know him better.

Ken stops about an hour outside Berkeley and buys a six pack of beer for him, two Double Colas and some beef jerky for me. I offer him a cap of mescaline, but he doesn't want to trip when he has to drive home. I drop both his and mine and down it with one of his beers.

We pull into Berkeley with plenty of time left before the show, which doesn't seem possible, the drive up was so long. The one white hyped me just enough not to sleep well. My mind buzzed the whole way. I'm so very tired of thinking, tired of trying to decide what I should do, what I want to do. I hope the double dose of mescaline will either bring me answers or make the questions go away—either is better than these endless mind trips about what is what and what is not.

We wait in line with freaks and local college kids and I wonder if anyone else traveled as far as we did to be here. Two guys right in front of us light a joint and cup it in their hands. Everyone starts looking around once the smoke carries the undeniable aroma of Maui-Wowie up and down the line. They don't share and I think the times they are a'changin'. Last year they would have been passing the joint to at least the folks in front and back of them.

We find our way to our seats way in the back, but that doesn't matter, no one ever stays in their seats at a Zeppelin concert. The first pulses of mescaline appear and then vanish, waiver and surge in time with the music and light show that precedes Zeppelin. I nudge Ken and motion towards the stage as soon as the lights go down. He follows behind me as I wind my way through the crowd and squeeze in close with others that left their seats—wait for Zeppelin to make this night special.

I push my way up the aisle, out through the glass doors, into the relative quiet of the stone courtyard that surrounds the theatre. Page is still screeching a bow across his guitar strings, and Plant is droning on and on like someone too drunk to come but not willing to give up trying.

My head is pounding and I can't stand another second of what should have been the perfect concert. But Zeppelin isn't Zeppelin tonight. Or maybe the double shot of mescaline showed me something I didn't want to see—me. Me dancing and tripping when all I felt like doing was running. I looked around and everyone looked phony, like they were trying too hard to be freaks, heads swinging with the sound, eyes eating Plant alive in his low cut jeans and bare chest, strutting and preening, his dick bulging in his pants.

I flash back to Morrison at the Shrine Auditorium all those years ago—back to when I was young and thought life would always treat me fair, thought I'd always be safe, thought I'd always be able to do just what I wanted—a lifetime ago.

Now Morrison is dead, and Hendrix, and Joplin—and here I am watching Plant prance around like he's the new Jim Morrison. I want to go back in there and scream at the top of my lungs that Plant isn't Morrison and no matter how hard Page humps his guitar, he can never be Hendrix—but I know I won't because none of it matters and none of it makes any sense anymore.

I take a few steps along the flat concrete slab, with its squares and triangle patterns, and look up at the night sky. I can just see the twinkle of a few scattered stars. The brightest of them, the one that is faintly blue and set off by itself from the others, I know is called the Dog Star, or so Terry told me before he died.

Is this all there is? I think. Is this it? Rock concerts and drugs? Ken? I look at the stars and remember another night, in the desert, when I thought they would all blink out of existence if I couldn't see them. I'd run through the night to save the stars. Now I know they'll always be there, but I won't. I could blink out of existence and the stars wouldn't even care. I saved the stars once, years ago. Now it's time to save me.

I think about winning all three scholarships, and Mr. Sundstrand telling me I have a quick wit, and a good mind. A part of me wants to believe him. I want to be a teacher like him—someone who cares, someone who helps kids, someone who makes a difference.

Soft, haunting chords drift out of the theatre, chords of a song I've never heard before. I'm tempted to go back inside, but I know if I do I'll be lost. Know that tonight my dreams have changed for good and all. Know I could never go back in that concert and do what I'm supposed to do. I wonder if that's why I took two caps of mescaline—to break on through and this time find myself on the other side.

I look around and realize the Sixties are gone, long gone. Realize I lived through them and have come out of them with ... what? We thought we could change the world, but in the end the world changed us.

I look up at the sky and the stars. Mr. Sundstrand's words come back to me: Allow for the possibility of change and it just might happen. I begin to feel excited about my prospects, about all the possibilities now that I'm not a kid anymore.

On the street a stream of bikers run the red light, their bikes roaring through the night, drowning out Plant and Page and Morrison and Hendrix, and all my fallen heroes.

I flash on Preacher and think, the times they are a changing—that maybe I will take that motorcycle ride after all.

Author's Notes

Suggested listening:
Single—*Slip Inside This House*, 13th Floor Elevators

The events recounted in *House of the Moon* took place more than forty-five years ago, so I have tried to capture the essence of what was said, if not the exact words. However, Jimi Hendrix's words, "You do not belong in this house with these men," are as clear to me as if he'd said them yesterday. The same is true for Jim Morrison's ramblings.

I have changed the names of most characters to protect their privacy. The exceptions are my family members and anyone notable or famous.

Several years after their divorce in 1971, Muzzie and Condie became friends. Condie would drop by with groceries purchased at a discount from the nearby military base and they would drink coffee and chat amicably for hours—something I never saw them do when they were married.

Although Muzzie successfully overcame her alcohol addiction she smoked herself to death in 1996 at the age of seventy-three. She continued smoking right up until her last day, saying that since she was dying anyway, she might as well enjoy herself. She went out with a smile at Shirley's home, surrounded by her daughters and granddaughters.

Condie remarried, and lived happily for several years with his new wife, Thelma, who died of cancer in 1984. To relieve her pain and suffering Condie procured illegal marijuana from his former buddies in the narcotics squad, a fact I razed him about unmercifully.

Thanks to my husband's efforts, I reconciled with my dad in 1979 and we enjoyed a good relationship the last ten years of his life. Condie was a heavy smoker, too. And while he didn't die of lung cancer, he died of complications due to smoking in 1991 at the age of seventy-three. Shirley had stopped speaking to him years before and refused to visit him in the hospital. I was with him at the end.

It was not until late in his life that I realized Condie suffered from post-traumatic stress syndrome, induced by years serving behind German lines during WWII; then working intelligence in Korea; and the many unspeakable things he did to maintain his cover and procure information to save the lives of Allied soldiers. He also never recovered from Terry's death, blaming himself for having called in favors that resulted in Terry's counter-intelligence assignment in Korea, instead of being sent to Viet Nam. I never gave him Terry's message that it wasn't his fault.

Shirley married "David" in 1969, and had two wonderful daughters, Michelle and Heleena. She returned to school in 1972 and received her high school diploma when she was twenty-three years old. She divorced David in 1976. She married and divorced three more times before deciding to live her own life, on her own.

She was instrumental in establishing the first domestic workers union in the country, SEIU local 585 in San Jose, California, and fought valiantly on behalf of disenfranchised people throughout her adult life. She was also a heavy smoker and succumbed to lung cancer while I was completing *House of the Moon*. She died at her youngest daughter's home in Hemet, California. She was sixty-three.

"Kathy" married while in her senior year in high school and almost immediately became pregnant. I have not heard from her in more than forty years. I hope she is doing well.

"Ken" and I went through a series of break-ups. The first time was his idea. He wanted to "play the field." He moved to Hawaii, but after six months of not getting laid, he begged me to take him back. I don't know why I did. As with Kathy, I have not heard from, or about, him in more than forty years.

I have been asked, "How did you survive?" I honestly don't know. I would say that knowing my mother and sister loved me kept me moving forward. They were imperfect, but their love was unconditional. I also credit my high school English teachers, first "Mrs. Andrews," and then Mr. Sundstrand (his real name), for pulling me out of the tailspin I was in by recognizing my potential and caring enough to help me to fulfill that potential.

I had always said that I'd stop taking acid if I ever had a bad trip. After the Hells Angels' party recounted in *Barking Mad*, I did exactly that. Although I continued doing other drugs for another eight years, I never dropped acid or mescaline again.

During my junior year in college, I returned to Charter Oak High to complete my teacher's training, just three years after I had graduated. Some students who had been freshmen when I was a senior, remembered me and couldn't believe I had "changed sides" and was now working for the establishment. Mrs. Andrews was still teaching there. I sincerely apologized for my behavior. She gave me a hug and told me I was her prize student, and she'd never been more proud of anyone in her life.

Mr. Sundstrand accepted a teaching job at a nearby Junior College. I saw him on several occasions, and depended on his guidance when I started teaching High School English. He is the most important mentor of my life.

The sixties were a turbulent time of social upheaval and internal investigation. I don't regret the drugs I took, nor the violence and cruelty I endured. I am who I am because of the times and the people that made up my early life. I look back in awe and wonder on my generation, a generation that faced down local, state, and federal government, and stopped a war by exercising their right to assembly, and their tenacious resistance to injustice.

I have been with the same man for forty years; have taught at High School, Elementary School, and College Prep Institutions; been a journalist and an accountant; I've studied and taught yoga, Middle Eastern dance, and karate. And in all the long hours of my life, I have never regretted living through the decade that changed the world.

In Peace and Love,
Donna D. Conrad
July 2016

Acknowledgements

The idea for this book came about during a conversation with Kent Sisson, my sister-in-law Kimberly's brother. I was working on a historical fiction manuscript about the life of Mary of Bethany, *The Last Magdalene*, and was talking about my writing with Kent. As conversations sometimes do, it turned to my encounters with Jim Morrison and Jimi Hendrix. When I assured him the stories were true he said, "You lived history … hell no! You are history!" To which Kimberly added, "Why don't you write about *your* life instead of people dead for two thousand years?" *House of the Moon* was born.

I have James, Kimberly and Kayla Anchell, as well as Jackie Yates, and Jacqui Davinroy Sullivan, to thank for reading the manuscript and giving invaluable feedback. To all the folks who showed up for live readings over the years: Knowing you'd be there and that you'd want to hear something new was incentive to keep me writing. And a special thank you to Marv Mattis for repeatedly admonishing me to write "real and raw." I hope I've done you proud, Marv.

Monica Dodd designed the cover and deserves accolades, not only for her design, but also for her patience and resolve in the face of a multitude of last minute changes, and dealing so well with my "artistic temperament."

Most of all, I have my husband of close to forty years to thank for the remarkable cover photograph, as well as his expert editing, patience, and understanding. He read and re-read dozens of drafts; held my hand and dried my tears; took me for long walks and talks when I was working through tough subjects. I would not have made it through the process of recounting my youth if it were not for his strength and enduring love.

In Memoriam
Shirley Yvonne Conrad
October 8, 1949 – January 8, 2013

My sister, Shirley Conrad, died during the writing of this book. She was sixty-three years old. We grew up in a madhouse and came of age in a time of miracles, when anything and everything was possible. We were "wild" and "incorrigible" according to adults; "liberated" and "hip" according to our peers. We weathered our youth and became women of courage, integrity, and independence. Shirley left two wonderful daughters and scores of devoted friends. The world is lessened by her passing.

Over the last year of her life we had many conversations about *House of the Moon*, some traumatic, most joyful and filled with laughter and awe at what we survived. I hope the reader will glean the deep bond and love we shared, and appreciate the strength and courage Shirley possessed during our youth, and the obstacles she overcame to become a woman loved by many.

Shortly before she died she told me that she hoped *House of the Moon* would help people realize they can survive abusive, destructive childhoods and make something of their lives if they choose to do so. She laughed and added, "Guess the old saying is true—What doesn't kill us, makes us stronger. Damn! I hate it when the old sayings are right!"

She was proud to be a survivor and encouraged people to live to their full potential, to strive to be stronger and more loving each and every day.

This book is possible because of my big sister, who saved my life, and my sanity, on more occasions than I can remember.

Suggested Listening

Aretha Franklin	Single—*Respect*
Big Brother and the Holding Company	Album—Cheap Thrills
Blind Faith	Single—*Can't Find My Way Home*
Blood, Sweat and Tears	Single—*Spinning Wheel*
Bob Dylan	Single—*Rainy Day Women*
Buffalo Springfield	Album—Buffalo Springfield Again
Buffy Sainte-Marie	Album—Little Wheel Spin and Spin
Canned Heat	Album—Living the Blues
Country Joe and the Fish	Album—Electric Music for the Mind and Body
Cream	Album—Fresh Cream
Crosby, Stills, Nash & Young	Single—*Déjà Vu*
	Single—*Ohio*
Dickey Lee	Single—*Patches*
Donovan	Single—*Season of the Witch*
H.P. Lovecraft	Single—*Mobius Trip*
Iron Butterfly	Album—In-A-Gadda-Da-Vida
Janis Ian	Single—*I'll Give You a Stone if You'll Throw It*
	Single—*There are Times*
Jefferson Airplane	Single—*White Rabbit*
Joan Baez	Album—Farewell Angelina
	Album—Joan Baez/5
John Lennon	Single—*Remember*
Joni Mitchell	Album—Ladies of the Canyon
Judy Collins	Album—Wildflowers
Led Zeppelin	Album—Led Zeppelin
	Single—*Stairway to Heaven*
Lesley Gore	Album—Lesley Gore Sings of Mixed-Up Hearts

Moby Grape	Album—Moby Grape
Scott McKenzie	Single—*San Francisco*
Simon & Garfunkel	Single—*Flowers Never Bend with the Rainfall*
	Album—Sounds of Silence
The Beach Boys	Album—Beach Boys' Party
The Beatles	Album—Magical Mystery Tour
	Album—Yellow Submarine
	Single—*A Day in the Life*
	Single—*Come Together*
	Single—*Birthday*
	Album—Revolver
The Chamber Brothers	Single—*Time Has Come Today*
The Doors	Album—The Doors
	Album—Strange Days
The Grateful Dead	Album—The Grateful Dead
The Jimi Hendrix Experience	Album—Are You Experienced
The Lovin' Spoonful	Album—Do You Believe in Magic
The Rolling Stones	Single—*Sympathy for the Devil*
	Album—Beggar's Banquet
The Stooges	Single—*We Will Fall*
The Who	Single—*Baba O'Riley*
The Yardbirds	Album—Over Under Sideways Down
13th Floor Elevators	Single—*Slip Inside This House*
Various Artists	Album—Easy Rider
Various Artists	Album—Woodstock
Velvet Underground	Single—*Venus in Furs*

Questions for Discussion

1. The book begins when the author is 18, then regresses to her early teen years. How does knowing what happens in the future add to the tension and foreshadowing throughout the book?

2. How does the graphic depiction of domestic and social violence influence your view of the 1960s?

3. What has changed since 1964 regarding the legal treatment of domestic violence? Do you think men today continue to abuse women without concern for legal ramification?

4. Has the legal and social treatment of rape victims changed since the 1960s?

5. Why do you think the author became so involved with drugs? Was it just the times, or were there other reasons?

6. How do you view the older sister's reluctance to introduce the author to drugs? How does your view of Shirley change when she later encourages the author's drug use?

7. What was the most disturbing section of the book?

8. What was the most empowering section of the book?

9. How does the author's father's involvement in the Brady Brother's arrest affect your perception of him as a father?

10. Would you be able to love and forgive your mother if she behaved as Helen did in *Glory Train*, and *Lunacy*?

11. Would you be able to forgive and accept your father if he behaved as Condie did throughout the book?

12. How do you explain the father forcing his children to participate in a game of Russian Roulette? Could you ever forgive him?

13. What one thing would you warn the young Donna about if you had the chance?

14. What is the turning point that provided Donna with the ability to change?

15. How would you explain the author ending the book where eighteen-year-old Donna is about to make another bad choice of deciding to take a ride with Preacher that lands her at the Hells Angels party?

16. How did the absence of quotation marks around dialog affect reading experience?

17. Do you feel the author's notes adequately address the changes that allowed her to mature and salvage her troubled life?

Donna Conrad spent her early childhood in Germany, where her father served as an undercover operative for the U.S. military. During the Sixties she lived in Covina, California, a suburb of Los Angeles. She has taught English and writing in public and private schools, and is an internationally published journalist. Her true passion lies in writing about women who have been marginalized throughout history. Her historical novel, *The Last Magdalene*, a first person narrative about the life and times of Miriam of Bethany, is scheduled for publication in 2017. Donna lives in the Pacific Northwest with her husband and their three cats.

www.donnaconrad.com

50613791R00209

Made in the USA
Middletown, DE
26 June 2019